Praise for *The Functional Art*

"Welcome to Alberto's world. Cairo has done it all in *The Functional Art: Theory, Practice, Examples*. And he's done it brilliantly. It is the most comprehensive and sensible book yet on real-world information graphics. We won't need another one for a long time."

> —Nigel Holmes

"If graphic designer Nigel Holmes and data visualizer Edward Tufte had a child, his name would be Alberto Cairo. In *The Functional Art*, accomplished graphics journalist Cairo injects the chaotic world of infographics with a mature, thoughtful, and scientifically grounded perspective that it sorely needs. With extraordinary grace and clarity, Cairo seamlessly unites infographic form and function in a design philosophy that should endure for generations."

> —Stephen Few, Author of *Show Me the Numbers*

"This book is long overdue. Whether you're just getting started visualizing information or have been doing it all your life, whether your topic is business, science, politics, sports or even your personal finances, and whether you're looking for a basic understanding of visualization or a detailed how-to reference, this is the book you were looking for. Alberto Cairo, a professional journalist, information designer and artist, shows how to visualize anything in a simple, straightforward, and intelligent way."

> —Karl Gude, former infographics director at *Newsweek* and graphics editor in residence at the School of Journalism, Michigan State University

"*The Functional Art* is brilliant, didactic, and entertaining. I own dozens of books on visual information, but Cairo's is already on the shortlist of five that I recommend to anybody that wishes to have a career in information graphics, along with those by Edward Tufte, Nigel Holmes, and Richard Saul Wurman. Cairo is one of those rare professionals who have been able to combine real-world experience with the academia."

> —Mario Tascón, director of the Spanish consulting firm Prodigioso Volcán

"Using his enormous professional and academic experience, Alberto Cairo offers a first-hand look at the revolution in visual communication. This book is key to understanding the current situation of print and online information design."

> —Javier Zarracina, graphics director at *The Boston Globe*

"*The Functional Art* is the perfect starting point for a career in information graphics and visualization, and also an excellent guide for those who already have some experience in the area. This is the first real textbook on infographics."

> —Chiqui Esteban, director of new media narratives at lainformacion.com, and blogger at *InfographicsNews*

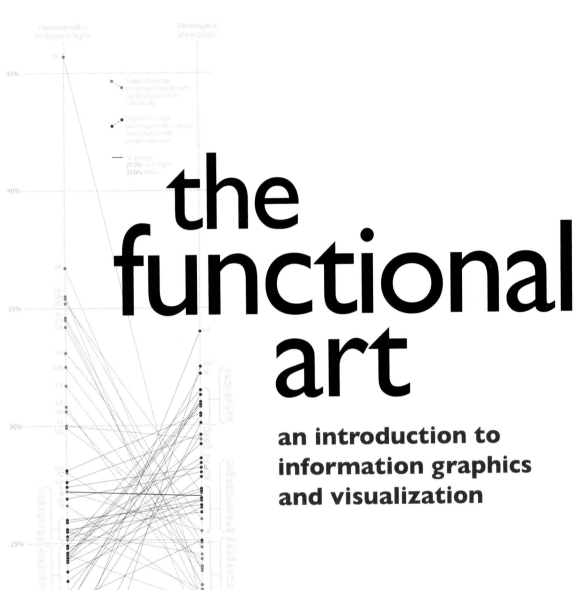

the functional art

an introduction to information graphics and visualization

alberto cairo

New Riders

VOICES THAT MATTER™

The Functional Art
An introduction to information graphics and visualization
Alberto Cairo

New Riders
1249 Eighth Street
Berkeley, CA 94710
510/524-2178
510/524-2221 (fax)

Find us on the Web at: www.newriders.com
To report errors, please send a note to errata@peachpit.com

New Riders is an imprint of Peachpit, a division of Pearson Education.

Acquisitions Editor: Nikki Echler McDonald
Production Editor: Tracey Croom
Development Editor: Cathy Lane
Proofer: Liz Welch
Composition: Kim Scott, Bumpy Design
Indexer: FireCrystal Communications
Interior Designer: Mimi Heft
Cover Designer: Mimi Heft, with Alberto Cairo
Media Producer: Eric Geoffroy
Video Producers: Amy Van Vechten, Andrew Wallace

ISBN 13: 978-0-321-83473-7
ISBN 10:   0-321-83473-9
9 8 7 6 5 4 3 2 1

Printed and bound in the United States of America

This book is for Alice, Elena, and Julio.
And for Erica, of course.

Acknowledgements

Experience teaches you that the archetype of the self-made man is a myth with roots in humankind's relish for delusion. Life's meanderings are determined by chance and luck, and the only thing we can do to funnel those factors is to ready ourselves to identify and seize opportunities when they pass by. We are the product of effort as much as we are shaped by the people who surround us. In this sense, I feel I am one of the luckiest individuals on Earth: I will start this book saying that curiosity is the most important trait any communicator should have. Therefore, I have to thank those who have ignited my curiosity throughout the years and have helped me focus it.

This book is, first, for my parents. When I was a kid, my dad prompted me to love books and good stories, both fictional and real, and to develop an insatiable hunger for new knowledge. Inadvertently, he also revealed to me how to summarize and convey information with images and how to be precise, concise, clear, and fun (or so I hope) when teaching others. In addition to being a medical doctor, my father is also an artist. He used to lecture on anatomy at a local university in Spain, and one of his former students once told me that, many years after graduating, the only classes he remembered from college were my father's. He told me it was because of the beautiful diagrams and cutaways Professor Cairo used to sketch out on the blackboard while he talked.

From my mother, I treasure a most relevant lesson: Don't give up pursuing and defending what you have been able to prove to be true, no matter what.

Thanks to my editors, Nikki McDonald and Cathy Lane, at Peachpit Press. They believed in this project from the very first day, and they encouraged me to keep writing in times of fatigue.

To Luis G. Prado, my editor and publisher in Spain, Óscar Fernández, from El País, and Ferrán Giménez and Laia Blasco, two colleagues at the Universitat Oberta de Catalunya: Years ago, they prompted me to put what I knew about information graphics and visualization into writing, and they aided me in making sense of it.

I wish to thank several students of mine. First, Patricia Borns, who read almost the entirety of The Functional Art and gave me valuable advice on how to improve its style. This book is much more readable because of her. Eileen Mignoni and Sophia Dengo read and edited very preliminary chapters, years ago. I also got suggestions from Lex Alexander, Mel Umbarger, and Lauren Flowers, and from many other of my undergraduate and graduate students at the University of North Carolina-Chapel Hill and at the University of Miami.

To Nigel Holmes, Stephen Few, and Karl Gude for their kind comments about the content of *The Functional Art*: Coming from them, their words mean a lot to me. They were three of my main sources when I was learning how to visually display information. They are giants with broad shoulders; I've taken advantage of that. Thanks also to Chiqui Esteban and Javier Zarracina, Spanish infographics masterminds.

Many of the examples in *The Functional Art* come from my two years as director of infographics and multimedia at *Época* magazine, in São Paulo, Brazil. I wish to thank the wonderful people I had the honor to work with. First, the infographics department: Marco Vergotti, David Michelsohn, Rodrigo Cunha, Rodrigo Fortes, Gerson Mora, Luiz Salomão, Gerardo Rodríguez, Erik Scaranello, and Pedro Schimidt. Also, *Época's* art director, Marcos Marques, author of some of the most impressive covers I've ever seen in a news magazine. Thanks also to Helio Gurovitz and his deputy, David Cohen, two managers with a background in computer science and engineering who understand what visualization and data journalism are about.

To my colleagues at the University of Miami and at UNC-Chapel Hill: Rich Beckman, Laura Ruel, Don Wittekind, Pat Davison, Charles Floyd, Kim Grinfeder, Michelle Seelig, and Jim Virga. Also, to the deans who, since 2005, have supported me in the teaching of graphics and visualization: Richard Cole, Tom Bowers, Jean Folkerts, and Gregory Shepherd.

To the people who, every year, organize and participate in the Malofiej International Infographics Summit (www.malofiej20.com): Javier Errea, Álvaro Gil, John Grimwade, Geoff McGhee, Juan Velasco, and so many others.

To Mario Tascón and Gumersindo Lafuente, makers of www.elmundo.es, where I was graphics director between 2000 and 2005. They both trusted a certain rookie more than a decade ago.

To all my colleagues at *La Voz de Galicia, Diario 16, El Mundo*, DPI Comunicación, and all the other newspapers and magazines I have worked for, both as a full-time employee and as a consultant. I wish to also thank all the organizations, companies, and friends who graciously gave me permission to use their infographics and visualizations in this book.

Finally, *The Functional Art* is, above all, for my wife and kids. In the past several months, they had to endure long hours of silence and deep concentration on my part. Patience has never failed them. Writing is the most solitary activity I know. I could not have survived without their support. I love you.

About the author

Alberto Cairo teaches information graphics and visualization at the University of Miami's School of Communication and serves as an advisor for the Master of Arts in Technology and Communication program at the University of North Carolina (UNC)-Chapel Hill.

In 2000, Cairo led the creation of the Interactive Infographics Department at *El Mundo*, the second largest printed and the largest digital daily newspaper in Spain. Between 2001 and 2005, Cairo's team won more Malofiej and Society for News Design (SND) infographics international awards than any other news organization worldwide.

Cairo was a professor at UNC-Chapel Hill between 2005 and 2009, and has been an invited lecturer and keynote speaker at all of the most influential international conferences on visual journalism and design. He has taught in the U.S., Mexico, El Salvador, Costa Rica, Venezuela, Ecuador, Peru, Brazil, Chile, Argentina, Spain, Portugal, France, Switzerland, Ukraine, Singapore, and South Korea. He has also been a consultant with many top news publications in those countries. Since 2006, he has been a lecturer at the Universitat Oberta de Catalunya, the first public university in Spain to offer online accredited degrees.

About the DVD

The video course in the DVD that accompanies *The Functional Art* expands on the contents of this book. The course is similar to the materials I've used in the past in my classes at UNC-Chapel Hill and at the University of Miami so, in case you are an instructor, they may be a good starting point to develop your own presentation slides. If you are a professional or a student, please be aware that many of the examples showcased in the video course are different than the ones included in the book.

The DVD is divided into three video lessons: First, there is an introduction to basic visualization concepts, followed by a discussion on the principles of graphic design, and finally, a section on how to plan for infographics projects.

In the first video lesson, I delve into the ideas outlined in the first section of *The Functional Art*. You will learn, for instance, why infographics should be "functional as hammers, multilayered as onions, and beautiful as equations." I also discuss what strategies you can follow to choose the most appropriate graphic forms to display your information.

In the second lesson, I explain the main principles of graphic design, such as unity, variety, and hierarchy, and how to apply them to create better layouts. I also give you some basic tips on how to better use type and color.

In the third lesson, I discuss an impressive visualization made by the British newspaper *The Guardian*. I also explain how I developed the chart on the front cover of *The Functional Art*. You will see how I use Microsoft Excel and Adobe Illustrator, and why I call my approach "low-tech visualization." This lesson is not a tutorial on software tools, but it may give you a clue or two about how to start a career in information graphics. If you work in this field already, this video may reveal a few tricks that you can apply in your own projects.

Contents

PART III practice

PART IV profiles

Introduction

Infographics and Visualization

The remarkable mechanisms by which the senses understand the environment are all but identical with the operations described by the psychology of thinking.

—Rudolf Arnheim, from *Visual Thinking*

The partnership of presentation and exploration

If you asked me to choose one mystery that has fascinated me through the years, it would be our brain's ability to create and understand visual representations with different degrees of abstraction: graphics that encode data, concepts, connections, and geographical locations. How is it possible that the brain, a wrinkled chunk of meat and fat squeezed into a cavity too small for its size, can accomplish such challenging tasks? This book is my personal attempt to answer that question.

The human brain has dozens of regions related to visual perception: densely interconnected groups of neurons devoted to the processing and filtering of information that we collect through our eyes. Evolution designed us such that no other activity demands more mental resources than visual perception and cognition. This fact permeates everything we do, and impacts the way we express ourselves. Go ahead and explain a difficult concept to a friend. In the moment she gets what you mean, she will exclaim, with a sparkle of relief and happiness in her eyes:

"I *see!*"

Her expression makes complete sense, because deep inside our minds, *to see* and *to understand* are intertwined processes. We understand *because* we see. This causal relationship is also true the other way around. As I will explain later, we see because we have previous understanding of certain things. Seeing precedes understanding, and this understanding precedes a better, deeper seeing down the road.

We are a visual species. We are also a *symbolic* species, if we follow Terrence W. Deacon's famous definition.[1] Everything our senses gather is transformed, deep inside our minds, into simple, manageable representations, or symbols. Some of those symbols are verbal or textual, encoded with one of the thousands of languages and dialects humanity has devised. They can also be expressed through what Harvard psychologist Steven Pinker called *mentalese*, the inner language the mind uses to talk to itself.[2]

---

1 *Terence W. Deacon,* The Symbolic Species: The Co-Evolution of Language and the Brain (New York: W.W. Norton & Company, 1998).

2 Steven Pinker, *The Language Instinct: How the Mind Creates Language* (New York: Harper Collins Publishers, Inc., 1994). Pinker builds on Noam Chomsky's hypothesis of an innate universal grammar.

But not all symbols are verbal. **The brain doesn't just process information that comes though the eyes. It also creates mental visual images that allow us to reason and plan actions that facilitate survival.** Imagine a bus. Picture it in your head. Now, examine it: Is it yellow, or blue, or red? Does it have a license plate? Is it a plate of the state you live in? That's it. That's a mental image. Understanding the mechanisms involved in these brain processes can help you become a better communicator, visual or otherwise.

This is the first theme of the book you have in your hands.

The second theme is the common nature of infographics and information visualization. Some professionals and academics have erected a sharp distinction between the two disciplines. According to them, infographics present information by means of statistical charts, maps, and diagrams, while information visualization offers visual tools that an audience can use to explore and analyze data sets. That is, where infographics tell stories designed by communicators, information visualization helps readers discover stories by themselves.

In the following pages, I take an unorthodox approach. **Infographics and visualization exist on a continuum.** Let me explain.

Imagine two straight, black parallel lines. On the top line, put the word "Infographics" on the left tip and "'Visualization" on the right. On the line at the bottom, write "presentation" on the left, and "exploration" on the right. All graphics present data and allow a certain degree of exploration of those same data. Some graphics are almost all presentation, so they allow just a limited amount of exploration; hence we can say they are more infographics than visualization (**Figure 1**), whereas others are mostly about letting readers play with what is being shown (**Figure 2**), tilting more to the visualization side of our linear scale. But every infographic and every visualization has a *presentation* and an *exploration* component: they present, but they also facilitate the analysis of what they show, to different degrees.

An excellent example: The beauty of Stefanie Posavec's *Literary Organism* is based on its organic appearance and careful selection of typefaces and colors, and also

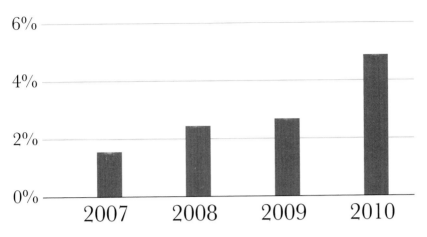

Figure I Unemployment rate in an imaginary country.

on the multiple readings you can extract from it. Each subdivision of this tree-like graphic represents a deeper, more granular level of organization in the book: chapters, paragraphs, sentences, and words. Colors correspond to the most common themes of the novel: travel, music, parties, sex, and so on.

After spending some time fathoming it, patterns emerge and convey a different message to each viewer. While the uninitiated in Kerouac's oeuvre will identify a big picture of the main topics the book discusses, the specialist or literary critic will be able to use this work of art as a tool to test hypotheses and intuitions. Is sex a prevalent theme in *On the Road*, for instance? What about the chapters that combine paragraphs about sex with paragraphs about work and survival?

A chart of mine in **Figure 3** also illustrates the complementarity between presenting and exploring. Each point of the color line represents a year between 1981 and 2010 in the history of Brazil. The position of a point on the horizontal axis is equivalent to the Gross Domestic Product, measured in billions of dollars. The position on the vertical axis is equivalent to the inequality level measured with the GINI index, developed by the UN. The farther to the right a point is, the bigger the GDP (adjusted for inflation and for purchase power parity); the higher the point is on the vertical scale, the higher the inequality in that particular year.

In other words, the graphic represents the covariation of economic development and social justice. The headline summarizes its central message: When the GDP

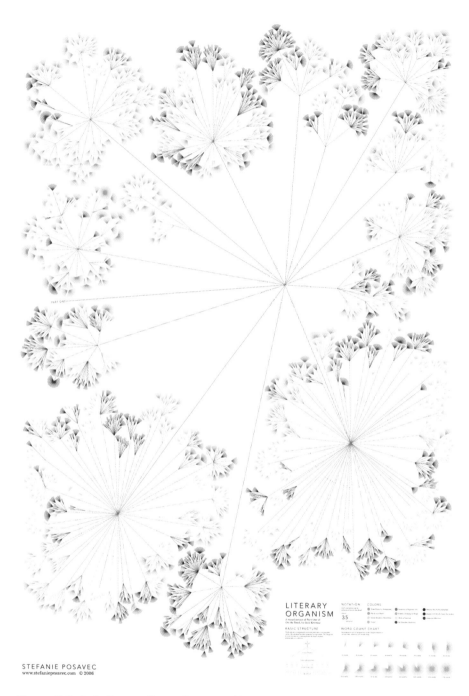

Figure 2 Stefanie Posavec *Literary Organism: a Visualization of Part 1 of "On the Road," by Jack Kerouac* (www.itsbeenreal.co.uk). Reproduced with permission.

When the Brazilian Economy Improves, Inequality Doesn't Drop

The graphic below shows the correlation between Brazilian GDP (horizontal axis) and inequality (vertical axis) between 1981 and 2010. The position of the points, each representing a year, depends on how high GDP and inequality were. You can notice, for instance, that the economy grew between 1986 and 1989 because the line tends to move to the right, but inequality also grew, as the point representing 1989 is much higher than the ones before. You can also see that, during Lula da Silva's government, the economy expanded almost as much as during the terms of the other presidents who preceded him combined.

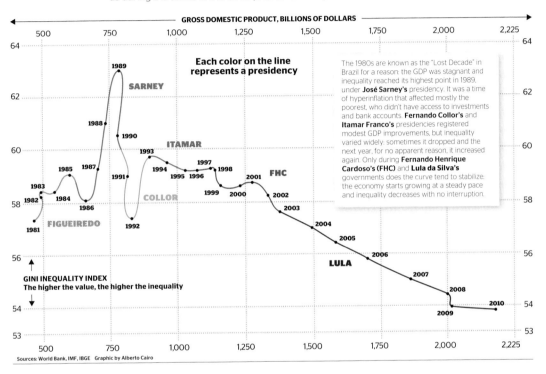

Figure 3 *Época* magazine. The co-variation of inequality and economic growth (Translated from Portuguese.) Reproduced with permission.

grows, inequality does not necessarily drop. It's one of the disgraces of recent Brazilian history that improvements in the economy don't always lead to a better living standard for everybody. In some years, particularly on the first half of the line, the opposite is true.

When I finished designing this project, I showed it to some middle-aged colleagues at *Época*, a weekly news magazine I worked for between 2010 and 2011. Their response was unanimous and encouraging. Although they were writers rather than designers or artists, all of them understood the graphic with a minimum of effort. It confirmed for them facts that every Brazilian older than 40 remembers: the constant and stable economic growth the country went through during Lula's administration (2003–2011), when the government promoted several income distribution programs; the instability of José Sarney's and Fernando Collor's years, when the GDP barely improved but inequality varied erratically; the stabilization forced by Fernando Henrique Cardoso (FHC), who took Brazil out of the black hole of inflation; and so on.

Some of them even told me that the multicolored line was history-making, because it revealed the correlation between the two variables, which had never been shown before. The line looks wildly erratic between 1981 and 1992 (the chaos years); it smooths between 1993 and 2002 (the stabilization period); and it becomes perfectly straight after 2003, revealing an almost perfect relationship between better economic output and more equality in Brazil. To see self-proclaimed nonvisual people in the process of unraveling such an uncommon graphic form, and getting satisfactory messages from it, was eye-opening for me.

- - ● - ◖● - ◖◖● - ●·● - - - - - - ● - - - - - - - - -

The surprise reaction of my "text" colleagues as they read the graphic, rather than merely looked at it, has deep roots. This is the third theme of *The Functional Art*: **Graphics, charts, and maps aren't just tools to be seen, but to be read and scrutinized.** The first goal of an infographic is not to be beautiful just for the sake of eye appeal, but, above all, to be understandable first, and beautiful after that; or to be beautiful thanks to its exquisite functionality.

If you are among those journalists, designers, and artists who think that infographics and visualization consist of a bunch of data shaped into a spectacular and innovative form, keep reading. I hope I will be able to make you forget that simplistic idea. As Ben Shneiderman wrote once, "The purpose of visualization is insight, not pictures."[3] Images are the vocabulary of a language. They are means, not ends. You will never hear a writing journalist say that her goal is to strive for a good literary style by using elegant sentences and sophisticated structures. Her style is just a tool to facilitate comprehension and to wake up emotions in readers' minds so they'll absorb difficult ideas with ease. Aesthetics do matter, but aesthetics without a solid backbone made of good content is just artifice.

---

3 Stuart Card, Jock Mackinlay and Ben Shneiderman, *Readings in Information Visualization: Using Vision to Think* (London: Academic Press, 1999).

In this book, you will see that I write quite a bit about visual journalism. That's because I am a journalist, and I am convinced that many of the challenges news media face in using graphics are common to other professions that also use them on a regular basis, such as marketing, advertising, business intelligence, data analysis, and so on.

In newspapers and magazines, infographics have traditionally been created within art departments. In all of those I'm familiar with, the infographics director is subordinate to the art director, who is usually a graphic designer. This is not a mistake *per se*, but it can lead to damaging misunderstandings. In Brazil, the country where I lived while writing part of this book, journalists and designers call graphics "art." They would say, with that charming musicality of South American Portuguese, "Vamos fazer uma arte!" ("Let's make a piece of art!") Thinking of graphics as art leads many to put bells and whistles over substance and to confound infographics with mere illustrations.

This error is at least in part the result of a centuries-long tradition in which visual communication has not been as intellectually elevated as writing. For too many traditional journalists, infographics are mere ornaments to make the page look lighter and more attractive for audiences who grow more impatient with long-form stories every day. Infographics are treated not as devices that expand the scope of our perception and cognition, but as decoration. As Rudolf Arnheim wrote, this tradition goes back to ancient Western philosophy, whose Greek thinkers such as Parmenides and Plato mistrusted the senses deeply.[4] Unfortunately today, 40 years after Arnheim's masterful *Visual Thinking* was published, the philosophy is still in very good health.

The fourth theme of the book, therefore, is **the relationship between visualization and art, which is similar to the linkage of journalism and literature.** A journalist can borrow tools and techniques from literature, and be inspired by great fiction writing, but she will never allow her stories to *become* literature. That notion applies to visualization, which is, above all, a functional art.

Let's get started.

Miami, Florida. June 2012

---

4 Rudolf Arnheim, *Visual Thinking* (Berkeley: University of California Press, 1969).

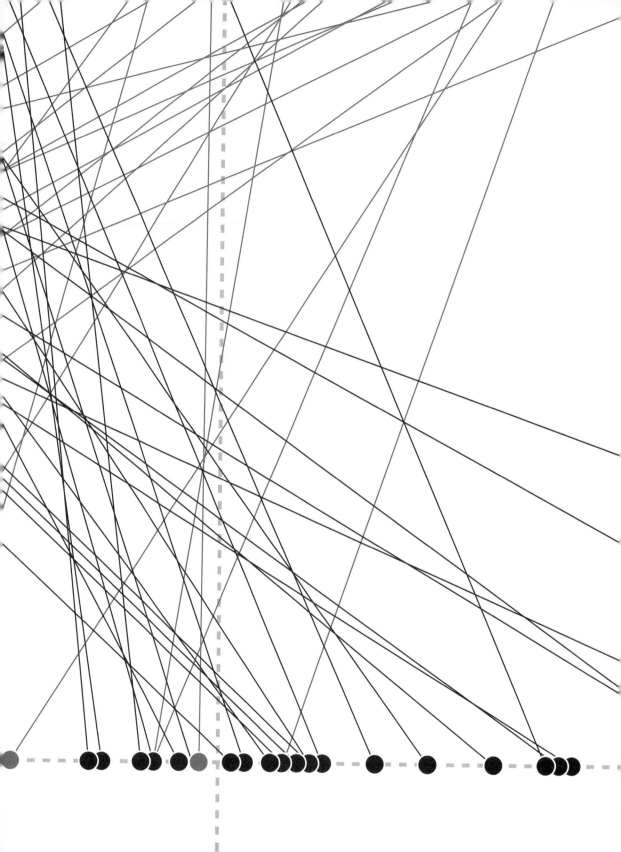

PART I

foundations

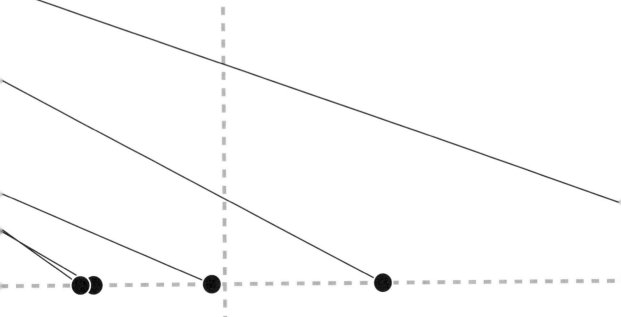

Why Visualize: From Information to Wisdom

My expertise has always been my ignorance, my admission and acceptance of not knowing….When you can admit that you don't know, you are more likely to ask the questions that will enable you to learn.

—Richard Saul Wurman, from *Information Anxiety 2*

Recently someone asked me what personality trait best characterizes those interested in a career in visualization and infographics. My answer: "An insatiable, childish curiosity."

Curiosity, combined with a tendency to try to explain everything using reason, led me to a career in journalism and, later, to specialize in information graphics. It is not possible to be a good communicator if you have not developed a keen interest in almost everything as well as an urge to learn as much as you can about the strangest, most varied, unrelated topics. **The life of a visual communicator should be one of systematic and exciting intellectual chaos.** In my case, it consists of regular shifts between journalism, cognitive psychology, international politics, and history. In your case, it might be sports, music, architecture, or just about anything else.

Let me give you an example of how far healthy curiosity can take you.

Rational Optimism

My original plan for this chapter was to open it with a few formal definitions for information visualization, information design, and infographics. But something changed my mind. While randomly navigating *The New York Times* website, I stumbled on a review of a book called *The Rational Optimist: How Prosperity Evolves*, by British science essayist Matt Ridley (2010).

The review[1] was mostly critical, but the hypotheses Ridley proposed sounded intriguing. The book honored its title, making a case for optimism about our future as a species. I had read other Ridley books in the past and had loved his *Genome: The Autobiography of a Species in 23 Chapters* (2006), so I was positively biased.

My curiosity ignited, I grabbed my Kindle and purchased the book. One minute later, it had finished downloading. For the rest of the day, I traded book writing for reading. (Note to my editor: I did it to make this chapter better, I promise!) The book is so well written that it was difficult to put down before the end.

One chapter about the fertility rate, or the average number of children born to women in each country, caught my eye. You may have heard or read the stories of Malthusian doomsayers who claim that rising fertility in poor regions is the reason the Earth has to support 7 billion people, with a forecast of 9 billion two decades from now, and even more in the far future.

Other doomsayers focus on the aging populations of developed countries where fertility rates are below 2.1 children per woman, a number that is known as the "replacement rate." If the replacement rate in a country is significantly below 2.1, the population will shrink over time. If it's much higher than 2.1, you'll have a much younger population down the road, which can cause problems. Younger populations, for example, show greater rates of violence and crime.

Ridley contradicts both kinds of apocalyptic thinking by discussing two interesting trends. On average, fertility in rich countries is very low, but in the past few years it has trended slightly upward. On the other hand, poor countries show a *decrease* in average fertility. Contrary to conventional wisdom, in many countries

---

1   William Easterly, "A High-Five for the Invisible Hand," *The New York Times*, June 11, 2010.

that verge on becoming first-world economies, such as Brazil, the drop is dramatic: the fertility rate has trended from more than six children per woman in 1950 to less than two in 2010.

Ridley suggests that, due to these two complementary trends, fertility rates everywhere will converge around 2.1 in a few decades, and the world population will stabilize at 9 billion people. It's counterintuitive, isn't it?

Ridley's case is compelling and supported by prospective data from reliable sources, such as the United Nations (UN) and The World Bank.[2] But something made me uncomfortable as I read his arguments. It took me a while to figure out what it was. Ridley writes about curves and lines and trends, but the chapter on fertility and population includes just one graphic, similar to the one in **Figure 1.1**.

Percentage increase in world population

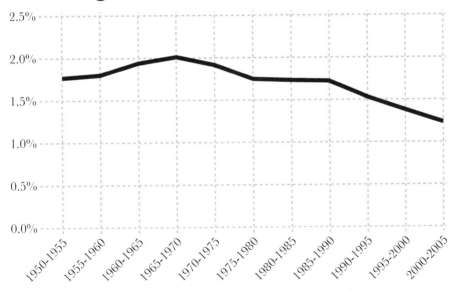

Figure 1.1 How much world population increases compared with the previous year.

The graphic is simple and clear, but also insufficient to support the claims Ridley makes. All it shows is that when you plot population change as a time-series chart, the trend is negative. The closer we get to the present, the lower the worldwide population growth. **The fact that the graphic is an aggregate of the data of all countries in the world impedes our ability to see the multiple patterns**

---

2 Matt Ridley, *The Rational Optimist: How Prosperity Evolves* (New York: Harper Collins).

Ridley discusses. Where are those rich countries whose fertility rate is slowly recovering? Where is the evidence for the assertion that developing countries such as Brazil, China, and India are stabilizing their populations?

I told you before that I am curious. I didn't just take a day off to read *The Rational Optimist*. I also looked for the data Ridley used for the chapter on population. With that data, would I be able to prove his hypotheses?

Low-Tech Visualization to the Rescue

The first thing I did was go to the United Nations website. If you search for "UN data," you will quickly find http://data.un.org/, which is a kind of paradise if you like to dig into huge databases on population, education, economics, and social development. Within the UN site, I searched for the fertility rate data. The UN's figures begin in 1950; the projections extend as far as 2100.

I decided to exclude the years after 2010, playing with actual data (at that time) rather than forecasts. Using the filters the site offers, I asked for a table that included the more than 150 countries on which the UN has complete research. **Figure 1.2** shows a screenshot of what I obtained.

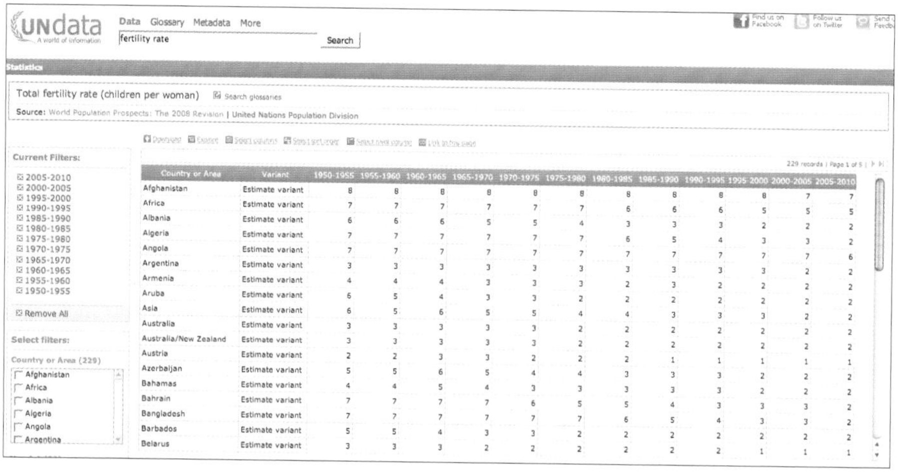

UNdata
A world of information
Data Glossary Metadata More
fertility rate
Search
Statistics
Total fertility rate (children per woman)
Source: World Population Prospects: The 2008 Revision | United Nations Population Division
Current Filters:
2005-2010
2000-2005
1995-2000
1990-1995
1985-1990
1980-1985
1975-1980
1970-1975
1965-1970
1960-1965
1955-1960
1950-1955
Remove All
Select filters:
Country or Area (229)
Afghanistan
Africa
Albania
Algeria
Angola
Argentina
229 records | Page 1 of 5

Country or Area	Variant	1950-1955	1955-1960	1960-1965	1965-1970	1970-1975	1975-1980	1980-1985	1985-1990	1990-1995	1995 2000	2000-2005	2005-2010
Afghanistan	Estimate variant	8	8	8	8	8	8	8	8	8	8	7	7
Africa	Estimate variant	7	7	7	7	7	7	6	6	6	5	5	5
Albania	Estimate variant	6	6	6	5	5	4	3	3	3	2	2	2
Algeria	Estimate variant	7	7	7	7	7	7	6	5	4	3	3	2
Angola	Estimate variant	7	7	7	7	7	7	7	7	7	7	7	6
Argentina	Estimate variant	3	3	3	3	3	3	3	3	3	3	2	2
Armenia	Estimate variant	4	4	4	3	3	3	2	3	2	2	2	2
Aruba	Estimate variant	6	5	4	3	3	2	2	2	2	2	2	2
Asia	Estimate variant	6	5	6	5	5	4	4	3	3	3	2	2
Australia	Estimate variant	3	3	3	3	3	2	2	2	2	2	2	2
Australia/New Zealand	Estimate variant	3	3	3	3	3	2	2	2	2	2	2	2
Austria	Estimate variant	2	2	3	3	2	2	2	1	1	1	1	1
Azerbaijan	Estimate variant	5	5	6	5	4	4	3	3	3	2	2	2
Bahamas	Estimate variant	4	4	5	4	3	3	3	3	3	2	2	2
Bahrain	Estimate variant	7	7	7	7	6	5	5	4	3	3	3	2
Bangladesh	Estimate variant	7	7	7	7	7	7	6	5	4	3	3	2
Barbados	Estimate variant	5	5	4	3	3	2	2	2	2	2	2	2
Belarus	Estimate variant	3	3	3	2	2	2	2	2	2	1	1	1

Figure 1.2 UN data table.

I downloaded the table and decided to try a low-tech visualization exercise to show my students—mostly journalists with no technology background—that learning to create information graphics is not all that difficult.

Using OpenOffice (an open source software suite that includes a spreadsheet program), I reorganized the data and cleaned up the table a little. Some cells were missing, so the process involved a bit of manual tweaking—no big deal. **Figure 1.3** shows an excerpt of the result.

	A	B	C	D	E	F
1	Country o▸ 1950-1955	1955-1960	1960-1965	1965-1970	1970-1975	
126	Senegal	5.97	6.46	6.75	7.25	7.50
127	Serbia	3.22	2.75	2.57	2.43	2.36
128	Sierra Leo▸	5.52	5.60	5.70	5.77	5.84
129	Singapore	6.40	5.99	4.93	3.46	2.62
130	Slovakia	3.52	3.27	2.89	2.50	2.51
131	Slovenia	2.80	2.39	2.32	2.32	2.19
132	Somalia	7.25	7.25	7.25	7.25	7.10
133	Spain	2.57	2.75	2.89	2.92	2.86
134	Sri Lanka	5.80	5.80	5.20	4.70	4.00
135	Sudan	6.65	6.65	6.60	6.60	6.60
136	Suriname	6.56	6.56	6.56	5.95	5.29
137	Swaziland	6.70	6.70	6.75	6.85	6.87
138	Sweden	2.21	2.23	2.32	2.16	1.89
139	Switzerlar▸	2.28	2.34	2.51	2.27	1.82
140	Syrian Ara▸	7.30	7.45	7.60	7.60	7.52
141	Tajikistan	6.00	6.20	6.30	6.72	6.83
142	Thailand	6.35	6.35	6.34	5.99	5.05
143	Timor-Les▸	6.44	6.35	6.37	6.16	6.15

Figure 1.3 My UN data table after tweaking.

Still with me? Now the fun begins. We have the table in the computer. Is it possible to make sense of it? Hardly. Extracting meaning from a table is tough. Can you see any interesting trends just by reading the figures? If you can, congratulations. You have an extraordinary memory. Most of us mortals have brains that didn't evolve to deal with large amounts of data. Let me prove it to you: Look at Figure 1.3 again and tell me in what years between 1950 and 1975 did the difference between the fertility rates of Spain and Sweden grow, and in what years did it drop?

This apparently simple task forces you to do something extremely difficult: look up a number, memorize it, read another one, memorize it and compare it with the previous one, and so forth until you get to the end of the series. I wouldn't bother.

But what if I designed a simple chart with the data in the spreadsheet? The result (**Figure 1.4**) is a visual tool that helps answer my question. The message in that graphic is clear: Spain started 1950 with an average number of children per woman higher than Sweden's. But then fertility in Spain fell drastically after 1970 and only recovered partially in the last five years of the series. On the other hand, Sweden's fertility rate has remained pretty stable over the last 60 years, although it is well below the replacement level of 2.1 children per woman.

By giving numbers a proper shape, by visually encoding them, the graphic has saved you time and energy that you would otherwise waste if you had to use a table that was not designed to aid your mind. **The first and main goal of any**

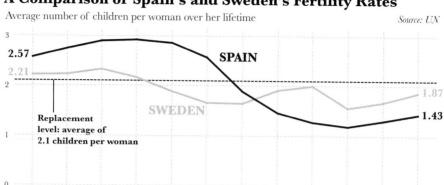

A Comparison of Spain's and Sweden's Fertility Rates

Average number of children per woman over her lifetime   *Source: UN*

Figure 1.4 So much for Spanish pride.

graphic and visualization is to be a tool for your eyes and brain to perceive what lies beyond their natural reach.[3]

However, presenting data for two countries is far simpler than presenting data for one hundred of them, which is what we may need to do in order to put some of Matt Ridley's ideas to the test. Once we represent the lines for all countries in our data set, we get something similar to **Figure 1.5**. This colorful spaghetti dish may look interesting, but it's totally useless for our purposes. This is what you get when you let a software program do the hard work for you.

Remember, what we want to reveal is the projected confluence of the lines of rich countries (trending slightly up in recent years) and those of poor countries (trending down) around the 2.1 children per woman line. If you look at Figure 1.5 long enough, you may be able to tell the lines apart, but it's more likely you will just give up.

The way to solve this problem is to add some visual hierarchy to the mix. Obviously it makes no sense for all lines to be equally visible. **In information graphics, what you show can be as important as what you hide.** I put the chart generated in OpenOffice into Adobe Illustrator, where I highlighted a few rich countries and a few developing and poor countries.

I made other countries' lines light gray, so they remain on the scene but don't obscure the message. Why not get rid of them? Because they provide context to

3 This idea has inspired some of the best books out there, including those of Edward Tufte, William Cleveland, Stephen Few, and Stephen Kosslyn, among others. See the Bibliography for references.

Fertility Rate

Average number of children per woman over her lifetime
Showing all countries for which complete data is available

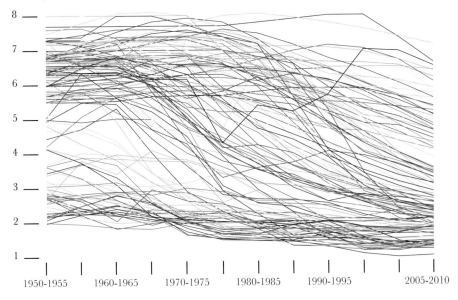

Figure 1.5 Too many lines obscure the message.

the cases that I highlight. While changing all the background lines to one color makes it impossible to see them as independent entities, collectively they show an overall downward trend in the data—you can see that many lines begin between the 6.0 and 8.0 children per woman point in 1950, but just a handful of them remain at that height in the vertical axis when they reach 2010. The final sketch in **Figure 1.6** looks much more user-friendly than the previous one.

Excited by what I was revealing, I explored other assertions made in *The Rational Optimist*. Ridley argues that a sudden drop in a country's fertility rate is usually precipitated by several factors: an increase in average per capita income, women getting better access to education, and the shrinking of infant mortality figures. The facts that more children survive their first years of life and that women are spending more time in school are positively correlated to better family planning.

On the economic side, Ridley explains that in rich countries, leisure options are everywhere, and they are cheap and accessible; the distractions of the modern world free us, albeit partially, of our primary impulse to reproduce with no control. We can explain this phenomenon in bogus academic jargon: the average number

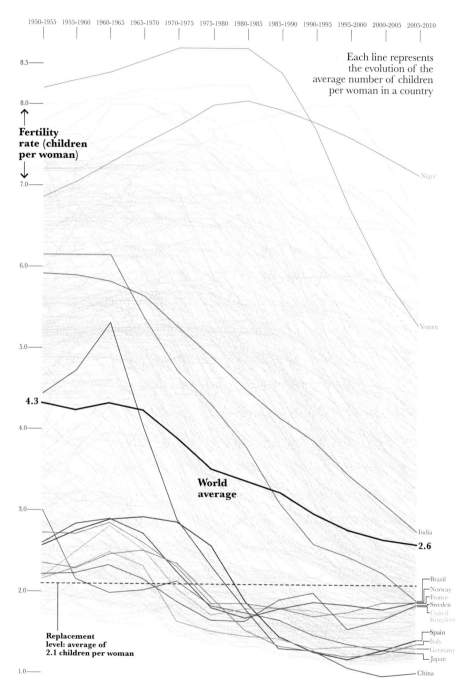

1950-1955 1955-1960 1960-1965 1965-1970 1970-1975 1975-1980 1980-1985 1985-1990 1990-1995 1995-2000 2000-2005 2005-2010

8.5—

Each line represents
the evolution of the
average number of children
per woman in a country

8.0—

↑
**Fertility
rate (children
per woman)**
↓

7.0—

Niger

6.0—

5.0—

Yemen

4.3

4.0—

**World
average**

3.0—

India

2.6

Brazil
Norway
France
Sweden
United
Kingdom

2.0—

Spain
Italy
Germany
Japan

**Replacement
level: average of
2.1 children per woman**

1.0—

China

Figure 1.6 Highlighting the relevant, keeping the secondary in the background.

of children per couple is inversely proportional to the average amount of hours each member of that couple spends in front of any kind of screen. No kidding.

To prove the correlation between fertility, income, and women's schooling, I designed two small scatter-plots in the same spreadsheet software I used before. In **Figure 1.7**, each little circle represents a country. The position of each country on the horizontal axis is proportional to its fertility rate. The position on the vertical axis equals average income per person (first chart) and the percentage of students in middle school who are female (second chart).

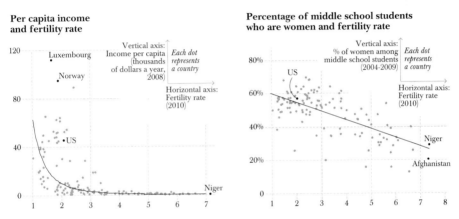

Figure 1.7 The more educated and rich you are, the fewer children you'll have.

The black line running between the dots is called a *trend line* or *regression line*: the closer the dots are to this line, the stronger the correlation between the two variables represented. You can see that the dots are pretty close to the line, so the variables are related. On average, the richer people are, the fewer children they tend to have; and the fewer girls who attend middle school, the more children on average they have in that particular country.

Here's the lesson I learned from this exercise: In just three or four hours of work, I completed a personal project that allowed me to see the evidence supporting Matt Ridley's discussion on the evolution of fertility. His hypotheses seem to have some basis after all. **But if you don't present your data to readers so they can see it, read it, explore it, and analyze it, why would they trust you?** This is a question many journalists, particularly those who write opinion columns, should ask themselves more often.

Drowning in Data? Only If You Don't Know How to Swim

The example I just gave you was not chosen randomly. It helps us delve into topics that are essential to understanding the present state of graphics as a form of communication. Isn't it amazing that we can read graphics at all, and use them to discover realities otherwise invisible to the bare eye? In the past two or three decades, psychology has unveiled many of the brain mechanisms involved in this kind of understanding. Another thought: Did you notice that the data I manipulated is available on the Internet *for free*? And isn't it wonderful that the tools I used to prove Matt Ridley's assertions are also broadly available to anyone and can be learned in a matter of hours?

Those three trends have converged to put visualization in the mainstream. The design of graphics is not just more democratic than it was a decade ago, when data was sparse and software expensive and difficult to use. We also have the potential to use graphics more intelligently because the principles informing their design have never been clearer.

Embracing graphics and visualization is no trivial endeavor. Citing research by International Data Corp (IDC), *The Economist* reported that the information generated in 2010 alone reached 1,200 exabytes,[4] an amount equivalent to thousands of billions of issues of the venerable British magazine. The story added that the total amount of extant digital information totals several zettabytes. Here's a simple explanation to help you grasp the challenge we're dealing with:

> **1 bit**, or binary digit, is the basic unit of information in computing. It represents either 0 or 1.
>
> **1 byte** (the amount of information necessary to encode a letter or a number) = 8 bits
>
> **1 kilobyte** = 1,000 bytes
>
> **1 megabyte** = 1,000 kilobytes or 1,000,000 bytes (10^6)
>
> **1 gigabyte** = 1,000 megabytes or 1,000,000,000 bytes (10^9)
>
> **1 terabyte** = 1,000 gigabytes or 1,000,000,000,000 bytes (10^{12})
>
> **1 petabyte** = 1,000 terabytes or 1,000,000,000,000,000 bytes (10^{15})
>
> **1 exabyte** = 1,000 petabytes or 1,000,000,000,000,000,000 bytes (10^{18})
>
> **1 zettabyte** = 1,000 exabytes or 1,000,000,000,000,000,000,000 bytes (10^{21})
>
> **1 yottabyte** = 1,000 zettabytes or 1,000,000,000,000,000,000,000,000 bytes (10^{24})

4 "All too much: monstrous amounts of data." *The Economist*, Feb. 25, 2010.

Confused? Don't worry. You're not alone. A yottabyte of information is such a huge number that it is impossible to imagine. In August 2010, Erich Schmidt, former CEO of Google, announced in a conference that between the beginning of time and 2003, humanity generated roughly five exabytes of data, whereas we now produce the same volume of bits *every two days.*

"The information explosion is so profoundly larger than anyone ever thought," said Schmidt. Five exabytes is more than 200,000 years of DVD-quality video.[5]

To be fair, not all that "information" is what you would call information in a colloquial conversation. Most of it is the product of automated processes and communications between computers, mobile phones, and other devices—nothing that a human brain can understand. But still.

Let's catch our breath here and move on.

From Information to Wisdom

In the 1970s, years before access to the Internet was universal, Richard Saul Wurman, then a professor of architecture in North Carolina, predicted that the oncoming information explosion would require the intervention of a new breed of professionals trained in organizing data and making sense of it. According to Wurman, the biggest challenge our species was about to face was to learn how to navigate the upcoming tsunami of bits that was cresting the horizon.

Wurman called these people *information architects.* Their discipline, *information architecture,* has been defined by others as:

- The structural design of shared information environments;
- The combination of organization, labeling, search, and navigation systems within websites and intranets;
- The art and science of shaping information products and experiences to support usability and findability;
- An emerging discipline and community of practice focused on bringing principles of design and architecture to the digital landscape.

Wurman suggests that one of the main goals of information architecture is to help users avoid *information anxiety*, the "black hole between data and knowledge."

> People still have anxiety about how to assimilate a body of knowledge that is expanding by the nanosecond.... Information anxiety is produced by the

---

5 Google Atmosphere 2010 conference.

ever-widening gap between what we understand and what we think we should understand.[6]

The gap is better represented through the diagram in **Figure 1.8**, which shows the steps separating the two extremes of Wurman's maxim. It is based on several models known as DIKW Hierarchies (Data, Information, Knowledge, Wisdom). Although the models have been criticized as simplistic and vague,[7] they are useful for explaining what visualizations and graphics are about.

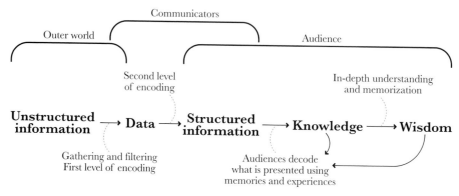

Figure 1.8 From reality to people's brains.

In the diagram, **unstructured information** means **reality**, the world out there in all its glorious complexity. Every phenomenon that can be perceived or measured can be described as information.

Data are records of observations. Data can be encoded as symbols (numbers and words) that describe and represent reality. In between unstructured information and data, you can see a **first level of encoding**. Imagine a researcher studying the fertility rate. The data would be the records the researcher makes in a spreadsheet, for instance: 2, 5, 6, 2, 2, 2, 1, 1, 4, 3, 3 (and so on) children per woman.

The **second level of encoding** takes us from data to **structured information**. This happens when a communicator (a researcher, a journalist, or whomever) represents data in a meaningful way, using text, visuals, or other means. We can also say that this communicator has given shape to data, so that relevant patterns become visible.

---

6 Wurman, p. 14.

7 David Weinberg, "The Problem with the Data-Information-Knowledge-Wisdom Hierarchy," *Harvard Business Review*, February 2010.

Information consumption can lead to higher **knowledge** on the part of the audience, if its members are able to perceive the patterns or meaning of data. It is not a passive process; our brains are not hard drives that store stuff uncritically. When people see, read, or listen, they assimilate content by relating it to their memories and experiences.

We reach **wisdom** when we achieve a deep understanding of acquired knowledge, when we not only "get it," but when new information blends with prior experience so completely that it makes us better at knowing what to do in other situations, even if they are only loosely related to the information from which our original knowledge came. Just as not all the information we absorb leads to knowledge, not all of the knowledge we acquire leads to wisdom.

Every step in our diagram implies higher **order**. When we see the world, we unconsciously impose organization on the unstructured information that our eyes gather and transmit to the brain. We create hierarchies. We don't perceive everything in front of us at once, as we'll see later in this book. A moving entity, for instance, attracts our attention more than a static one, because movement may suggest an approaching threat. We therefore process the position and identity of the moving object before paying attention to anything else. Our brain gives **meaning** to the object, even if we are not aware of the reason why.

In the words of Kevin Kelly, a famous philosopher of technology, in his book *What Technology Wants* (2010):

> Minds are highly evolved ways of structuring the bits of information that form reality. That is what we mean when we say a mind understands; it generates order.

So, without conscious effort, the brain always tries to close the distance between observed phenomena and knowledge or wisdom that can help us survive. This is what cognition means. **The role of an information architect is to anticipate this process and generate order before people's brains try to do it on their own.**

Making Reality Visible

Today, *information architect* refers broadly to professions with very different sets of tools and theoretical traditions. Outside academic circles, an information architect can be someone who writes technical handbooks, a software engineer, a web developer, a wayfinding designer (yes, that's a profession; who do you think creates public spaces that can be navigated with ease?), and that nerdy guy who makes charts on fertility just for the fun of it.

All of those professions share the goal of making the world easier for audiences and users, but that's too broad a goal to put them all in the same bag. For my purposes in this book, information graphics and visualization is a form of information architecture. But how can we be more precise in describing the relationship between the branch and the trunk?

Look at **Figure 1.9** and imagine information architecture as a big circle. Inside is the set of disciplines devoted to dealing with information. Among the most relevant disciplines is *information design*, defined by Stanford University's Robert E. Horn as "the art and science of preparing information so that it can be used by human beings with efficiency and effectiveness."[8] The goal of the information designer is to prepare documents (both analog and digital) and spaces so they can be navigated effortlessly.

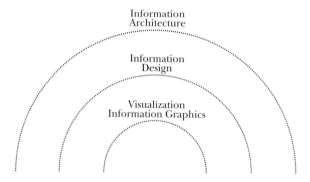

Figure 1.9 Information graphics is a form of information design. Information design branches from information architecture.

A significant part of information design is information graphics and visualization. Academic literature sometimes separates infographics from visualization and defines the latter as "the use of computer-supported, interactive, visual representations of data to amplify cognition,"[9] but I prefer the more straightforward take of Joan Costa, a famous Spanish professor of design: To visualize is "to make certain phenomena and portions of reality visible and understandable; many of these phenomena are not naturally accessible to the bare eye, and many of them are not even of visual nature."[10]

---

8 Robert Jacobson, ed. *Information Design*, (Cambridge: MIT Press, 2000).

9 Card, Stuart, Jock, Mackinlay, and Ben Shneiderman. 1999. *Readings Information Visualization: Using Vision to Think*. San Francisco: Morgan Kauffmann.

10 Joan Costa, *La esquemática: visualizar la información* (Barcelona: Editorial Paidós, Colección Paidós Estética 26, 1998). One of the best books I've read on the visual representation of information. No English version available, unfortunately.

Why does Costa add that second part about not being necessarily of visual nature? Because graphical displays can be either figurative or non-figurative. To understand figurative displays, think of a map as a scaled portrait of a geographical area, or a manual that explains through illustrations how to use your new washing machine, or a news infographic on a catastrophic plane crash, like the one in **Figure 1.10** (pages 20 and 21), a superb project by *Público*, a medium-sized Spanish newspaper with a small but extremely talented graphics desk.

Other graphics that display abstract phenomena are **non-figurative**. In these, there is no mimetic correspondence between what is being represented and its representation. The relationship between those two entities is *conventional*, not natural (see **Figure 1.11**). The unemployment rate doesn't really resemble a grid of multicolored rectangles, does it?

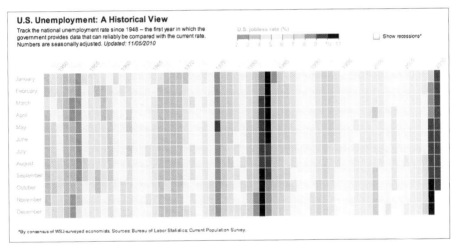

Figure 1.11 *The Wall Street Journal.* Web chart U.S. Unemployment: A Historical View. (Reprinted with permission of *The Wall Street Journal*, Copyright © 2010 Dow Jones & Company, Inc. All Rights Reserved Worldwide.)

Visualization as a Technology

Let me introduce an idea crucial to the premise of this book: **Visualization should be seen as a technology.** That may sound odd. When someone mentions technology in a routine conversation, we usually think of machines: MP3 players, cars, refrigerators, electric toothbrushes, lawn mowers, computers. But what do all those devices have in common? I don't mean *physically*, but in their very essence:

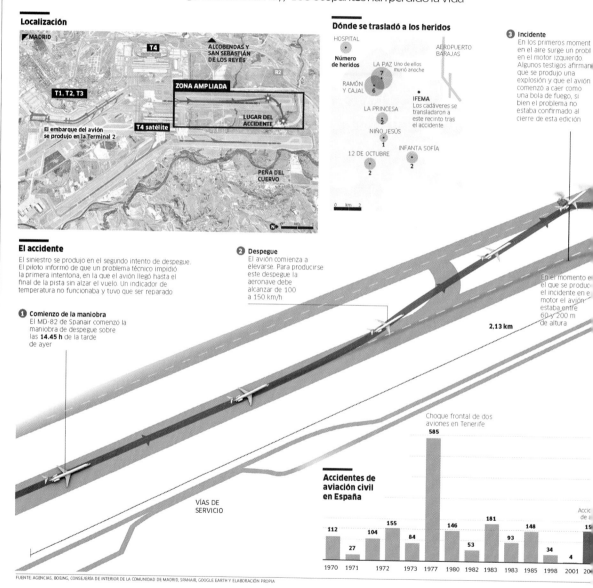

Radiografía de la catástrofe

El vuelo 5022JK de Spanair se salió de la pista de despegue a las 14:45 con 172 personas a bordo // El accidente activó todos los servicios de emergencias de Madrid // 153 ocupantes han perdido la vida

Localización

MADRID
T4
ALCOBENDAS Y SAN SEBASTIÁN DE LOS REYES
R2
T1, T2, T3
ZONA AMPLIADA
LUGAR DEL ACCIDENTE
El embarque del avión se produjo en la Terminal 2
T4 satélite
PEÑA DEL CUERVO

Dónde se trasladó a los heridos

HOSPITAL
AEROPUERTO BARAJAS
Número de heridos
LA PAZ Uno de ellos murió anoche 7
RAMÓN Y CAJAL 6
IFEMA Los cadáveres se trasladaron a este recinto tras el accidente
LA PRINCESA 2
NIÑO JESÚS 1
12 DE OCTUBRE 2
INFANTA SOFÍA 2

0 km 2

❸ **Incidente**
En los primeros moment en el aire surge un probl en el motor izquierdo. Algunos testigos afirman que se produjo una explosión y que el avión comenzó a caer como una bola de fuego, si bien el problema no estaba confirmado al cierre de esta edición

El accidente
El siniestro se produjo en el segundo intento de despegue. El piloto informó de que un problema técnico impidió la primera intentona, en la que el avión llegó hasta el final de la pista sin alzar el vuelo. Un indicador de temperatura no funcionaba y tuvo que ser reparado

❷ **Despegue**
El avión comienza a elevarse. Para producirse este despegue la aeronave debe alcanzar de 100 a 150 km/h

En el momento e el que se produc el incidente en e motor del avión estaba entre 60 y 200 m de altura

2,13 km

❶ **Comienzo de la maniobra**
El MD-82 de Spanair comenzó la maniobra de despegue sobre las **14.45 h** de la tarde de ayer

Choque frontal de dos aviones en Tenerife
585

Accidentes de aviación civil en España

VÍAS DE SERVICIO

1970	1971	1972	1973	1977	1980	1982	1983	1983	1985	1998	2001	20
112	27	104	155	84	146	53	181	93	148	34	4	15

Acci de a

FUENTE: AGENCIAS, BOEING, CONSEJERÍA DE INTERIOR DE LA COMUNIDAD DE MADRID, SPANAIR, GOOGLE EARTH Y ELABORACIÓN PROPIA

Figure 1.10 *Público* (Spain). Plane crash in Barajas airport, Madrid, August 21, 2008. Infographic by Chiqui Esteban, Mónica Serrano, Álvaro Valiño.

El dispositivo de emergencia

150 SANITARIOS

4 HELICÓPTEROS

35 AMBULANCIAS

5 VEHÍCULOS DE INTERVENCIÓN RÁPIDA

24 PSICÓLOGOS Y PSIQUIATRAS

5 AUTOBOMBAS DE BOMBEROS

24 UVI MÓVILES

2 PUESTOS DE ATENCIÓN MÉDICA AVANZADA

Balance de víctimas

En el avión viajaban **172** personas, **163** eran pasajeros y los otros **nueve**, miembros de la tripulación

153 muertos

12 graves

19 heridos

2 muy graves   2 leves   3 con pronóstico reservado

Dos personas no llegaron a embarcar por llegar unos minutos tarde a facturación

4 Caída
La nave se precipita hacia la derecha de la pista en la que despegó

5 Impacto
El avión termina en una zona arbolada entre las dos pistas de despegue y aterrizaje más cercanas a la Terminal 4. El avión queda destrozado y partido en varios pedazos y comienza a arder

6 Incendio
El fuego se propaga por la zona arbolada, produciendo una gran columna de humo negro

Los restos de la nave fueron a parar a un arroyo

Los restos de la nave fueron a parar a un arroyo

CARRETERA DE SERVICIO
Por ella accedieron gran parte de los equipos de emergencia que acudieron a socorrer a las víctimas

El historial negro del MD-82

La nave, que ya se ha dejado de construir, cuenta con un historial de cerca de 500 muertos en estos últimos seis años

112	CHINA 2002	Incendio en la cabina. Pudo tratarse de un sabotaje
160	VENEZUELA 2005	Se estrelló en una zona montañosa
91	PHUKET, TAILANDIA 2005	El avión se partió en dos al aterrizar
153	BARAJAS, AYER	Problema en el motor izquierdo

El avión

El avión iba bastante cargado de combustible para cubrir la distancia del itinerario previsto

MADRID

1.800 km

1.800 km

LAS PALMAS DE GRAN CANARIA

MD-82
CONFIGURADO PARA 172 PASAJEROS

Construcción 1994
Operando con Spanair desde 1999

Velocidad de crucero
811 km/h

Autonomía
3.798 km

INTERIOR

Cabina

2.04 m

Bodegas

3,34 m

12,2 m

32,8 m

9,05 m

45,1 m

MOTORES
Modelo Pratt & Whitney JT8D-217 A/C

Peso
9.072 kg

GRÁFICO: CHIQUI ESTEBAN, MÓNICA SERRANO, ÁLVARO VALIÑO

1. **They are extensions of ourselves.** Canadian media thinker Marshall McLuhan was the first to advance this notion half a century ago. A lawn mower helps us keep our garden neat without having to use our bare hands. An electric toothbrush reaches small spaces in between our teeth that would be impossible to reach with a toothpick—which is also a technology, by the way. An MP3 player is not just a player, but also a device that helps us remember the songs that define the best and worst moments of our lives.

2. **They are means to reach goals.** Sometimes it's just one goal—a freezer keeps food fresh—but it can be several. Think of a computer, whose functionality depends on other technologies such as software that we install. Technologies can harbor other technologies.

Visualization as technology has these same traits. Also, the word *technology* has various meanings and is potentially open to interpretation. I use it here with the sense given by W. Brian Arthur in his foundational *The Nature of Technology* (2009). According to Arthur, we can use the word *technology* in three different senses, illustrated in **Figure 1.12**: Technologies-singular, technologies-plural, and technology-general.

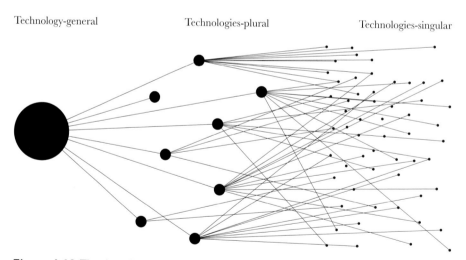

Technology-general   Technologies-plural   Technologies-singular

Figure 1.12 The three kinds of technology: general, plural, and singular.

What Arthur means is that technology can be, first, any object, process, or method devised to aid in a task, "a means to fulfill a human purpose." This can be called *technology-singular*. The refrigerator and other devices described above are examples. The algorithms that run a software program as well as the letters, sentences, and paragraphs that help me communicate with you are also technologies-singular. Even a humble nail is a technology.

Technologies-plural describe "assemblages of practices and components." In other words, they are groups of technology-singular items that, when put together, make something new emerge. Electronics, biochemistry, and the varieties of engineering are all technologies-plural. Arthur also refers to technology-plural groups as "bodies of technology."

The third meaning of technology is "the entire collection of devices and engineering practices available to a culture," or *technology-general*.

How is this relevant for information graphics and visualization? First, as emerging disciplines, they are still a formative hodge-podges of concepts, methods, and procedures borrowed from many areas: the principles of map design (from cartography); guidelines on how to better display data on a chart (from statistics); rules on best practices for the use of type, layout, and color palettes (from graphic design); principles of writing style (from journalism); and more, including a wide array of software tools.

Second, and more important, **individual information graphics are also technologies, means to fulfill purposes, devices whose aim is to help an audience complete certain tasks**. This apparent no-brainer will have consequences later on. If you accept that a visualization is, above all, a *tool*, you are implicitly accepting that the discipline it belongs to is not just art, but *functional art*, something that achieves beauty not through the subjective, freely wandering self-expression of the painter or sculptor, but through the careful and restrained tinkering of the engineer.

2

Forms and Functions: Visualization as a Technology

The usefulness of a graph can be evaluated only in the context of the type of data, the questions the designer wants the readers to answer, and the nature of the audience.

—Stephen M. Kosslyn, from *Graph Design for the Eye and Mind*

The fact that an information graphic is designed to help us complete certain intellectual tasks is what distinguishes it from fine art. Rather than serving as a means for the artist to express her inner world and feelings, an infographic or visualization strives for objectivity, precision, and functionality, as well as beauty. In short:

The function constrains the form.

In this chapter I will explore this idea and its usefulness for infographics and visualization, starting with the original phrase "form follows function," and the critiques and iterations it has undergone over time. The original idea remains the same, but these iterations contribute to a more nuanced understanding of what the relationship between forms and functions entails.

An Information Graphic on Defense

Let's start with a real-life example to illustrate what I mean. Although Brazil is a huge country and the main power in South America, its armed forces are not on par with its status as the sixth-largest economy in the world. Proportionally, some of Brazil's neighbors, such as Venezuela and Chile, invest much more each year in keeping their armies, naval fleets, and air forces up to date. And that's an issue: Brazilians are proud of their newly earned status as an almost-developed nation, and they want the world to know about it. So, in August 2008, the Brazilian government announced a new strategic defense plan, the culmination of a public discussion that had begun many years before.

Brazil's main newspaper is *Folha de São Paulo*. It has the biggest information graphics staff in the country, full of great talent. *Folha* dedicated an entire page to then-President Lula da Silva's new strategic plan. It was a critical story, explaining that some of the defense investments were not well planned, and that some of Brazil's rivals in the region were better focused on what was really needed to defend their territories and offshore waters.

Two information graphics accompanied the story. The first detailed the Brazilian defense budget for 2009. The second, which was the source for **Figure 2.1**, was titled "The Defense of the Neighbors: An overview of the armed forces of countries surrounding Brazil."

I will use Figure 2.1 to demonstrate an exercise I recommend you try whenever you see an information graphic in a newspaper, magazine, book, or website. Practice this exercise and it will help you become an infographics and visualization expert. The first part is simple. Ask yourself:

What does the designer want me to do with this graphic?

In other words: **If we accept that an infographic is, at its core, a tool, what tasks is this one intended to help me with?** Here is my personal list for the Brazilian defense graphic:

1. The graphic must ***present*** several variables—armed forces personnel, population to be defended, defense budget, and so forth—so that I have the proper information in front of me.

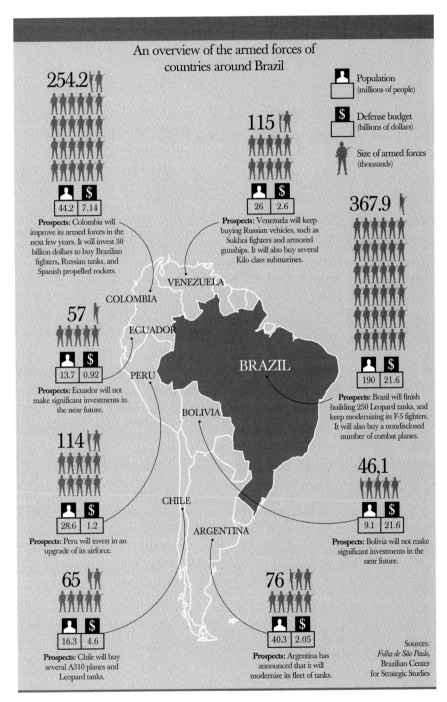

Figure 2.1 A portrait of the power balance in South America.

2. It should allow *comparisons*. At a glance, I should be able to tell which country has the biggest and the smallest army, is more or less populated, or invests more heavily or lightly in its military.

3. It should help me *organize* countries, from the biggest to the smallest, based on the variables and the comparisons.

4. It should make *correlations or relationships* evident to me. For instance, are population and size of defense forces directly and perfectly proportional?

Of those four possible tasks—present, compare, organize, correlate—the graphic accomplishes *just one* satisfactorily. It presents tons of variables and values. But it doesn't show them in proportion to one another. This makes it impossible for readers to dig into the data.

Imagine you're a concerned Brazilian patriot. Your first impulse will probably be to compare your country with Venezuela and Argentina, Brazil's main commercial and strategic rivals in the region. See how difficult this operation is? If you want to compare, say, population, you will have to read all the numbers, memorize them, and then organize them in your head. The same thing happens when you try to compare the countries' defense budgets.

You need a pretty powerful memory to do that. From a functional standpoint, there's little difference between this graphic and a simple table. The graphic may be prettier, but it still makes you work too hard to extract basic meanings.

There's something else: Does the map need to be the main visual element in the composition? I doubt it. Using so much real estate for the map suggests that the main goal of the graphic is to show where Brazil's neighboring countries are—and likely most or all of *Folha de São Paulo*'s readers know that already.

To be fair in my remarks, I know that a single *Folha de São Paulo* designer had just two hours to produce this infographic after obtaining the data from a reporter. That's how things work in newspapers. Turnaround times for breaking-news projects are tight. Still, I believe that the graphic could have been greatly improved with 10 or 15 minutes of planning.

Here's where the second part of our exercise begins.

What Shape Should My Data Have?

Once we have listed the goals our graphic should help accomplish, it's time to consider what shape the numbers should adopt.

Let's start with the comparison. As originally published, the infographic doesn't make our lives easy. The numbers are there, but populations and budgets are not visually represented. Comparing the figures mentally—which is what we are forcing readers to do if they want to get an idea of the proportional sizes of those variables in different countries—is too hard.

Military personnel are represented by tiny silhouettes, each equivalent to 1,000 soldiers. But in the original, the symbols are useless because the bars formed by the little soldiers do not sit on the same horizontal axis. This makes comparisons more difficult than they should be. See how much easier things are if we place the columns of soldiers side by side, as shown in **Figure 2.2**.

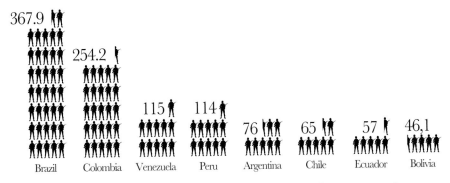

Figure 2.2 Simply placing the bars on the same horizontal axis allows you to make more accurate comparisons.

If you accept that bars facilitate comparison better than other ways of encoding the variables, let's represent the countries' military personnel as bars and organize them from biggest to smallest amounts. In **Figure 2.3** you can see the result: Readers can now easily identify the winners and losers in the South American arms race (I'm being a bit hyperbolic), a task that required far more cognitive energy in the original *Folha de São Paulo* graphic.

At this point we face a challenge. It would seem Brazil will be the winner in all of the rankings, because the bigger the population a country has, the bigger its military forces and heftier its defense budget will be. But is this relationship perfectly proportional? In other words, if population is *n* times bigger in one country than in another, will armed forces also be *n* times larger?

This question is related to the fourth task, *correlation* among variables. The bars in the previous figure don't address that goal. That is because they encode *absolute* figures.

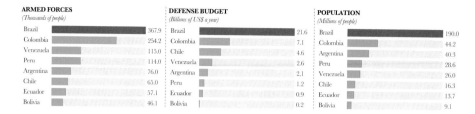

Figure 2.3 Let's get rid of the pictograms and use a traditional bar chart.

Think about it this way: What if you want to compare violent crime in Detroit, Michigan, against figures in Poughkeepsie, New York? You would never use an absolute variable, such as the *total* number of people killed, because Detroit is much bigger than Poughkeepsie, so the total number of crimes will also be enormous.

Instead, you would choose a *derived* variable; that is, you would obtain the number of homicides in each city, divide it by the population, and then multiply the result by 100,000. You would then get the *homicides per 100,000 people*.

The same can be applied to our Brazilian defense graphic. See what happens when we control the armed forces sizes by population, or when we calculate per capita spending in defense? The rankings look much different. Compared with Figure 2.3, **Figure 2.4** gives readers an additional and useful level of depth and understanding: The biggest armies in *absolute* terms may not be the biggest ones in *relative* terms. In relative terms, our Brazilian patriot would surely be alarmed, because her country ranks second *from the bottom*. Countries like Venezuela and Bolivia are more militarized, and Colombia is far ahead because of its war on narco-guerrillas.

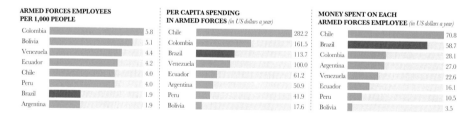

Figure 2.4 The country rankings change quite a bit when you encode secondary variables instead of absolute numbers.

Are there ways of representing correlations using absolute variables? Sure. You could design a scatter-plot, a type of chart mentioned in Chapter 1. In the redesign

I put together after thinking about *Folha de São Paulo's* original graphic (**Figure 2.5**), I included another version titled, "A different look at the data." If this were a real project, I would not have done this because it tells essentially the same story as the two sets of bar charts, but it illustrates an important point: **In most cases, there is not just one way of encoding a particular set of data properly.** You may have more than one option, but your goal must be always to think first about what kinds of questions readers are more likely to want answered by your infographic.

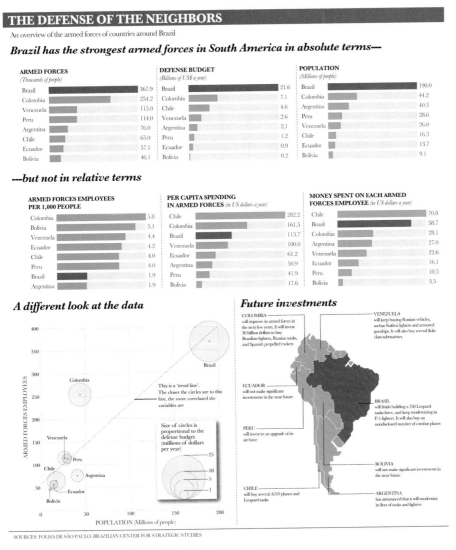

Figure 2.5 A different take on the defense infographic.

The Origins of "Form Follows Function"

The maxim "form follows function" was born in 1896 when the American architect Louis Sullivan wrote an article titled, "The Tall Office Building Artistically Considered." In it, Sullivan discussed the needs of the occupants of big office buildings, which had begun to proliferate at the end of the nineteenth century. The most widely cited paragraph is:

> All things in nature have a shape, that is to say, a form, an outward semblance, that tells us what they are, that distinguishes them from ourselves and from each other. Unfailing in nature these shapes express the inner life, the native quality of the animal, tree, bird, fish, that they present to us; they are so characteristic, so recognizable, that we say, simply, it is "natural" it should be so (...) It is the pervading law of all things organic and inorganic, of all things physical and metaphysical, of all things human and all things superhuman, of all true manifestations of the head, of the heart, of the soul, that the life is recognizable in its expression, that **form ever follows function**. This is the law.[1]

Those highlighted words were defining for twentieth-century architecture and had an enormous influence on contemporary masters, either because they embraced them (the Bauhaus school), or because they rejected them or introduced their own nuances (Frank Lloyd Wright). Some of the most renowned ideas of luminaries like Le Corbusier, who defined a house as "a machine for living in," connect directly to Sullivan.

Today, we interpret Sullivan's idea as a call to center any design, regardless of its nature—a building, a tool, a software program—on the user. However, that was not exactly what Sullivan had in mind when he wrote his article. His "function" is not a goal in the sense of a task that the tool is designed to help achieve, but rather, an intrinsic property of both artificial and natural entities, a kind of essence. According to Sullivan, the form of a thing is a clue to its nature.

The fact that we misinterpret Sullivan is one of those fortunate paradoxes that make history colorful. Taken in a literal sense, the original paragraph includes several fallacies worth discussing before we can understand the relationship between form and function in visualization.

---

1 Louis Sullivan, "The Tall Office Building Artistically Considered," *Lippincott's Magazine*, March, 1896, accessed Feb. 11, 2012, http://academics.triton.edu/faculty/fheitzman/tallofficebuilding.html.

Consider this:

> All things in nature have a shape ..., an outward semblance, that tells us what they are .... Unfailing in nature these shapes express the inner life, the native quality of the animal, tree, bird, fish, that they present to us.

If you remember something from your high school biology classes, you'll understand why this is appealing at first but ultimately absurd. If we follow Sullivan's rationale, we could hypothesize, as pre-modern thinkers did, that fishes and dolphins belong to the same animal order, because the shapes of their bodies are pretty much identical. Or we could say that hippopotami are cousins of elephants and rhinoceros, since all three share features such as thick legs and bodies, and tons of body fat under hard skins. But, as always happens in science, evidence (in this case, genetics) contradicts appearances. The hippopotamus descended from whales that evolved to return from the sea to the land.[2] Never trust your intuitions without testing them.

Even in the world of technology, the idea that the shape of an object is unequivocally connected to its functions is not valid. True, a spoon is concave and solid so no liquid can fall through it, so one can deduce that we can use it to bring liquid food to our mouths. But what about an iPod? Does the shape of its central wheel naturally suggest the way it should be used? Hardly. In this case, the connection between form and function must be learned. It is in reflections such as these that we see that Sullivan's law cannot be strictly applied.

More about Functions in Nature

Another problem with Sullivan's law is that the sentence "form follows function" indicates that the relationship between the two components is unidirectional. At first this seems intuitive. After all, what are a couple of feather-covered wings for, if not for flying? If wings have evolved, it must be because some animals felt the need to flee from predators or to reach fruits growing on treetops.

The problem is that the world doesn't work that way. A species doesn't *feel* a need first (the *function*) and then develops an organ to fulfill it (the *form*). If you've ever had this kind of thought—some people still do—you've fallen prey to what is known as the *Lamarckian Fallacy*.

Jean-Baptiste Lamarck, who lived between the nineteenth and twentieth centuries, was one of the first scientists to describe the mechanism that guides evolution. In his time, evidence existed linking living species to usually extinct ancestors,

2 Carl Zimmer, *At the Water's Edge* (New York: Touchstone, 1999).

who in turn were heirs of even older ancestors, and so on, in a chain dating to the beginning of time. What Lamarck and other scientists had not discovered was the hidden logic of this phenomenon, the underlying force that leads one animal or vegetable to become a completely different one given enough time.

Lamarck proposed a scientific theory called "inheritance of acquired characteristics." To understand it, let's consider giraffes, a descendant of ancient creatures that supposedly were similar to modern antelopes. How did the giraffe evolve its long neck?

According to Lamarckian logic, thousands and thousands of years ago, some antelopes felt the need to feed on tree leaves beyond the reach of their mandibles. They began stretching their necks to get them. As a consequence, they were born with slightly longer necks than the previous generation. But this is like saying that if I start doing heavy bodybuilding today and become a clone of Sylvester Stallone, my kids will be born with steel muscles. To the followers of Lamarckism, form *literally* follows function. The former pushes the latter.

Thanks to Charles Darwin, though, we now know that evolution doesn't work that way. Darwin's *On the Origin of Species* was published in 1859 and offered an alternative to Lamarck's hypothesis. The force that moves evolution forward is not the acquisition of characteristics and skills inherited by kin, but the natural selection of traits that help an organism survive in its environment. What Darwin did was to invert Lamarck's logic: Function doesn't *determine* form. In fact, in many cases, the opposite is true.

First, let's be clear about what Darwin meant by *natural selection.* Back to our friend the giraffe, a Darwinian narrative of its origin might run like this:[3] Many generations ago, the ancestors of the giraffe lived in grasslands and forests and fed on vegetation. Every time a new calf was born, it could have a neck that was slightly longer or shorter than its parents because of tiny mutations in its DNA (Darwin didn't know about DNA, but it doesn't matter; he did know that children look very much like their parents.) This is called *variation.*

In a particular moment in time—maybe because a drought made grass scarce, or because some pre-giraffe families moved to savannahs where food was difficult to find—having a slightly longer neck than your kin suddenly became an advantage. You could feed on tree leaves that were far from the ground.

---

3 The giraffe story has not been confirmed but is plausible. See "On the origin, evolution and phylogeny of giraffes *Giraffa camelopardalis,*" by G. Mitchell and J. D. Skinner, Transactions of the Royal Society South Africa, 58 (1), 2003, pp. 51-72. Accessed Feb. 11, 2012 from http://www.bringyou.to/GiraffeEvolution.pdf.

The pre-giraffes that had longer necks tended to live longer and have better health (on average) than their congeners. They also reproduced more and passed the longer-neck gene mutations to their offspring. Successive mutations leading to even longer necks may have given subsequent generations an even bigger competitive advantage, in a fortuitous circle.

In other words, the need to reach higher every day (the *function*) didn't force the development of longer necks (the *form*). Longer necks were the result of random genetic mutations that were *nonrandomly* filtered (that is, selected) by the environment. In nature, then, relationships between forms and functions are much more complex than what Sullivan thought.

Another factor also counters the idea of a cause-effect relationship between functions and forms. Remember our question, "What are a couple of feather-covered wings for, if not for flying?" Well, wings were certainly not for flying at first. Birds descended from dinosaurs that began to evolve feathers not for flight, but for maintaining body temperature and attracting mates. The functions of feathers—that is, their competitive advantages—were to keep their owner warm and make the creature more handsome.

But evolution eventually crossed paths with another possible function: to control the movement of air around the feathered extremities, which allowed a primitive form of gliding. This is an example of what paleontologist Stephen Jay Gould called *exaptation*, by which a trait that evolves in response to an environmental challenge is used for an entirely different purpose (flying).[4]

Exaptations are common in technology as well. The Internet could be analyzed as an exaptation. Designed to enhance communication between scientists, it ended up being adopted by the public as a virtual world that facilitates many kinds of human sharing. Guttenberg's printing press was based on technologies previously used to crush grapes and make wine. The original function of presses was to crush grapes, and their form was well suited to that function. It just happened that someone eventually saw that the form of those machines could have an entirely different function.[5]

Cases such as these help us understand that the relationship between forms and functions is *bidirectional*. Form doesn't *always* follow function; in many cases, the function follows a form that previously followed another unrelated function. It is

4 Stephen Jay Gould and Elisabeth Vrba, "Exaptation - A Missing Term in the Science of Form, Paleontology," 8(1), Winter, 1982, 4-15.

5 Steven Johnson, *Where Good Ideas Come From: The Natural History of Innovation* (New York: Penguin Group, 2010).

easy to imagine one of our ancestors, hundreds of thousands of years ago, walking through the woods and finding a sharp triangular rock. Our ancestor picks up the rock and notices that it perfectly fits the palm of his hand. What is the function of that form? None, until our ancestor sees a goal that matches what the rock's shape suggests: *It may be used for cutting fur, flesh, and bone.* Nature becomes technology through the eyes and mind of an intelligent agent.

Functions Constrain Forms

The fact that Louis Sullivan was misguided in his coarse essentialism doesn't disprove the idea that forms and functions are and must be closely related. It is true, as we just have seen, that function doesn't necessarily determine form. But it is also true that **the form of a technological object must depend on the tasks it should help with.** This is one of the most important principles to remember when dealing with infographics and visualizations: **The form should be constrained by the functions of your presentation.** There may be more than one form a data set can adopt so that readers can perform operations with it and extract meanings, but the data cannot adopt *any* form. Choosing visual shapes to encode information should not be based on aesthetics and personal tastes alone.

In general, **the better defined the goals of an artifact, the narrower the variety of forms it can adopt**. Let me illustrate this principle with several real-world examples.

More than a decade ago, I worked for several print newspapers in Spain and became familiar with the templates used for stories that repeat on a regular basis. This is common practice in news media: If you know that you will publish, say, an infographic on the unemployment rate every month, or a weather page every day, why would you design a new graphic for each occasion? Using templates saves time. Unfortunately, it also encourages inertia. Bringing up the template file over and over again invites you not to think deeply about its structure and appropriateness. Just open it, update it with the new data, save it, and move on to more interesting stuff.

The infographic in **Figure 2.6** is similar to the template many newspapers in Spain use to publish monthly government data on unemployment. It presents all the numbers and includes a layer of information that aggregates them, offering a quick overview of the data. Three different tones of gray represent the higher-than-average, on-average, and below-average employment regions. But let's apply a little question-based critique to test it. Try to answer these questions in less than five seconds each:

1. In which region has unemployment grown the most?

2. In which one has it dropped the most?

3. Has the unemployment change been bigger in Madrid, La Rioja, or Canarias?

4. Has unemployment dropped more in Extremadura, Andalucía, or Baleares?

Likely, you can't do it. I did not ask myself such questions when I was designing these kinds of graphics, but I do now. My perspective has changed. I no longer think like a designer, but like a reader. And, as a reader, those are the kinds of answers that I want to get using this kind of tool.

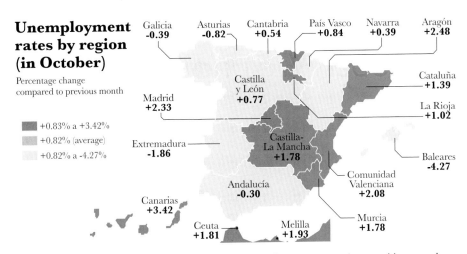

Figure 2.6 A type of graphic very common in Spanish newspapers: the monthly unemployment rate change.

The challenge of this graphic is similar to the one we analyzed in the first pages of this chapter. Here's what happens when you try to complete any of the operations above:

1. Your eyes look for the numbers mentioned in the question.

2. Your brain memorizes them.

3. Your brain organizes the numbers from biggest to smallest (or vice versa).

4. Your brain compares the reorganized numbers.

That's too much work. If we know that readers are likely to look for how their own region fits into the big picture, *why not anticipate it?* **Figure 2.7** represents exactly the same data, but offers more options to explore them.

Again, the map: Is it necessary? Perhaps. In this case, the geographical location of the regions may be relevant, as it shows that unemployment is getting worse in the southeast of Spain.

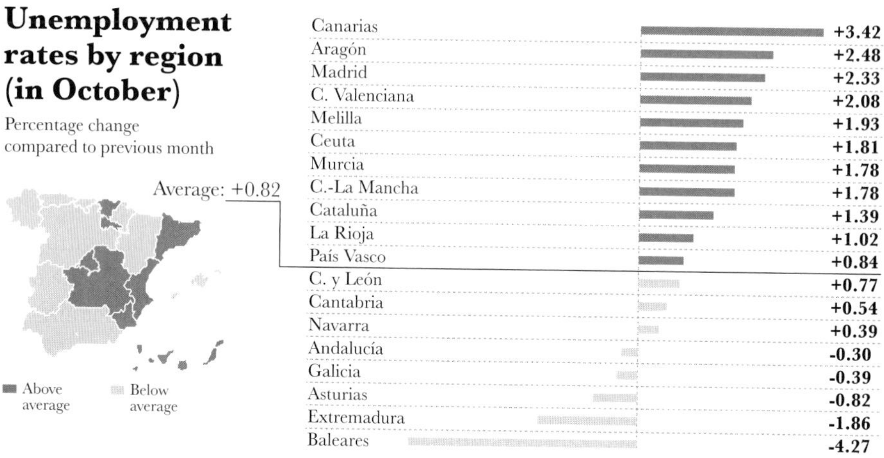

Unemployment rates by region (in October)

Percentage change compared to previous month

Average: +0.82

Above average   Below average

Canarias	+3.42
Aragón	+2.48
Madrid	+2.33
C. Valenciana	+2.08
Melilla	+1.93
Ceuta	+1.81
Murcia	+1.78
C.-La Mancha	+1.78
Cataluña	+1.39
La Rioja	+1.02
País Vasco	+0.84
C. y León	+0.77
Cantabria	+0.54
Navarra	+0.39
Andalucía	-0.30
Galicia	-0.39
Asturias	-0.82
Extremadura	-1.86
Baleares	-4.27

Figure 2.7 This variation of the unemployment rate graphic allows you to compare and rank Spain's regions.

In an interview with *Technical Communication Quarterly* in 2004, Edward Tufte, arguably the most influential theoretician in visualization and information design (which he prefers to call *analytical design*), defined the relationship between form and function succinctly:

> Effective analytic designs entail turning thinking principles into seeing principles. So, if the thinking task is to understand causality, the task calls for a design principle: "Show causality." If a thinking task is to answer a question and compare it with alternatives, the design principle is: "Show comparisons." The point is that analytical designs are not to be decided on their convenience to the user or necessarily their readability or what psychologists or decorators think about them; rather, design architectures should be decided on how the architecture assists analytical thinking about evidence.[6]

6 Mark Zachary and Charlotte Thralls, "An Interview with Edward Tufte," *Technical Communication Quarterly*, 2004, 13(4), 447-462. Accessed Feb. 11, 2012 at http://www.edwardtufte.com/tufte/s15427625tcq1304_5.pdf.

Clear enough. But this idea is not as obvious as it should be, as the previous examples prove. A simple Google search on *infographics* will return thousands of links to projects in which the designer didn't choose graphic forms according to how well they assist thinking, but because they looked cool, innovative, or funny. Designers who don't develop the crucial skill of asking themselves, "What is my graphic for?" are easy victims of fashion. No fashion plague is more prevalent as I write this book than the bubble.

The Bubble Plague

The overuse of bubble charts in news media is a good example of how infographics departments can become more worried about how their projects look than with how they work. When I give presentations, I often use charts like the one in **Figure 2.8**, which I made up based on a real project by *Bloomberg News.*

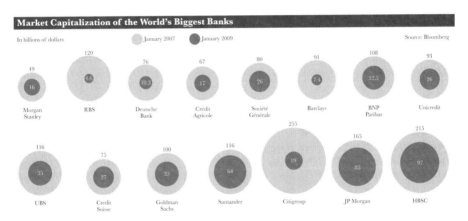

Figure 2.8 Banks as shrinking bubbles. How appropriate. This example is inspired by an article by Stephen Few: "Our Irresistible Fascination with All Things Circular": http://www.perceptualedge.com/articles/visual_business_intelligence/our_fascination_with_all_things_circular.pdf

When I ask the audience for their reaction to the graphic, the answer usually is, "I don't see a problem. It is clear that the value of all banks in the chart fell dramatically during the 2007–2008 economic meltdown." I agree; that's what I see as well. Immediately, I show a different slide, **Figure 2.9**, and ask, "If you know that Société Générale's market capitalization was $80 billion in 2007, how much was it in 2009?" (Try to answer the question without looking at Figure 2.8.)

Market Capitalization of Société Générale

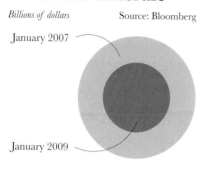

Billions of dollars   Source: Bloomberg

January 2007

January 2009

Figure 2.9 The first bubble represents $80 billion. What percentage of that does the second bubble represents? Half, perhaps?

According to my informal records, more than 70 percent of attendees guess that the answer is slightly more than $40 billion. In other words, they see the smaller bubble as being *half* the size of the bigger one.

Then I switch to **Figure 2.10** and tell them that the length of the bars display *exactly* the same numbers as the areas of the bubbles. This figure makes it clear that the value of Société Générale in 2009 was around *one third* of what it was in 2007. The surprised looks I get when they see this are a lot of fun.

Market Capitalization of Société Générale

Billions of dollars   Source: Bloomberg

January 2007

January 2009

Figure 2.10 Our friend, the bar chart, comes to the rescue.

Why do so many people overestimate the number for 2009 in the bubble chart? Because the human brain is not good at calculating surface sizes. It is much better at comparing *a single dimension* such as length *or* height. As we'll see in the second section of this book, the brain is also a hopelessly lazy machine. When faced with the question of whether that bear running toward you is big enough to pose a threat, the brain doesn't waste time or energy analyzing if the bear is tall *and* wide. Seeing if it's *just tall* is good enough. In **Figure 2.11**, what you want your readers to compare (the areas) is on the left; what they *actually* compare (the diameters) is on the right.

Figure 2.11 You want readers to compare areas, but they tend to compare heights.

The objection I usually hear when I build my case against bubbles as a means to facilitate *precise* comparisons between magnitudes is, "I understand your point, but you're cheating. You've hidden all the values. If you hadn't done so, there'd be no problem." Granted, but in that case, *what do you need the bubbles for?* Bubbles are misleading. They make you underestimate differences. In Figure 2.8, consider Santander Bank. Can you tell without reading the numbers that its value in 2009 was *half* what it was in 2007? I'll bet you can't. If you are as absent-minded as I am and don't pay close attention to the graphic, you may walk away with the idea that Santander didn't suffer much during the crisis.

If the bubbles have no functional purpose, why not design a simple and honest table? Because circles *look good*. They are decorative.

Are there other ways to design this chart respecting Edward Tufte's principle of transforming thinking principles into design principles? Certainly. As we discussed earlier, function doesn't dictate form. It constrains your options, but you still *have* options. You can design a chart that not only allows comparisons, but also focuses on changes that occurred between the two years. (See **Figure 2.12**.)

Is it always wrong to represent numbers with bubbles? No. Let's return to our most cherished principle of the infographic as a tool whose shapes should be chosen according to intended goals. The banks infographic is supposed to help us make precise comparisons between values. But see the map in **Figure 2.13**, published by *The New York Times* after the 2004 presidential elections. Each circle represents the margin of votes in those counties won by John Kerry (blue) or by George W. Bush (red). In cartography, this kind of map is called a proportional symbol map.

Why was the bank infographic ineffective, whereas this map works? The reason lies in their goals. The goal of the election map is not that readers should be able to accurately compare Manhattan's bubble with Houston's. It would take a different kind of chart to facilitate that task. The goal here is to help readers *identify general patterns of concentration* of Democratic and Republican votes.

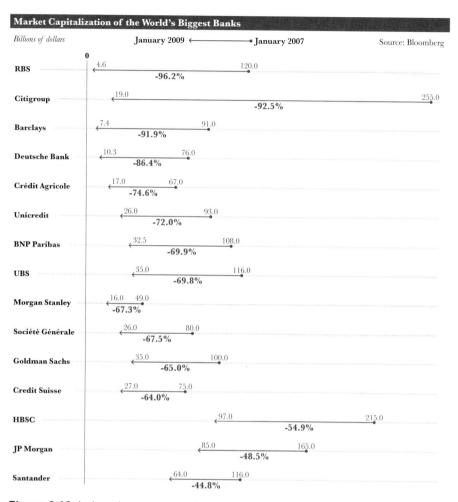

Figure 2.12 A chart that represents change.

Red and Blue, the Divided Electorate, in All Its Shades

The simple formula for winning an election is to get more votes than your opponent in as many counties as possible. It worked for President Bush. The map below, which uses the size of circles to indicate a candidate's winning margin, shows how it played out. Senator John Kerry had huge margins in many counties with large cities, and those margins were enough for him to win some of those states. However, Mr. Bush's relatively smaller but consistent margins in suburban and rural counties, in much of the South and West, helped him overcome Mr. Kerry's urban-county margins.

Figure 2.13 A proportional symbol map is appropriate when your goal is to visualize the big picture. It allows you to perceive general patterns and trends.

More Flexible Than It Seems

I don't want you to leave this chapter with the impression that choosing the right graphic forms for each story is an easy task. It is tempting to propose rock-solid rules—if you want to show change through time, use a time-series chart; if you need to compare, use a bar chart; or to display correlation, use a scatter-plot—because some of these rules make good common sense. There is even evidence supporting the use of certain kinds of charts for particular goals. (See **Figure 2.14**.)

But reality is complex, and hard-and-fast rules can transform sound advice into immovable law. Exceptions and nuances can arise with the particularities of each project. What is really important is to remember that no matter how creative and innovative you wish to be in your graphics and visualizations, the first thing you must do, before you put a finger on the computer keyboard, is **ask yourself what users are likely to try to do with your tool**.

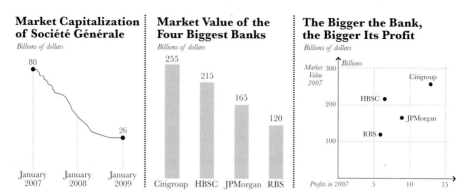

Figure 2.14 Three very common kinds of charts: (from left to right, time series chart, bar chart, and scatter-plot chart.

3

The Beauty Paradox:
Art and Communication

No one can write decently who is distrustful of the reader's intelligence, or whose attitude is patronizing.

—E. B. White, from *The Elements of Style*

Learning to deal with frustration is part of professional life. So is being able to explain what you do and why you do it. I kept repeating those maxims to myself on November 1, 2010, after the weekly news magazine I worked for, *Época*, published what I considered a decent graphic about the prison population in Brazil.

It all began two weeks before. As the magazine's infographics director, one of my responsibilities was to coordinate a two-page section called "Diagram," a news story told through short pieces of text, statistical charts, maps, and illustrations. "Diagram" was our big infographic of the week, and we put a lot of effort and resources into it.

From January 2010, when I was hired, to that moment in November, we had published more than 30 "Diagrams," each a detailed visual description of subjects as diverse as demographics; spaceships; boats made of thousands of recycled plastic bottles (its name is *Plastiki*); *and* election results, with a wide assortment of other data-based stories besides.

Part of my job was to dream up potential stories for "Diagrams," so I read several newspapers a day looking for inspiration. An item published by *Estado de São Paulo*, one of Brazil's three largest newspapers, caught my eye. It contained data recently released by the Ministry of Justice revealing a surge in the number of prison inmates over the previous four years. Surprisingly, although *Estado* cited the ministry's exhaustive database, it did not include a chart.

Stories about packed prisons in Brazil are nothing new. The problem dates to a military dictatorship that ruled the country between 1964 and 1985, and, paradoxically, it has only gotten worse as the police and judiciary have become more efficient. More efficiency leads to more criminals behind bars, which is good, but it also pressures federal and state governments to keep up by building more facilities. There's never enough money for that.

When dealing with a story that people are already familiar with, what you lack in novelty must be compensated for with depth. After all, **journalism is not just about covering the news, but also about providing context for the news**.

Building a Narrative Structure

As I was downloading and organizing the data from the Brazilian Ministry of Justice, Humberto Maia, a talented young reporter, telephoned sources who could explain what the numbers meant. He spoke with public officials, sociologists, and human rights advocates.

We decided to create a stand-alone graphic with four parts:

1. A comparison of Brazil's prison system and those of other countries between 1997 and 2007. We had found a United Nations report showing that Brazil ranked fifth in prison population growth over those years and first in the Americas. Its number of inmates grew 150 percent in that decade.

2. A list of the Brazilian states with the most drastic inmate increases between 2007 and 2010, based on the Ministry of Justice data. We decided to calculate the number of inmates per 100,000 people in each state, as this measure allows a fair comparison of regions with different-sized populations. Had we used absolute numbers, the states with more inhabitants, such as São Paulo and Rio de Janeiro, would always rank first.

3. A graphic that showed the imbalance between the number of prison inmates and the number of spaces for them in jails. In the worst cases, like the state of Acre, there were more than two prisoners per space. We included those figures.

4. Explanations highlighting the most surprising numbers. Designers sometimes forget that in many cases an infographic is a narrative based on charts, maps, and diagrams, in which text is crucial.

Our next step was to devise a structure that would make sense of the data. We decided to use headlines to guide readers through the information:

1. Between 1997 and 2007, Brazil experienced the fifth-largest increase in prison population in the world;

2. The trend has continued since 2007; and

3. Government has not kept pace with the growing prison population by building sufficient accommodations.

Figure 3.1 shows the infographic we published.

We ended up with a two-page, graphics-based story told in several layers of increasing depth and complexity that readers could explore at their leisure. While we could have restrained ourselves and merely summarized the data, I reasoned that readers living in Rio Grande do Norte, Tocantins, or Amazonas would want to analyze how their home states compared with others and with the country averages. They would want details in terms of granular data. On seeing the story in print, I believed we had created an acceptable and interesting graphic.

Not everyone agreed.

An Unexpectedly Controversial Chart

The *Época* newsroom finishes working on each issue by Friday evening. The magazine hits the newsstands Saturday morning. That gives executive editors—myself among them at the time—a chance to look over the stories and prepare for a critique meeting that takes place every Monday morning before the next edition is planned.

On Monday, November 1, 2010, I arrived in the newsroom five minutes before the meeting started. Anticipating a routine critique, I basked in the lingering feeling of peaceful drowsiness after a particularly nice, quiet weekend. **Nothing prepared me for what happened next.**

Diagram
NEWS IN PERSPECTIVE

Brazilian Population Grows More in Prisons
With 258 inmates per 100,000 people, Brazil has one of the largest prison populations.

Alberto Cairo, Humberto Maia Junior

BRAZIL IS THIRD in the worldwide ranking of countries with the largest prison populations. Data released by Ministry of Justice this week reveal that Brazil had 494,237 inmates in June 2010. Only the US, with 2.3 million, and China, with 1.6 million, have larger prison systems. According to the United Nations Office on Drugs and Crime, Brazil is one of the countries where the prison population has grown most rapidly in the world. Between 2007 and 2010, it increased by 13.3% (see chart on the right), while the overall population growth was 0.98% in the same period. Even considering the new prisons that are being built, Brazil has reached a deficit of 200,000 jail spaces.

Sources: Ministério da Justiça, IBGE, United Nations Office on Drugs and Crime

1 Between 1997 and 2007, Brazil experienced the fifth largest increase in prison population in the world.

WORLDWIDE RANKING

		Percentage change
1º	Cambodia	+ 255.3%
2º	Indonesia	+ 209.1%
3º	Cyprus	+ 155.1%
4º	Israel	+ 152.6%
5º	**BRAZIL**	**+ 150.5%**

RANKING OF AMERICAN COUNTRIES

1º	**BRAZIL**	**+ 150.5%**
2º	Uruguay	+ 101.3%
3º	Ecuador	+ 91.6%
4º	Mexico	+ 86.1%
5º	El Salvador	+ 85.5%
6º	Haiti	+ 81.4%
7º	Argentina	+ 76.7%
8º	Chile	+ 68.2%

2 The trend continued since 2007...
The rate of inmates per 100,000 people has gone down in just eight of the states plus the Federal District.

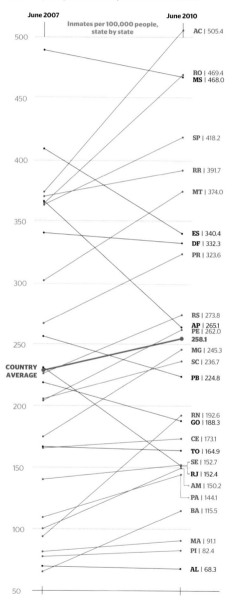

| June 2007 | Inmates per 100,000 people, state by state | June 2010 |

AC | 505.4
RO | 469.4
MS | 468.0
SP | 418.2
RR | 391.7
MT | 374.0
ES | 340.4
DF | 332.3
PR | 323.6
RS | 273.8
AP | 265.1
PE | 262.0
258.1
MG | 245.3
SC | 236.7
COUNTRY AVERAGE
PB | 224.8
RN | 192.6
GO | 188.3
CE | 173.1
TO | 164.9
SE | 152.7
RJ | 152.4
AM | 150.2
PA | 144.1
BA | 115.5
MA | 91.1
PI | 82.4
AL | 68.3

Figure 3.1 *Época* magazine (São Paulo, Brazil). Originally published in Portuguese on November 1, 2010.

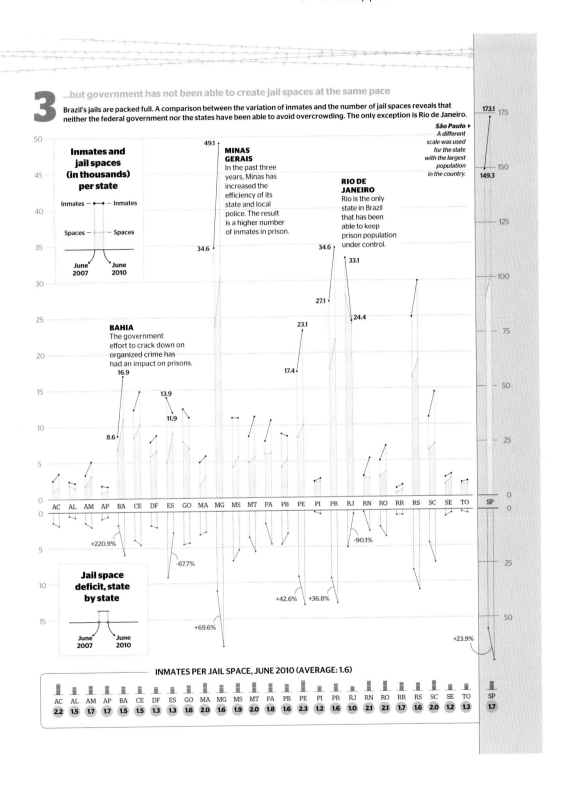

3

...but government has not been able to create jail spaces at the same pace

Brazil's jails are packed full. A comparison between the variation of inmates and the number of jail spaces reveals that neither the federal government nor the states have been able to avoid overcrowding. The only exception is Rio de Janeiro.

Inmates and jail spaces (in thousands) per state

Inmates —•—•— Inmates

Spaces .... Spaces

June 2007   June 2010

MINAS GERAIS
In the past three years, Minas has increased the efficiency of its state and local police. The result is a higher number of inmates in prison.

RIO DE JANEIRO
Rio is the only state in Brazil that has been able to keep prison population under control.

São Paulo ▶
A different scale was used for the state with the largest population in the country.

173.1 175

149.3 150

125

100

BAHIA
The government effort to crack down on organized crime has had an impact on prisons.
16.9

49.1

34.6

34.6

33.1

27.1

24.4

23.1

17.4

13.9

11.9

8.6

75

50

25

AC AL AM AP BA CE DF ES GO MA MG MS MT PA PB PE PI PR RJ RN RO RR RS SC SE TO   SP   0

+220.9%

-67.7%

-90.1%

+42.6%   +36.8%

+69.6%

+23.9%

Jail space deficit, state by state

June 2007   June 2010

25

50

INMATES PER JAIL SPACE, JUNE 2010 (AVERAGE: 1.6)

AC	AL	AM	AP	BA	CE	DF	ES	GO	MA	MG	MS	MT	PA	PB	PE	PI	PR	RJ	RN	RO	RR	RS	SC	SE	TO	SP
2.2	1.5	1.7	1.7	1.5	1.5	1.3	1.3	1.6	2.0	1.6	1.9	2.0	1.8	1.6	2.3	1.2	1.6	1.0	2.1	2.1	1.7	1.6	2.0	1.2	1.3	1.7

"I feel compelled to say that this week's 'Diagram' is horrible," said one of the executive editors. "We should strive to become more popular. Our average reader is not going to be able to understand something as complex as this."

The comment unleashed a firestorm. "I think this graphic is not friendly enough. No one will read it," said another colleague.

The director took a turn: "The problem is not complexity. The infographic is not hard to understand. The problem is that it is ugly."

"In my opinion, it has too much information," another colleague said.

Holy *crap*! I was flabbergasted. Patiently, I waited for everyone to finish tearing our project down, giving myself a chance to cool off. Then, I explained the reasoning behind the piece: the gathering of the data, the structure, the narrative, the depth. No one was convinced. It really wasn't my goal to convince them. The critique meeting is not the place to persuade others of how good your work is, but to hear suggestions for how to improve it.

Even if I disagreed with the objections, and even if, one year later, the graphic would go on to win a Malofiej Infographics award, the highest honor in the infographics field, I took the comments to heart. In fact, they led me to revisit a question that generations of designers have pondered:

What does "ugly" mean when used to describe an infographic?

That is, what did my colleagues, whose combined journalism experience totaled more than 100 years, really mean when they said that the graphic was *horrible, too complex*, and that *it could scare readers away*?

The Visualization Wheel

After the meeting, I took a couple of hours off to reflect. I grabbed a pen and paper and began sketching and taking notes, which helps me think. I listed my colleagues' opinions. According to them, our graphic was:

1. Too complex

2. Too abstract

3. Too far from the aesthetics a majority of our readers expect ("ugly")

4. Too dense

I discovered their critique could be summarized using a conceptual device I had developed while writing my first book, *Infografía 2.0* (2008, no English version available): **the visualization wheel**. See **Figure 3.2**.

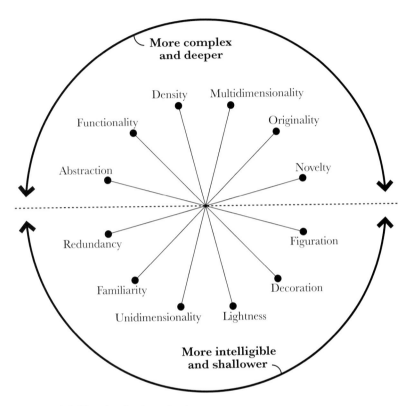

Figure 3.2 The visualization wheel.

The visualization wheel's axes correspond to the main features you need to balance when you design an information graphic. For this reason, I also refer to it as the *tension wheel*. The idea isn't so original: It's based on a similar wheel in Chapter 1 of Joan Costa's *La Esquemática* (see bibliography). My wheel includes several changes and more axes.

A word of warning before we move on: The visualization wheel is an aid I use for thinking about my own graphics. The position along each axis is therefore very subjective, so it is unlikely you'll be able to use it for academic or quantitative analyses. It is an exercise in meta-visualization: *a visualization for planning visualizations*.

Let's see how the wheel works.

The outer layer is divided into two hemispheres, each with six features. The upper hemisphere's features define graphics that are deeper and more complex. By complex I mean the amount of effort readers have to invest in deciphering a particular graphic. Depth is the number of layers of information a graphic includes.

It is possible for a graphic to be complex *and* shallow if you use a funky graphic form to encode irrelevant data, or simple *and* deep if you encode tons of data with common graphic forms. But, in general, complexity and depth are related variables in information graphics and visualizations. Graphics containing a good amount of data tend to be more difficult to read, but are also more rewarding and enlightening.

Let's look at the axes.

Abstraction-Figuration

An information graphic (or a portion of it) is completely *figurative* when the relationship between the referent and its representation is perfectly mimetic. The more distant the representation and its referent are, the more abstract the infographic will be: For example, a realistic illustration of a person is more figurative than a pictorial symbol of the person. In extreme cases, there will be no natural relationship between the two, and in those cases we would say that the connection between referent and representation is *conventional*.

You can see this axis at work in two scenes of a single interactive graphic of mine about the NASA Cassini-Huygens Mission to Saturn. See **Figure 3.3**.

The graphic in the top image is more figurative. The illustration resembles the object it intends to explain. The graphic at the bottom displaying the distances between planets in the solar system is much more abstract. In general, the more closely a graphic reproduces a material reality, the more figurative it will be.

On the other hand, if the representation involves significant conceptual manipulation on the part of the designer, it will tend to be more abstract. In the case of the Saturn mission graphic, I consciously reduced the realism of the planets to transform them into simple color circles, and I placed them on top of a distance scale—another conceptual item device.

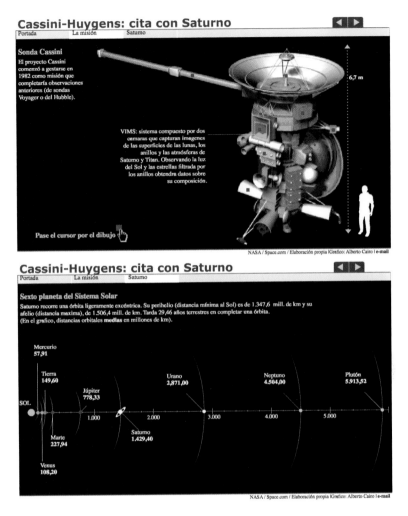

Figure 3.3 Cassini-Huygens Mission: http://www.elmundo.es/elmundo/2004/graficos/jun/s4/ cassini.html.

Functionality-Decoration

A graphic can be functional and visually pleasing, obviously, but here I am not considering stylistic elements that improve readability, such as the correct use of elegant fonts and carefully crafted color palettes. This axis refers to the inclusion of visual elements that are not directly used to enhance the comprehension of the material.

Take another look at the Brazilian prison graphic (Figure 3.1). Do you see the barbed wire? That's what I would call a non-functional visual element. It's decoration. Decoration is not bad per se, but it can interfere with the information in a chart if not handled well.

Density-Lightness

The position an infographic occupies on this axis is related to the amount of data it displays in relation to the space it uses. See the two graphics in **Figure 3.4**, which my colleagues and I created at *Época* magazine. Although almost equal in size, the graphics offer very different amounts of information. The first graphic is very dense; the second, very light, although still informative.

Multidimensionality-Unidimensionality

This axis is a measure of two related variables: the number of layers of depth a graphic lets readers navigate, and the different forms it uses to encode the data.

Consider our prison graphic. I believe that this one leans toward the *multidimensionality* side of the wheel, because it gives readers the opportunity to dig into the data quite deeply. Also, in the case of the relationship between number of inmates and jail spaces in different states, it lets them see the same data in different ways.

Another example of multidimensional infographics is **Figure 3.5**, published by *The New York Times* right after the 2004 U.S. presidential elections. The popular vote is represented by county and by population density. The electoral vote is shown state by state in a standard *choropleth map* (a map that uses different colors and shades) and in a *cartogram* (a map that distorts the relative size of regions proportionally to a variable—in this case, the number of electoral votes each state has). On top of the composition is the proportional symbol map I discussed at the end of Chapter 2, "Forms and Functions: Visualization as a Technology."

Originality-Familiarity

Some graphic forms have become so common that they are almost as readable as text. Think of bar charts, line charts, and pie charts. This has not always been so, of course. In the late eighteenth century, when the use of such charts was first systematized and theorized by polymath William Playfair, they were considered revolutionary, albeit understandable.

Figure 3.4 "Megaramp: Skate Boarding Competition in São Paulo," and "How the Brown Capuchine Macaque Hunts Termites."

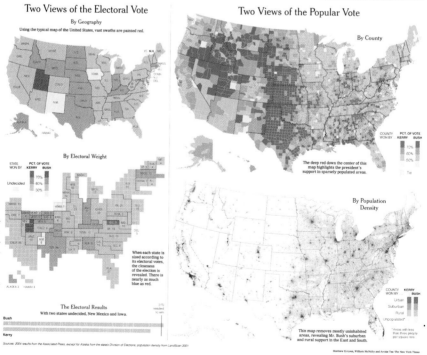

Figure 3.5 *The New York Times.* Reproduced with permission.

However, the explosion of the use of information graphics and visualization in many areas—from academic computer science departments to PR and marketing companies and more—has fueled a desire to innovate new graphical forms. An example of a form that today some people would find new or challenging is *theme rivers* (also called stream graphs), for instance. See one in **Figure 3.6**, made by Periscopic, an information visualization firm, for Yahoo!. It shows the keywords processed by Yahoo! Mail over a 30-second period. Word size and line width denote volume of occurrence. Spam keywords are shown in gray.

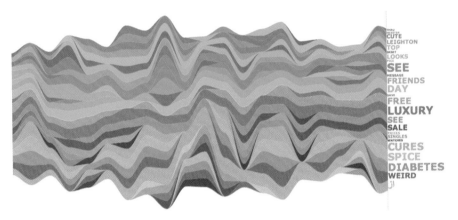

Figure 3.6 An example of a stream graph. ©2011 Yahoo! Designed by Periscopic (http://periscopic.com/).

Novelty-Redundancy

An information graphic can explain many different things once (novelty) or it can explain the same things several times, by different means (redundancy). Striking a balance between novelty and redundancy is critical. Novelty is important to avoid boring your readers, but a certain level of redundancy is necessary if you want to be understood.

See **Figure 3.7**, which shows a portion of an infographic about giant waves that I'll discuss later on in this book. The copy accompanying each step of the explanation repeats some of the information encoded in the illustration. In this case, the text not only complements the image (or vice versa), it also *strengthens* the message by clarifying what the image shows. Another example: In a complex statistical chart, you could add necessary redundancy by highlighting relevant data points.

Figure 3.7 Realistic illustrations accompanied by redundant copy.

If I had to visualize my Brazilian prisons infographic using the visualization wheel, the result would be **Figure 3.8**. I consider the graphic more abstract than figurative, for an obvious reason: The charts don't resemble physical reality but are conceptual tools that allow me to encode quantitative data.

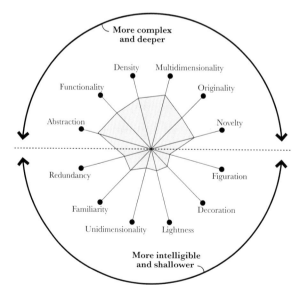

Figure 3.8 Visualization wheel of the Brazilian prisons infographic.

In a conventional sense, the chart is more functional than beautiful. It contains almost no decoration, although we paid attention to color palettes and the consistency of typographical style.

The chart is multidimensional: It has at least five layers of information that readers can explore.

It's not very original. All of the graphic forms are in common use—the bar chart, the slopegraph (used for the second part), the tables, and so on.

The charts contain quite a bit of redundancy. Notice on the second page, where the number of inmates is compared to jail spaces, that the same data is encoded in different formats. It also includes explanatory text to clarify the most striking figures.

Is this an adequate combination of factors? I believe it is. Despite the comments from my colleagues, I don't think that this information graphic is overloaded or excessively difficult to read. It's not the prettiest thing in the world, I concede. But it's not very ugly, either. (I've done worse!)

It is true that, according to my own terms, the Brazilian prisons project leans toward the upper half of the visualization wheel: It is complex and deep. This should be no obstacle for readers of a quality publication such as *Época*. If we assume that our audience is willing to read 8,000-word stories about convoluted corruption schemes in the upper echelons of government, why not apply the same expectation to graphics? It would be strange to publish stories for adults illustrated with graphics for kids, which is what happens when publications underestimate what their readers can absorb.

Identifying your audience

The complexity of a graphic should be adapted to the nature of your average reader. This sounds easier than it really is. **Figure 3.9** explains that at least two factors influence the communication between a designer and an audience through information graphics and visualizations: first, how well the visual forms used to encode the information are adapted to the nature of the story the graphic should tell; and second, the previous knowledge the user has about the topic and about how those visual forms work (e.g., bar charts are more common than scatter-plots).

The more specialized your audience niche, the more you can take for granted, and the more you can rely on what your users presumably already know.

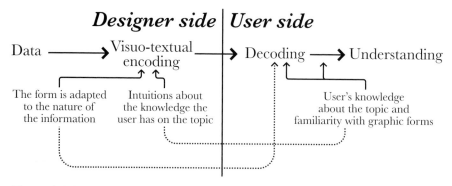

Figure 3.9 Designers encode, users decode.

Consider the charts in **Figure 3.10**. They display the co-occurrence of neuropsychiatric disorders within families, drawn from an academic paper published in the online magazine *PlosOne*.[1] Do you know what it all means? I don't (well, actually, only to a point). That is not criticism of the charts: It's just that the researchers didn't have me in mind when they plotted their graphics. They were thinking of their peers, people with so much knowledge of psychiatry and neuroscience that they can decode these graphics in the blink of an eye. They don't need extra explainers, legends, or any other artifice that designers ordinarily employ to make readers' lives easier.

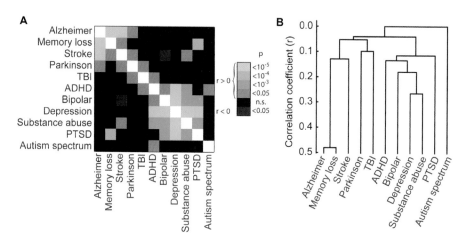

Figure 3.10 Try to figure out what these charts mean. It's not easy, is it?

1 B.C. Campbell and S.S. Wang, "Familial Linkage between Neuropsychiatric Disorders and Intellectual Interests," *PLoS ONE* 7(1): e30405. Accessed Feb. 23, 2012 from http://www.plosone.org/article/info%3Adoi%2F10.1371%2Fjournal.pone.0030405.

Few designers have the privilege of working for scientific publications, where it is easy to base decisions on assumptions about one's audience. Most of us work for general publications and face questions such as, "Is this graphic too complex for the majority of our readers?" or "Will our readers feel overwhelmed by the amount of data we've given them, or by the way we've presented it?"

Sadly, when faced with these challenges, **too many communicators dumb down the data**, simplifying it rather than *clarifying* it, and they add cutesy illustrations and icons that, to their way of thinking, will make the graphic presentations less dry.

The mind-set behind this approach is captured in a statement that I've heard, with minor variations, in three different newsrooms from three different managers who didn't know one another: "Our readers are idiots." The quote that opens this chapter, taken from E. B. White's great classic on writing, *The Elements of Style*, is the perfect antidote against this deleterious nihilism:

> No one can write decently who is distrustful of the reader's intelligence, or whose attitude is patronizing.

Do you respect your audience's intelligence? How do you know if you are over-estimating it (not likely) or underestimating it (most common)?

Engineers vs. Designers: Edward Tufte and Nigel Holmes

There has always been a fundamental clash in information graphics and visualization between those who favor a rational, scientific approach to the profession, emphasizing functionality, and those who consider themselves "artists," placing emphasis on emotion and aesthetics.

There is a middle ground between the two groups, and the boundary between the two philosophies is blurry. But, in general, it is my perception that those in the first group typically come from technical backgrounds (statistics, cartography, computer science, and engineering), while those in the second group are graduates of graphic design, art, and journalism programs. The first group would be drawn to visualization wheels like the one shown on the left in **Figure 3.11**. The second group would prefer to deliver graphics similar to the wheel on the right.

War between the factions was more or less formally declared by Edward R. Tufte in 1990. A professor emeritus of political science and statistics at Yale University, Tufte is arguably the most influential theoretician in information design and visualization, and deservedly so. His books *The Visual Display of Quantitative Information* (1983), *Envisioning Information* (1990), *Visual Explanations* (1997), and *Beautiful Evidence* (2006) are must-reads in our field.

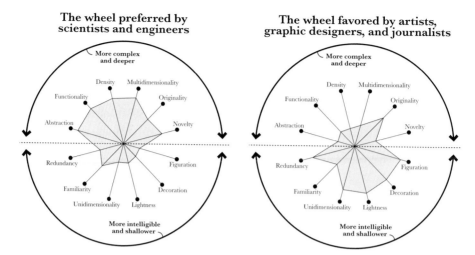

Figure 3.11 Different professional backgrounds, different ways of facing projects.

In *Envisioning Information,* Tufte attacked an infographics tradition that took shape in the United States in the late 1980s and early 1990s. Thanks to the success of the visual style of *USA Today* (launched in 1982) and *Time* magazine, illustrated charts and pictorial maps became very popular.

Tufte coined a term to define pictograms and illustrations within charts and maps: *chartjunk.* To make his case, he chose a *Time* chart (**Figure 3.12**) designed by renowned artist Nigel Holmes, the magazine's art director at the time. Holmes himself recognizes that this is not one of his most inspired works, but also contends that Tufte picked just one graphic among hundreds and elevated an isolated anecdote to a category level to make his case.

Tufte explained why he despised decorative ideology represented by the graphic this way:

> Lurking behind chartjunk is contempt both for information and for the audience. Chartjunk promoters imagine that numbers and details are boring, dull, and tedious, requiring ornament to enliven. Cosmetic decoration, which frequently distorts the data, will never salvage an underlying lack of content. If the numbers are boring, then you've got the wrong numbers (...) Worse is contempt for our audience, designing as if readers were obtuse and uncaring. In fact, consumers of graphics are often more intelligent about the information at hand than those who fabricate the data decoration (...) The operating moral premise of information design should be that our

Figure 3.12 Chart by Nigel Holmes for Time magazine. (Reproduced with permission.)

readers are alert and caring; they may be busy, eager to get on with it, but they are not stupid.[2]

Minimalism and Efficiency

A cherished notion of Tufte's is a principle of efficiency: **A visual design project is good if it communicates a lot with little**. In his own words, in his principles of graphic excellence:

- Graphical excellence is the well-designed presentation of interesting data—a matter of substance, of statistics, and of design.

2 Tufte, *Envisioning Information*, p. 34.

- Graphical excellence consists of complex ideas communicated with clarity, precision, and efficiency.

- Graphical excellence is that which gives to the viewer the greatest number of ideas in the shortest time with the least ink in the smallest space.[3]

This efficiency principle is defined with more precision by Tufte as the *data-ink ratio*: a measurement of the amount of ink that is used to represent data in a chart. Tufte defines data-ink elements as those that cannot be removed without destroying the integrity of the presentation. The other items, those that amount to decoration, can be eliminated because they are either redundant or they distract the reader from what really matters. Tufte even proposed a little formula:

> Data-ink ratio = Ink that encodes data / Total amount of ink used to print the graphic

Nigel Holmes's diamonds graphic scores low in this formula. Let's say that 1,000 drops of color ink were used to print it. Of those, around 150 are the ones that define the line, the headline and subtitle, the scale, and the specific values. Those are the elements that encode data. The woman illustration is non-data ink. So:

> Data-ink ratio = 150 / 1,000 = 0.15

According to Tufte, the closer the data-ink ratio is to 1.0, the better the graphic is. The less ink you use for ornamental effects, the better. Tufte doesn't just consider mere decoration erasable. In his first book, he also proposed removing gridlines and even portions of bars in a bar chart. See **Figure 3.13**.

Tufte's books imposed sanity at a time when flashy prevailed over functional, when pictorial and fun presided over abstract and intellectual. His writing style is as austere and economical as the graphics he favors, and many of his best quotes and soundbites (including "chartjunk" and "chartoon") became conceptual weapons in many discussions on what is appropriate in information graphics and visualization. But are Tufte's rants against *redundant* and *unnecessary* visual junk always right?

Is All "Chartjunk" Junk?

The problem with Tufte is that he tends to write in aphorisms and epigrams rather than building a continuous argument cover to cover. John Grady, a Wheaton College professor, observed in 2006 that Tufte's books are neither guides nor analytical

---

3 Tufte, *The Visual Display of Quantitative Information*, p. 51.

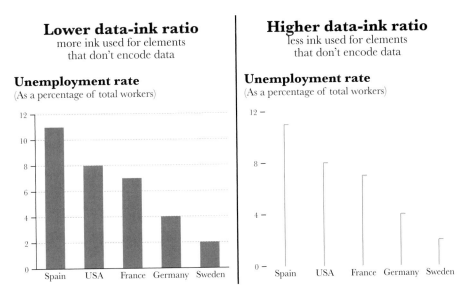

Figure 3.13 A traditional bar chart and its minimalist version.

texts, but "meditations" or essays: "Each chapter of his books consists of loosely integrated discussions of the merit of particular displays."[4] **That is why so many readers of Tufte's work** (in the past, myself among them) **feel a bit disoriented when they try to transfer his abstract principles to the real world.**

Another challenge of Tufte's writing is that he doesn't indicate whether an opinion is based on research or derived from personal views. The writing is matter-of-fact, as if the ideas are self-evident and grounded in reason. There are no cracks in the armor that would allow you to sense whether the author has any doubts. This minimalism is not purely a rational choice, it is also an aesthetic one. As much as I agree with Tufte on being serious about the data you handle, respecting the reader's intelligence, and reducing clutter and increasing elegance, his lack of differentiation between evidence-based assertions and personally informed intuitions is a weakness.

The data-ink ratio is paradigmatic. His assertion that a higher efficiency—the lowest amount of visual resources to communicate the highest possible amount of content—*always* facilitates understanding is dubious. This doesn't mean that designers should feel free to start cramming charts with cartoons and illustrations, but it does mean that resources considered by Tufte to be non-data ink—for

---

4 Luc Pauwels, ed. *Visual Cultures of Science*. (Hanover, NH: University Press of New England, 2006), pp. 222-265.

instance, gridlines in a time-series chart, or unobtrusive and subtle icons that identify the topic the chart discusses—might not be junk at all. Far from obstacles to understanding, they may *enhance* understanding.

In the past decade, academic papers have tested Tufte's hypotheses with mixed results. A 2007 study from Ben-Gurion University presented 87 students with traditional bar charts and maximized data-ink ratio charts similar to those in **Figure 3.14**. The minimalist version was rejected by many of the participants, perhaps because the bar chart is such a common graphical form. More importantly, when researchers tested to see if readers interpreted the minimalist chart better and faster than the more cluttered one, they found no significant difference. In this case, radically reducing the bar chart to its main constituents was not a matter of functionality, but of visual style.[5]

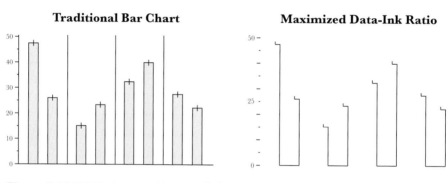

Figure 3.14 Which chart would you prefer?

In another study at the University of Saskatchewan (Canada),[6] 20 students read four old Nigel Holmes graphics and their corresponding minimalist versions designed by the researchers. One was our well-known diamonds chart in **Figure 3.15**.

The study was divided into three stages. First, the researchers used eye-tracking devices to register eye movements as each participant read each pair of graphics.

5 Ohad Inbar, Noam Tractinsky, Joachim Meyer, "Minimalism in Information Visualization: Attitudes Towards Maximizing the Data-Ink Ratio," *ECCE '07: Proceedings of the 14th European Conference on Cognitive Ergonomics* (New York: ACM, 2007).

6 S. Bateman, R.L. Mandryk, C. Gutwin, A.M. Genest, D. McDine, C. Brooks. "Useful Junk? The Effects of Visual Embellishment on Comprehension and Memorability of Charts," *Proceedings of the 28th International Conference on Human Factors in Computing Systems,* (New York: ACM, 2010).

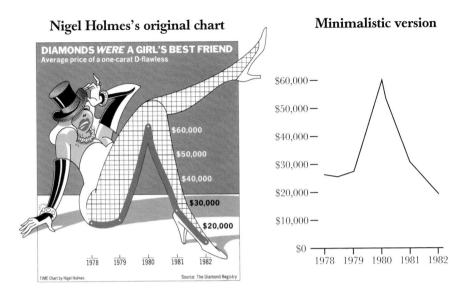

Figure 3.15 The original graphic is not very appealing, but the stripped-down version was not easily remembered.

In the second phase, each subject answered a questionnaire about the charts' contents, answering questions such as:

1. What is its central topic?

2. What phenomena and variables does the graphic show?

3. What changes does the graphic highlight in the data it represents?

4. Does the graphic present information in an objective manner, or does the author editorialize about the content?

As in the Ben-Gurion University paper, the researchers detected no significant differences in the effectiveness of the embellished and minimalist graphics. The components of each pair of charts conveyed the message equally well.

The most interesting part of the study was the third phase, in which the researchers tested the level of short- and long-term recall for each graphic. The participants were divided into two groups of equal size. They were not informed that they would be questioned about the graphics later on. The first group was tested five minutes after phase two questioning was completed, while the second group was asked to return to the lab three weeks later.

In all cases, the participants were better able to recall the topics and contents of the chartjunk-filled graphics. Apparently, their coarse humor ("coarse" is the adjective Tufte used to refer to Holmes's work) enhanced memory.

Fun and Functionality

To call these two studies conclusive would be a mistake. Both have been justly criticized by experts such as Stephen Few, author of two essential books on statistical charts,[7] for their methodologies, for the small number of subjects tested, and for the lack of socioeconomic and cultural diversity among subjects. While it would be risky to extract general lessons from the papers, I personally believe they suggest compelling reasons to doubt that always reducing charts to their barest bones facilitates comprehension and memorability. It depends on the audience's nature, knowledge, tastes, and expectations.

This idea coincides with what other critics of Tufte's approach, including Nigel Holmes, have observed: Tufte's influence in the visualization and information graphics communities has led many publications to adopt a style that is serious, cold, and stripped bare of aesthetic attributes that may be gratuitous to the statistician but that are useful for readers. This is not to say that we should not strive for economy of style and respect the integrity of the data, but that, as Donald A. Norman pointed out in *Emotional Design* (2003), beautiful things are more functional, and beauty is as much in the eye of the designer as it is in the eye of the beholder. Feeling good about an artifact makes us better at using it to accomplish a goal.

Holmes anticipated a similar idea in his early writings. He has always been an advocate of humanizing information graphics and using humor to instill affection in readers for numbers and charts. In *Designer's Guide to Creating Charts and Diagrams* (1984), he wrote in what appears to be a direct reference to Tufte's *Visual Display of Quantitative Information*, published the year before:

> If you belong to the school of people who believe that charts should only present statistics in the most straightforward, plain way, with no other visual help to the reader, for example, than the bar of the bar chart, the line of the fever graph, the circle of the pie chart, or the rules of the table, then move on to another part of the book. As long as the artist understands that the primary function is to convey statistics and respects that duty, then you can have fun (or be serious) with the image; that is, the form in which those statistics appear.[8]

7 Stephen Few, "The Chartjunk Debate," accessed Feb. 23, 2012 at http://www.perceptualedge.com/articles/visual_business_intelligence/the_chartjunk_debate.pdf.

8 Nigel Holmes, *Designer's Guide to Creating Charts & Diagrams* (New York: Watson-Guptill Publications, 1984), pp. 72-76.

Holmes also referenced this passage from *A Primer of Visual Literacy* (1973), a classic book by Donis A. Dondis:

> Boredom is as much a threat in visual design as it is elsewhere in art and communication. The mind and eye demand stimulation and surprise.

And Holmes praised the power of humor:

> Humor is a great weapon in your visual arsenal. As long as it is not malicious, making people laugh with you will usually help them remember your image and therefore the point of the chart. Even a smile will encourage a reader to look into the statistics if he or she might not have thought of reading in a less-embellished chart.

Many of the examples Holmes includes in his book are problematic from a structural standpoint because, as in **Figure 3.16**, integrating lines and bars with

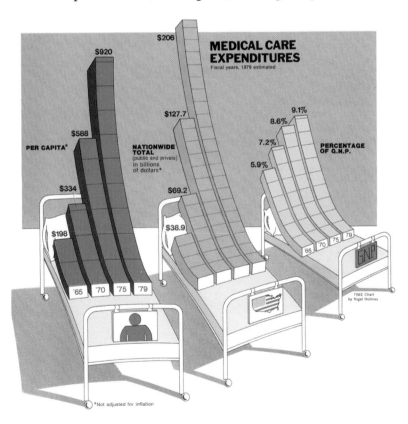

Figure 3.16 Too much expense on medical care makes bars feel sick. Chart by Nigel Holmes for *Time* magazine, 1979.

illustrations sometimes leads to misleading distortions. But they do use humor, and they are memorable. Most of the graphics would not be publishable today, as Holmes himself acknowledges, but we must remember that *Designer's Guide to Creating Charts and Diagrams* was marketed almost 30 years ago and is a product of its times.

Holmes's style has evolved. Without losing its humorous appeal, it has become more restrained, as is evident in his wonderfully illustrated *Wordless Diagrams* (2004), which is witty, funny, and informative. (See **Figure 3.17**.) His work has become closer to the man he calls his main inspiration, Otto Neurath, one of the great thinkers of the twentieth century.

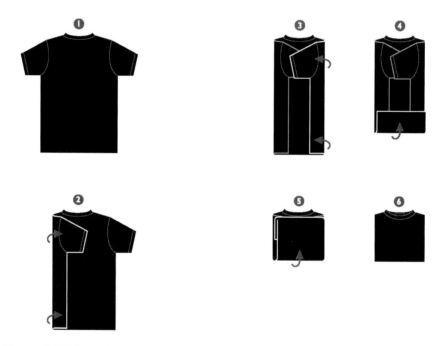

Figure 3.17 My mother was very happy after I read *Wordless Diagrams* (2005) by Nigel Holmes. After more than 30 years, I finally learned how to properly fold a T-shirt.

Otto Neurath and the Visual Education of the Masses

Otto Neurath was an Austrian philosopher, mathematician, sociologist, and political scientist born in 1882. He forged his fame in the world of information graphics in the Vienna of the first quarter of the twentieth century.

At the time, the capital city of Austria was a scientific and philosophical power-house. Besides Neurath, geniuses like Karl Popper, Niels Böhr, and Kurt Gödel walked Vienna's streets. Together, these intellectuals would be known as The Circle of Vienna, and their ideas gave rise to the philosophical tradition of logical empiricism.

Neurath combined the virtues of a rigorous, rational, and logical mind with the humanitarian concerns that emerged from his leftist leaning. He was a democratic socialist, a rare species in a time of ideological extremes. Neurath didn't want to communicate solely with his peers. He wanted to promote mass education. He defended the idea that abstract and mathematical thought could be conveyed with clarity and ease to people regardless of their social, cultural, and economic backgrounds.

Around 1925, as director of the Museum of Society and Economy in Vienna, Neurath devised *Isotype* (International System of Typographic Picture Education), a universal language based on pictograms whose goal was the "humanization of knowledge" and the overcoming of cultural barriers. Over many years, he worked with Gerd Arntz, a German graphic designer, and Marie Reidemeister (who would become Mrs. Neurath in the 1940s) to create many displays of information, charts, and maps of beautiful simplicity and clarity. See **Figure 3.18** representing the amount of fabric produced in Britain between 1820 and 1880. The chart shows a paradigm change: At the beginning of the century, production was small and mainly a family venture; later, it became industrialized.

In his professional autobiography, written between 1943 and 1945 and titled *From Hieroglyphics to Isotype* (2010 edition), Neurath explained what his pictographic language was intended to achieve:

> We started our visualization in adult education by making exhibitions for museums and preparing sheets for classes and diagrammatic films in the Isotype style. We tried to evolve a new type of exhibition to attract the masses immediately. The subject of the exhibition should be serious but it should be combined with a charm and direct appeal to everybody. As many people should be persuaded to visit it as would go to some public show of purely entertainment value. Education has to compete with entertainment (...) It would be dangerous if education were to become a purely occupational matter and something boring in itself.[9]

---

9 Otto Neurath, *From Hieroglyphics to Isotype*, p. 113.

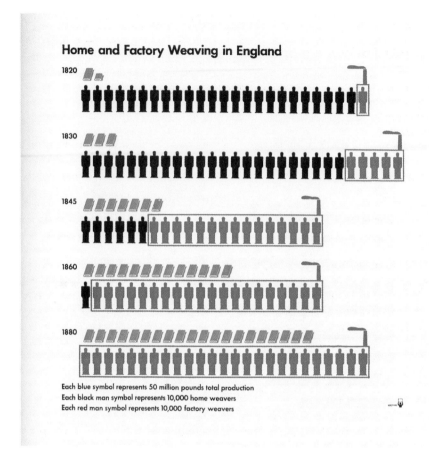

Figure 3.18 Otto & Marie Neurath Isotype Collection, University of Reading.

Charm and direct appeal. Those words resonate deeply in Nigel Holmes's work, which, like Neurath's, tends to be tightly edited and to convey a few ideas with clarity and power. That goal is not opposite to Tufte's approach, but it is different. Tufte favors highly detailed, multivariate presentations that allow careful exploration on the part of the reader.

So who is right—Tufte in his defense of dense graphics, bereft of trivial "junk"? Or Holmes and Neurath and their populist graphics, encoding just a few easily digestible messages with friendly looking pictograms and humorous illustrations? Is it possible to reach a synthesis between the two approaches, or at least to choose one of them without despising the other? I believe it is. After all, even if it may seem otherwise, Tufte's and Holmes's *ideologies* are more similar than different. This is the focus of the next chapter.

4

The Complexity Challenge: Presentation and Exploration

A data visualization should only be beautiful when beauty can promote understanding in some way without undermining it in another. Is beauty sometimes useful? Certainly. Is beauty always useful? Certainly not.

—Stephen Few, from "Should Data Visualization Be Beautiful?"

The first step to finding the middle ground between radical minimalism and a more playful approach to information graphics and visualization is to remember that a good graphic realizes two basic goals: It **presents** information, and it allows users to **explore** that information. In other words, an information graphic is a tool for the designer to *communicate* with readers, and a tool for readers to *analyze* what's being presented to them. It doesn't matter if you see yourself as an engineer or as an artist: If you create infographics and visualizations, the balance you achieve between these two dimensions will define whether or not your work is good.

It's Not the Style, It's the Content

Figure 4.1 contains a graphic I made about the economic performance of the Games&Toys Company (which doesn't exist, of course). If we apply the visualization wheel (see Chapter 3) to it, we can see that it's pretty dense, albeit one-dimensional. It gives just one piece of information—how Games&Toys's after-tax revenue changed between 2006 and 2011—but lets you do little else, other than enjoy the bright colors and irrelevant eye candy surrounding the data line. **The graphic presents information, but barely allows exploration.**

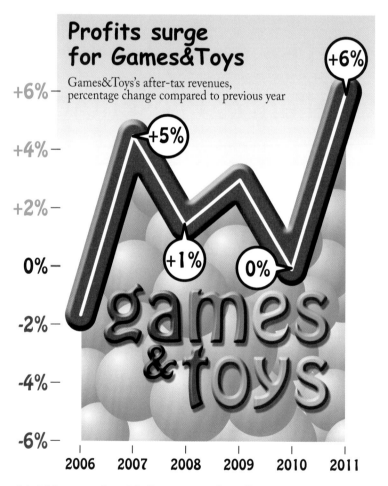

Figure 4.1 Adding tons of special effects to a graphic will not make it any better if it lacks good information.

Now see **Figure 4.2** which shows three scatter-plots I designed based on data taken from *The Spirit Level*, by Richard Wilkinson and Kate Pickett. The book's main thesis is that income inequality is related to negative socioeconomic indicators such as pregnancies among teenage women, rates of homicide, mental disorders, and so on. These two plots tend to the other side of the visualization wheel spectrum: They are spartan in appearance, very abstract, and encode a lot of data. In this case, while the charts also present facts, their main goal is to allow readers to visualize relationships and perhaps compare their own country with others.

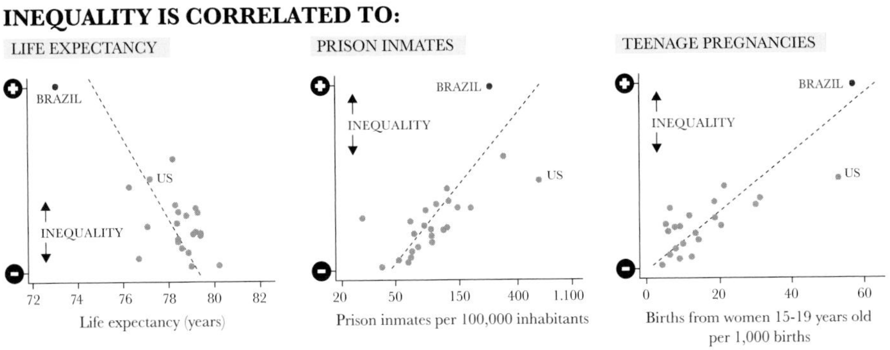

INEQUALITY IS CORRELATED TO:

LIFE EXPECTANCY   PRISON INMATES   TEENAGE PREGNANCIES

Figure 4.2 Inequality is correlated with negative socioeconomic indicators.

The differences between Figures 4.1 and 4.2 are deep. The designer who made Figure 4.1—that would be me—assumed that readers don't care about information if it's not surrounded by bells and whistles. On the other hand, when I designed Figure 4.2, I assumed that the people reading my work were interested in inequality beforehand.

Do I believe Figure 4.2 is better than 4.1? I do, not because of the decorative nature of the eye candy, but **because the special effects take away space that could have been used to highlight other angles of the story**; for example, to explain the erratic changes in Games&Toys's performance. How was the company doing in comparison to its competitors and with the market in general? What caused the surge in revenue: computers and video games, perhaps? Could I have visualized the covariation between Games&Toys's after-tax revenue and the penetration of digital games at home?

Figure 4.1 is not a so-so graphic because of its style. The reason it's not good enough is **because it wastes too much real estate (and the designer's time) on things that don't help readers understand the figures**.

Seek Depth

My advice is: **No matter what style you choose**—whether you decide to follow Tufte and become a hardcore minimalist or adopt a friendlier approach—always **take advantage of the space you have available to seek depth within reasonable limits. After that, *and only after that*, worry about how to make the presentation prettier.**

Take a look at the series of maps titled *Dangerous Germany* in **Figure 4.3**. They were produced by a company called Golden Section Graphics for *SZ Wissen Magazine*. Sure, those maps *present* information, encoding tons of data by means of colors and shapes, but they also allow readers to compare what goes on in the places they live with other areas. In this case, the designer doesn't force the data to adopt a particular shape just to make a point. The designer works as a facilitator, someone who designs a visual device that readers can use to navigate the figures, freely interpret them, and make their own points.

This is more clearly seen in interactive graphics, where the exploration component of visualization becomes crucial. *The New York Times*'s coverage of the 2010 midterm elections (**Figure 4.4**) lets readers dig through several layers of data. The project is not only a synthesis of the most important figures, but also an analytical tool that can be applied to the results. In this case, **the designer is no longer just a designer. He has begun to think and act as a software engineer**, someone who designs interactive tools rather than simple displays of data.

The reason I emphasize seeking depth, whenever possible, is that **too many journalists express distrust for their readers' interest in relevant issues**. I have been unfortunate to hear sentences like these too many times in my career:

> "Our readers want just snippets, not long stories."

> "Our readers just want to be told what to think about issues; they don't want to put effort in figuring things out."

> "Our readers will only understand stories written at the level of a 12-year-old."

> "Our readers don't read complex graphics."

There's a grain of truth in all of those statements, but it's a small one. Like all partial truths, they are context-dependent. If readers refuse and avoid complexity, why do publications such as *The New York Times, The Guardian, El País, The Economist, The New Yorker, Bloomberg BusinessWeek,* and their equivalents worldwide still survive and, in some cases, even thrive? Because, first, readers are smarter than you think, and second, because not all readers are equal.

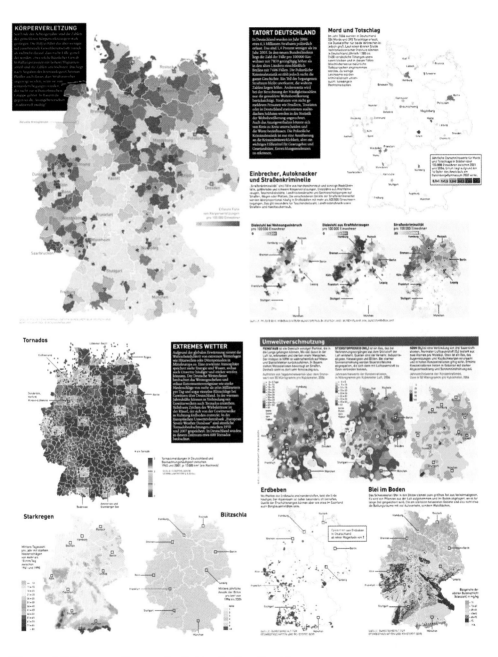

Figure 4.3 *Dangerous Germany,* by Golden Section Graphics.

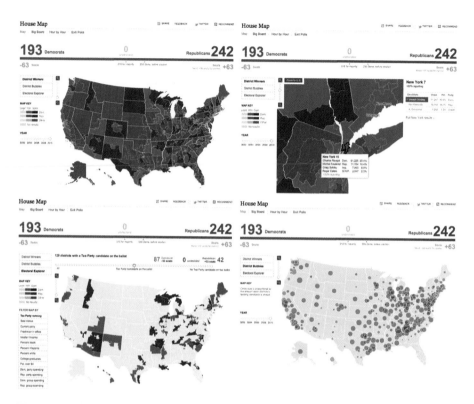

Figure 4.4 An example of how to organize an infographic that allows the deep exploration of data. *The New York Times* online. (http://elections.nytimes.com/2010/results/senate).

Graphics Don't "Simplify" Information

A common misconception related to this discussion is that information graphics and visualizations are means to *simplify*. This idea, popular among news managers, PR professionals, and marketing gurus, leads to infographics of disproportionate size that are informatively poor and weak, with no sophistication and depth. **Figure 4.5** is an example of what happens when you surrender to this philosophy. I made it up, but I assure you it is possible to see similar graphics every day in newspapers, business reports, and ads: It's something that could be reduced to one-third or even one-fourth of its current size without sacrificing anything relevant.

When I discuss graphics of this kind with media executives, the reaction I usually get is: "But its impact is undeniable. It'll grab the reader's attention. And it's beautiful!" Sure it will, but, after that, it delivers a message better told with

Profits falling!
Millions of dollars, 2005-2010

60
50
40
30
20
10

Figure 4.5 Three-dimensional effects are popular in business presentations, but they are hardly appropriate when the goal is to communicate, as they distort proportions.

a single line of text. Infographics like this are the equivalent of writing a huge, catchy headline followed by a single paragraph of trivial copy. The headline should not be an end on its own. It's a means to get readers interested in the relevant content that follows it.

In other words, **graphics should not simplify messages**. **They should *clarify* them**, highlight trends, uncover patterns, and reveal realities not visible before. My objection to graphics that put impact before depth is not that they are visually interesting and fun—they may well be. But **having spent so much space and resources on being impactful, they end up being shallow**. They don't allow inquiry or reflection on what they show. As much as I feel thrilled by eye-grabbing visualizations and concede that superficial beauty may be a laudable goal, I must insist that it's a secondary one, compared to that of building a visual structure that the human mind can understand, which is a major theme in the second part of this book.

Focusing too much on making things pretty can also lead to poor decisions, Stephen Few points out:

> Making a data visualization beautiful in a way that compromises the integrity of the data always works against you. Even when the information is not compromised, however, beauty can work against you by drawing attention to the design of the visualization rather than the information that it seeks to communicate. Think back over your life and ask: "Were the people who influenced and taught me the most all physically beautiful? If they were wrapped in a different physical package, would that have affected their

ability to influence me or my ability to listen to them? Did I ignore information that wasn't delivered by stunningly attractive people?" Beauty is not
the goal of visualization and it is usually not required to achieve the goal
(...) Remember that the goal is to enlighten.[1]

Finding Balance: Density and Multidimensionality

This takes me back to the visualization wheel. Is it possible to use it to find the right
balance between density and lightness, novelty and redundancy, functionality
and decoration? Yes, it is. But it is hard work and depends on the project you are
designing, the audience your graphic is aimed at, and the publication you work
for. Nonetheless, there are some generic personal rules of thumb that I apply to
my own work. They are based on intuition and experience, so don't expect them
to have any scientific validity.

Think of a project of your making and where it might sit on the visualization wheel.
Focus first on the Density-Lightness and Multidimensionality-Unidimensionality
axes, as in **Figure 4.6**. Try to define how dense and dimensional your graphic is.

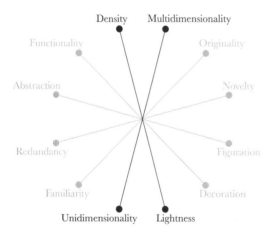

Figure 4.6 Let's focus
first on these two axes.

---

1   Few, February 1, 2012, blog post, "Should Data Visualizations Be Beautiful?," *Perceptual Edge*, http://
www.perceptualedge.com/blog/?p=1169.

Then try this: move the position of your graphic at least 10 percent toward the multidimensionality *and* density end of the axes. I do this to compensate for the fact that we usually underestimate what our readers are capable of. Next:

1. Organize your graphics in layers. First, offer a summary of the data, such as a good intro, some averages, or highlights of the main figures. This will be the entry point into the graphic, clueing readers into how to read what follows.

2. Beneath the outer layer of your onion-like graphic, on the next level, include as many inner layers of information as possible. Don't include everything, of course. Make editorial decisions based on the story and your focus.

3. Structure the layers in a logical order. In some cases, the structure will be linear. In others, you can organize the navigation (regardless of whether you are doing a print or an interactive project) so that readers can explore as they wish.

The interactive visualization in **Figure 4.7** illustrates how to apply these abstract principles in the real world. It is a complex, deep, interactive presentation analyzing how much each of the 513 Brazilian congressional representatives spends per month on telephone calls, along with the aggregates for 2011 and the averages and totals by party.

The headline "298 Years of Speaking," along with the huge R$ 13.902.425,16 figure, is the eye-catching element. This is the first layer of information, the one that will make readers interested: That's a lot of money by Brazilian standards. The first layer also includes the worst offenders: a ranking of the top 10 spenders.

After that, readers can follow a navigation path of their own. They may want to see only the representatives from their state (several filters are built into the graphic to allow this), or see how much a particular congressman spent over 2011 (clicking on any of the circles will reveal the specifics). This is the exploratory component of the visualization. We are not just showing stuff—we are providing tools to let our readers manipulate that stuff.

Functionality and Abstraction

Let's go to the next two axes in the visualization wheel (**Figure 4.8**). The more space you devote to decoration, the less room you will have to explain your story properly, to develop it with different angles, and to give necessary context to your data. When building your graphic, **think about structure first and eye**

Figure 4.7 How Much Brazilian Representatives Spend On Telephone a Month. Revista *Época*: http://revistaepoca.globo.com/diagrama/noticia/2011/10/diagrama-298-anos-de-falacao.html.

candy later. If decorative flourishes leave you without enough real estate for your substance, you'll be in trouble.

Unfortunately, designers and journalists often worry too much about visual styles and illustrations before they think about how the data should be organized and hierarchized to make sense. We saw examples of this previously, but let me give you another.

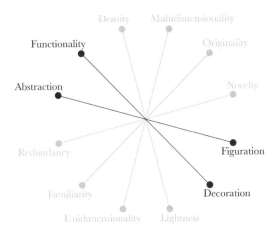

Figure 4.8 Moving on to decide where to define our graphics using the visualization wheel.

Figure 4.9 contains a graphic by *Good* magazine, a fun and nice-looking presentation, one of those this publication is deservedly famous for. But can you easily see patterns in it? Try to identify the states with a higher obesity rate, or states where people use more public or private transportation. You will have to actively search for your answers and memorize a good deal of data to accomplish these tasks. In other words, the graphic is all about presentation. It's not good at all when it comes to helping us explore the data.

One reason for this is that the map may not be the best way to display the data, and the little pictograms, fun as they are, do not help us perceive variations in obesity rates between states. It's hard to see how fat or thin each figure is compared to the others. In this case, traditional graphic forms—a bar chart for comparisons or a scatter-plot for correlations between obesity and car use—might work better.

We'll return to the relationship between abstraction and figuration in Part 2, which deals with visual cognition. For now, let me just add that using illustrations and pictograms à la Neurath is more than acceptable, depending on your audience and where your project is published. Highly abstract statistical charts may not always be the best answer (see **Figure 4.10**). That said, by taking the figurative road, you could end up infantilizing your data, patronizing readers by treating them as though they aren't very bright, rather than enlightening them. **Never, ever dumb down your data just because you think your readers will not "get it."**

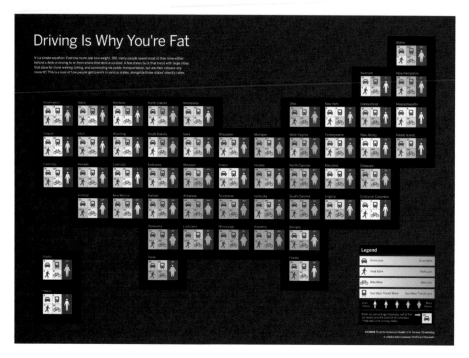

Figure 4.9 "Driving Is Why You Are Fat," a nice-looking project by Hyperakt for *GOOD* magazine.

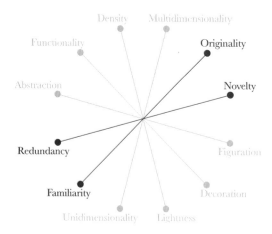

Figure 4.10 The last two axes of the visualization wheel.

Fun-tionality

Does this mean that you can't have fun with your projects, go a little crazy every now and then, and experiment with unusual or even wacky graphic forms? Not at all. **Experimenting (carefully) with novel forms is not just a whimsical impulse, it's a necessity.** By pushing the boundaries every so often, we help readers increase their visual vocabulary. A decade ago, scatter-plots, slopegraphs (like the one used in the prisons project in Chapter 3), and proportional symbol maps were rarities in the media. Today, they are almost as mainstream as bar charts and time-series plots.

In general, the rule of thumb I apply, based on the axes of my own visualization wheel, is: **The less common the graphic form I choose for my visualization, the more redundancy I should include**. In other words, if you intend to display your data in a novel way, make sure you include an explanation of how it works, with enough clues for readers to understand its mechanism.

Figure 4.11 shows an example of this approach. It is one of many information graphics that *Época* magazine published right after the November 2010 Brazilian

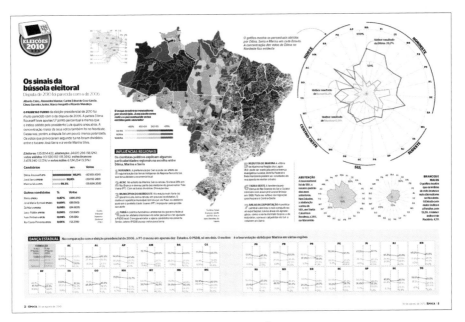

Figure 4.11 "The Signs of the Electoral Compass." *Época* magazine. See the text on the next page for a full explanation.

presidential elections. The central visual element, the map, with its colors identifying the winner in each district, is easy enough to read. But what about the bizarre compass on the right, which someone in the newsroom jokingly referred to as a "horoscope chart"?

The compass—from which the project took its headline, "The Signs of the Electoral Compass"—is a *radar chart*, and there is a specific reason why we chose to use it.

Each radius of the wheel corresponds to a state in Brazil, organized according to its position in the map. Notice that the northeastern states appear on the top-right quadrant of the wheel, the southeast states on the bottom-right, and so on. You can also see this in the grouping of the states: Northeast (Nordeste), Southeast (Sudeste), South (Sul), Central West (Centro-Oeste), and North (Norte). This is a traditional way of clustering states in large regions.

Within the wheel are three color lines: the red representing results for Dilma Rousseff, candidate of the Brazilian left; the blue for José Serra, candidate of the center-right; and the green for Marina Silva, candidate for the (surprise) Green Party.

The position of the vertices of the color lines on each of the radii is proportional to the percentage of votes won by the candidate in that state. The farther from the center the vertex is, the more votes the candidate received.

You can see at a glance that the left has a disproportionally high percentage of votes in the northeast, the poorest region in Brazil, whereas the center-right has much better results in the richer southern states, such as Santa Catarina, Paraná, and São Paulo. This is exactly what we wanted to highlight by positioning the states according to their place on the map. We wanted to suggest that Dilma Rousseff's red line was stretching out like a rubber band toward the northeast, while Jose Serra's line was undergoing a similar pull toward the south. In other words, we were more interested in the bigger trends and patterns than in the specifics.

The "Boom" Effect

My friend Luiz Iria, the infographics director at Abril Group, South America's largest magazine publisher, describes the emotional power of a good infographic with irrepressible Brazilian wit and enthusiasm: "I want my readers to flip the page and, *boom!* The infographic shows up as an explosion!"[2]

Luiz's infographics are spectacular displays of visual pyrotechnics, perfectly adapted to the publications he works for: *Superinteressante* (popular science), *Mundo Estranho* (science for kids), and *Aventuras na História* (popular history). These publications are full of short texts, eye-catching special effects and headlines, with no pretense of depth. They are great at what they do, which is to provide basic educational tools for the masses.

You can see an example of Luiz's work in **Figure 4.12**, on Brazilian rodeos.

The boom effect Luiz speaks of is an aspiration of every professional in this field. You *do* want to attract readers. But not all readers respond to the same kinds of booms; one type of boom can be beneficial for a particular project, but counterproductive in another one. It would be inappropriate, for instance, to transfer *Superinteressante*'s style to *The Economist* or *Bloomberg BusinessWeek*—and vice versa. Their readers are different, and so should be their graphics styles. Emotions matter, but not all emotions are aroused by identical phenomena. Sometimes you can stimulate the viewer's feelings through a beautiful illustration; at other times, by making sophisticated type and color choices.

In Chapter 3, I mentioned Donald A. Norman's *Emotional Design* (2004), a book in which the famous information designer confessed that the approach he had taken in his previous and classic *The Design of Everyday Things* (1988) had missed a crucial element. He wrote:

> In writing *The Design of Everyday Things* (1988) I didn't take emotions into account. I addressed utility and usability, function and form, all in a logical, dispassionate way—even though poorly designed objects infuriate me. But now I've changed. Why? In part because of new scientific advances in our understanding of the brain and of how emotion and cognition are thoroughly intertwined. We scientists now understand how important emotion is to everyday life, how valuable. Sure, utility and usability are important, but without fun and pleasure, joy and excitement, and yes, anxiety and anger, fear and rage, our lives would be incomplete.[3]

Beauty and functionality are intertwined, or should be. Beautiful and intriguing objects leave us in a better mood and predispose us to have patience when the

---

2 When I lived in Brazil, Luiz's style and mine were considered at opposite sides on what I would call a "bombastic-restrained" spectrum. The fact that I admire his style so much is an indication that I do believe the quality of an infographic is context-dependent—after it has fulfilled certain requirements, such as respecting what the human eye and brain can do.

3 Donald Norman, *Emotional Design: Why We Love (or Hate) Everyday Things*: Basic Books, 2004, p. 17.

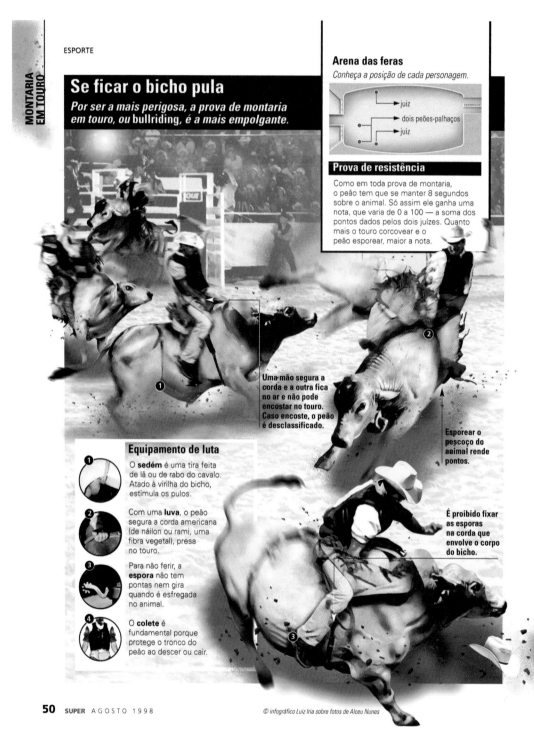

Figure 4.12 Luiz Iria's infographic for *Superinteressante* magazine, Editora Abril (Brazil).

Botando pra quebrar

Um estudo do preparador físico Denilson Santiago, da Federação Nacional do Rodeio, mostra que são freqüentes as distensões enquanto o peão está montado, e as torções e fraturas quando ele cai.

Tipos de acidentes mais freqüentes:

fratura		56%
torção		30%
distensão muscular		14%

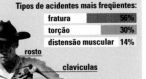

rosto

claviculas

cotovelos

braços

costelas   mãos

virilha

coxas

pernas

joelhos

tornozelos

pés

Ao final da prova, o peão escolhe o melhor momento para pular fora.

Gigante com chifres

É preciso muita força e agilidade para dominar o touro, que pode ser quinze vezes mais pesado que o peão.

Raças: nelore, holandês, caracu, *red bull*
Peso: de 600 a 1 100 quilos
Comprimento: 2,3 metros
Altura: 1,6 metro

Tranco pesado

Cada pulo do animal é sentido pela coluna do peão como se ele tivesse caído sentado no chão. A repetição dos impactos pressiona os **discos gelatinosos** que separam as vértebras, principalmente as da região lombar. Por isso, é comum ele ter hérnia de disco.

O peão-palhaço é também chamado de salva-vidas. Fica na frente do touro, distraindo o animal depois que o peão desmonta. Isso é que é herói.

E o bicho, o que pensa?

"Os homens se divertem às custas do **sofrimento** do animal", afirma a veterinária Irvênia de Santis Prada, da Universidade de São Paulo. "Além da dor física, eu estou convencida de que o barulho, as luzes, e as cordas causam estresse." O ponto mais polêmico é o sedém, a faixa amarrada perto da virilha do touro e do cavalo para fazê-los pular. Mas, segundo um laudo da Universidade Estadual Paulista (Unesp), a amarra não causa lesão alguma. Só que, para Irvênia, mesmo sem machucados aparentes é impossível provar que o bicho não sinta dor. De acordo com ela, o sistema nervoso dos bovinos e dos eqüinos é parecido com o humano. E um homem, com uma faixa espremendo o baixo-ventre, ficaria bem incomodado. Os organizadores dos rodeios se defendem: "Nenhum dono de tropa quer que seu animal sofra e, sim, que permaneça saudável", raciocina Flávio Silva Filho, presidente do grupo Os Independentes, que organiza a festa de Barretos. Para ele, o touro e o cavalo pulam porque o sedém incomoda um pouco, como se fosse um relógio de pulso apertado demais. "Com certeza, esses bichos são mais bem tratados do que os que não participam de competições", garante Flávio.

RESPOSTAS

Como se faz uma cirurgia de mudança de sexo?

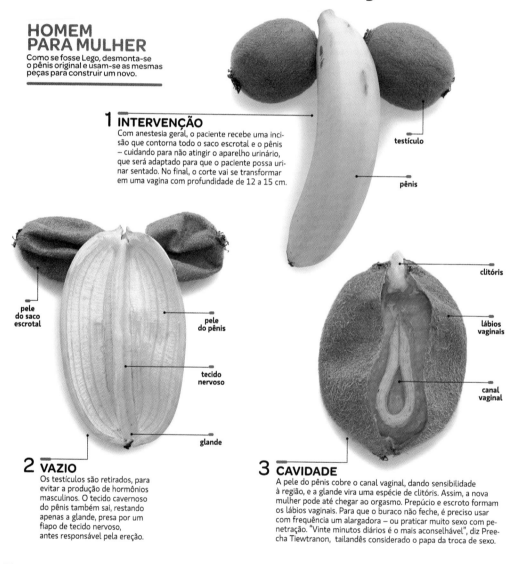

HOMEM PARA MULHER

Como se fosse Lego, desmonta-se o pênis original e usam-se as mesmas peças para construir um novo.

1 INTERVENÇÃO

Com anestesia geral, o paciente recebe uma incisão que contorna todo o saco escrotal e o pênis – cuidando para não atingir o aparelho urinário, que será adaptado para que o paciente possa urinar sentado. No final, o corte vai se transformar em uma vagina com profundidade de 12 a 15 cm.

testículo

pênis

clitóris

lábios vaginais

pele do saco escrotal

pele do pênis

tecido nervoso

canal vaginal

glande

2 VAZIO

Os testículos são retirados, para evitar a produção de hormônios masculinos. O tecido cavernoso do pênis também sai, restando apenas a glande, presa por um fiapo de tecido nervoso, antes responsável pela ereção.

3 CAVIDADE

A pele do pênis cobre o canal vaginal, dando sensibilidade à região, e a glande vira uma espécie de clitóris. Assim, a nova mulher pode até chegar ao orgasmo. Prepúcio e escroto formam os lábios vaginais. Para que o buraco não feche, é preciso usar com frequência um alargadora – ou praticar muito sexo com penetração. "Vinte minutos diários é o mais aconselhável", diz Preecha Tiewtranon, tailandês considerado o papa da troca de sexo.

Figure 4.13 "How sex change surgeries work." Renata Steffen, William Vieira, Alex Silva and Sergio Gwercman. *Superinteressante* magazine, Editora Abril (Brazil).

Com convicção: no Brasil, é preciso ter mais de 21 anos e encarar 24 meses de acompanhamento médico até que a cirurgia seja autorizada – sem contar a fila do SUS. Entenda como são feitas as transformações nesta versão censura livre – acredite, você não quer ver as fotos. ➤INFOGRÁFICO **EMILIANO URBIM, RENATA STEFFEN, WILLIAN VIEIRA E ALEX SILVA**

MULHER
PARA HOMEM
Bem mais raro que o processo anterior, este se baseia no aumento do clitóris por causa de hormônios masculinos.

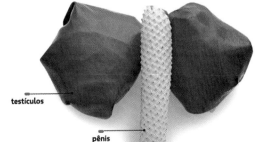

lábios vaginais

clitóris

canal vaginal

1 TESTOSTERONA
A paciente tem de tomar diariamente 200 mg de testosterona. Os resultados são: fim da menstruação, voz mais grave, mais massa muscular, às vezes calvície, mais pelos e o desenvolvimento do clitóris – que tem a mesma origem embrionária do pênis (só que um cresce e o outro não).

clitóris aumentado com hormônios

testículos

pênis

2 CRESCIMENTO
Quando o clitóris alcança 6 cm, o órgão é "despregado" do púbis para que possa ter autonomia de movimento. A uretra é aumentada com tecido extraído da antiga vagina. "O paciente sai daqui urinando em pé", diz a responsável pelo ambulatório de transexuais do Hospital das Clínicas de São Paulo, Elaine Costa.

3 PSICOLOGIA
Os testículos são formados com o tecido dos grandes lábios vaginais, que passarão a envolver duas próteses esféricas de silicone. Fica bem parecido. Quanto ao neopênis, o resultado é mais psicológico: além de minúsculo, quase não serve para penetração.

time comes to learn how to use them. The perception of meaningful beauty is a lubricant for the mind's gears and a boost for memory. If you don't believe me, take a look at **Figure 4.13**. I'll bet the way you think about sex change surgery will never be the same from this moment on.

It is crucial to remember our priorities as visual communicators. Here's Tufte, once more:

> All the history of information displays and statistical graphics—indeed of any communication device—is entirely a progress of methods for enhancing density, complexity, dimensionality, and even sometimes beauty.[4]

In the end, and above all, avoid being true to one of the saddest, cruelest, but also most accurate quotes on journalism I have read in the past few years. It comes from Evgeny Morozov, a critic of new media:

> Journalists, always keen to sacrifice nuance in the name of supposed clarity.[5]

4 Edward Tufte, *Envisioning Information*: Graphics Press, 1990, p. 33.

5 Evgeny Morozov, *The Net Delusion: The Dark Side of Internet Freedom*: Public Affairs, 2011.

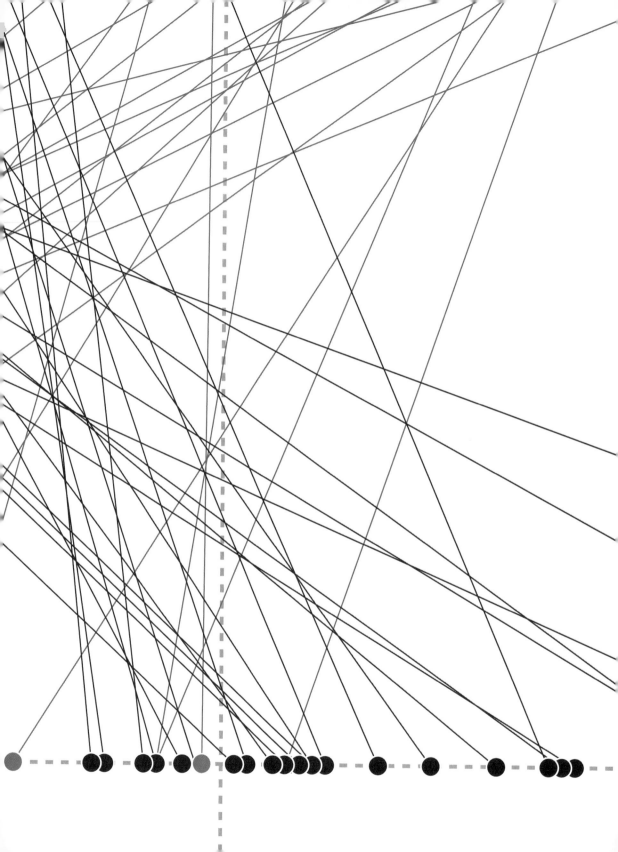

cognition

5

The Eye and the Visual Brain

The distinctive feature of brains such as the one we own is their uncanny
ability to create maps.

—Antonio Damasio, from *Self Comes to Mind: Constructing the Conscious Brain*

Imagine yourself sitting on a bench in your favorite park. Your eyes are focused on
a long story in the newspaper. Maybe you are reading it on your tablet computer,
or maybe you are old-fashioned, as I am, and prefer the newsprint version. No
matter. Either way, the world around you blurs and becomes unimportant. The
storyline flows. You feel enthralled. You barely notice a group of children playing a few yards away. Your mind is off and wandering in a better place, chasing
fleeting words.

Suddenly, you notice a movement in the corner of your eye: Something is flying
toward you at high speed. Your hands drop the newspaper. Your heart pounds
harder and faster. Your arms instinctively position themselves in front of your
face in a protective shield of skin, flesh, and bone.

A soft object hits your elbow and falls to the ground. Your body relaxes. A plastic
ball bounces in front of you, harmless.

To say that *a part of you* noticed a movement is a manner of speaking, for that part
was not really *you*. Your conscious self didn't know what your eyes were seeing
until the ball was already at your feet. The first lesson we can extract from this

is that vision is fast, but reason is slow. The second lesson is that, as the famous neuroscientist Antonio Damasio wrote, "The human brain is a natural-born cartographer." In our story, in a fraction of a second and without your conscious awareness, your brain devised a map calculating the precise position of the potential flying threat—and prompted your arms to react.[1]

The third lesson of this story is that **seeing, perceiving, and knowing are different phenomena**. You can see without perceiving and without knowing that you are seeing. The eye and the visual brain are more complicated and fascinating than you may have ever thought. **Exploring their inner workings is crucial if we want to approach information graphics and visualizations as communicators, not simply as traditional graphic artists.**

The Unexplained Eye

If you are my age, the biology textbook you used during high school probably included a diagram similar to **Figure 5.1**, which shows how human visual perception works.

Light coming from a source—the sun, a light bulb—hits an object. In my diagram, that object is my friend Mike Schmidt, a talented multimedia producer who graciously agreed to be part of this teaching experience.

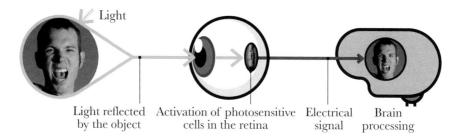

Light

Light reflected   Activation of photosensitive   Electrical   Brain
by the object   cells in the retina   signal   processing

Figure 5.1 This is what I learned about the eyes and the brain when I was in high school.

Mike's skin absorbs some of the photons—the particles light is made of—and reflects some of them. The photons bouncing off his face pass through my eyes and stimulate certain photosensitive cells on my retina. Those cells transform

1 Antonio Damasio, *Self Comes to Mind: Constructing the Conscious Brain* (Toronto Pantheon Books, 2010).

the light stimulus into an electrical impulse that reaches the brain through the optic nerves.

So far, so good. Up to this point, the process is almost mechanical: a dancing game of light particles and cell activation patterns. But as a teenager, I found the last part of the diagram confusing. A photograph shows up in the middle of a picto-graphic brain? How mysterious. At the time, the end of the perceptual process seemed like magic to me.

The best metaphor to explain human visual perception is that of a digital video camera, where our eyes are the camera lens, our optic nerves are the cables, and our brains are the microprocessor and the hard drive. The only problem with this model is that, **while our eyes truly act as lenses, the brain is certainly not a hard drive, as we'll see**.

Let There Be Light

The next part of the perception equation is light. Understanding a bit of how it works can be useful for design and graphics, so stick with me.

Light is electromagnetic radiation. It can be described as waves that scatter in different lengths, frequencies, and energy charges. See **Figure 5.2**. The frequency of a light wave is a measure of the number of waves that cross a particular point within a given time frame. Frequency is inversely proportional to length: The shorter a wave of light is, the higher its frequency.

The energy of a ray of light is related to those two physical properties: frequency and length. The shorter the wavelength and higher its frequency, the more energy the light carries. Our mother's insistence on smearing us with sun protection cream before exposing our skin to the sun's mid-day rays has a solid scientific basis: Ultraviolet light, even after it's been filtered by the earth's atmosphere, can burn you.

As Figure 5.2 shows, our eyes can detect only a tiny fraction of the electromagnetic spectrum. The visible range for humans runs from violet (high frequency and energy, short wavelength) to red (low frequency and energy, long wavelength). Other species' visible ranges are different. Bees, for instance, can see ultraviolet light, and many predators can see infrared.

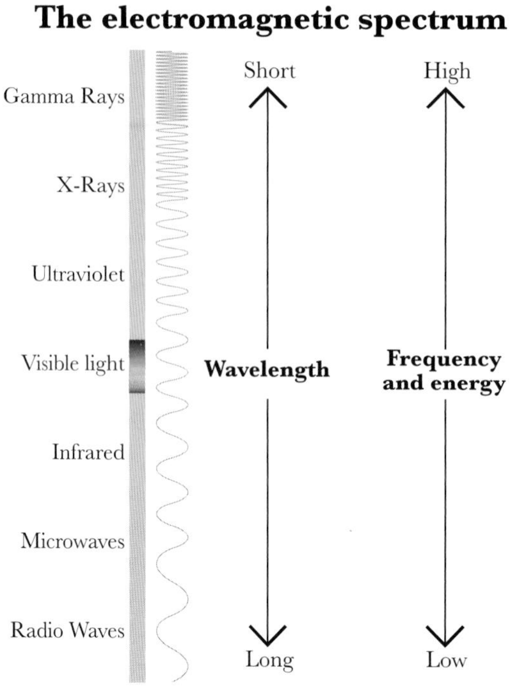

The electromagnetic spectrum

Gamma Rays

X-Rays

Ultraviolet

Visible light

Infrared

Microwaves

Radio Waves

Short

Wavelength

Long

High

Frequency and energy

Low

Figure 5.2 The electromagnetic spectrum.

As explained before, when light hits any object, the surface absorbs some of the light and reflects the rest. An object that appears white reflects all wavelengths of light, while a black object is one that absorbs all light visible to the eye. Between those two extremes is a vast range of possibility. We see a blue chair not because the chair oozes an intrinsic bluish quality, but because its surface swallows all frequencies of light except those that our brain identifies as belonging to blue. Without light, nothing is blue, green, yellow, black, or white.

Light and Photoreceptors

Figure 5.3 shows the main components of the human eye. Starting at the left, the pupil controls the amount of light that enters the eye. It contracts when there's too much light and opens when there is very little.

After light has entered the eye and is filtered and adjusted, it reaches the retina, a thin sheet of nerve tissue on the back side of the eye. (The retina, by the way, is not part of the eye but part of the brain—one of those factoids that proves it is not a good idea to trust your intuitions when it comes to science.) During embryonic development, the cells of the retina and optic nerve are born in the encephalus, and, little by little, like tiny, thin tentacles, they stretch until they find the right place to attach.

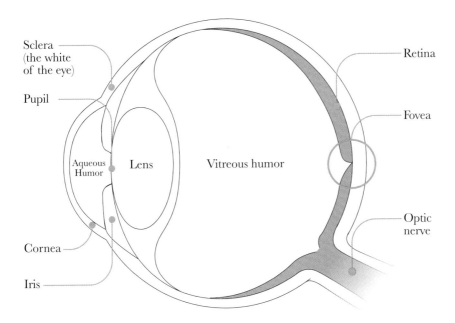

Figure 5.3 The structure of the eye.

The retina is covered with several kinds of cells. The most relevant for light detection are called **photoreceptors**. They come in two main groups: rods and cones, so called because of their shapes. Each retina has around 100 million *rods* that see in black and white and are active when light is dim. *Cones* (7 million, more or less) are in charge of color detection.

To understand how rods and cones work, wake up in the middle of the night. Open your eyes and wait until your pupils dilate enough for your surroundings to become visible. You will see the bed, the chair where you left your clothes, and the bedroom door as monochrome objects, perhaps with a very subtle blue tone. Your rods are active. Your cones are just whispering.

Now, turn on the lights. In all probability, the sudden, bright explosion of light will blind you for the second it takes for your pupils to contract. Now, what was monochrome and barely visible appears bathed in vivid hues and shades: the blue sheets on the bed, the red plastic of the chair, your green jeans and flowery shirt (I live in Miami, mind you), the white door. Cones have taken over.

Foveal, Peripheral Vision, and Animated Infographics

One of the first illusions we suffer when our eyes are open is that the acuity of our vision is the same throughout our entire visual field. You are as much a victim of this illusion as everyone else. Try this: Go for a walk. Stop on the sidewalk and close your eyes for 10 seconds. Open them and make an effort to fix them on something static in front of you: a parked car or a street sign. It is important that you keep your eyes focused on that object: Don't move them.

Now, try to identify the objects closer to the outer limits of your vision field. Remember, don't allow your eyes to move. You will not only find it is impossible to make out the surrounding objects, but also to tell *what color they are.*

The reason is that although each of our eyes is capable of taking in everything within a 180-degree angle, as shown in **Figure 5.4**, we only see with full acuity the things that lie in a very narrow field in front of us, an angle around two degrees wide. This angle is centered around the retinal region called the *fovea* (see Figure 5.3). The fovea contains only cones on a tiny surface of just one square millimeter. The cones grow sparser as we move away from the fovea to another small, surrounding region called the *parafovea.* Outside the parafovea, the retina is covered only with rods.

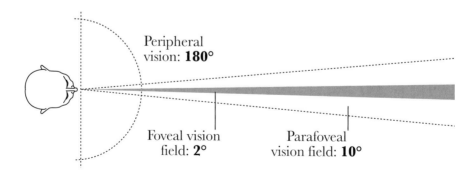

Figure 5.4 You may think that you see in a 180-degree angle in front of you with absolute acuity, but that is just a convenient illusion.

This limitation has consequences that affect perception. In order for us to identify an object, the rays of light that bounce off of it must stimulate the cones on the fovea; otherwise, we will see only a blurry mass. What is it then that creates our very convincing illusion of acuity, which leads us to believe that we see everything in our vision field with equal accuracy, as if it were a picture?

We enjoy this illusion because our eyes don't remain still, even when we are consciously forcing them to. They jerk around scenes with great speed, two or three times a second, fixing on different points of whatever is in front of them. These ocular movements are called *saccades*, and each stop your eyes make on a particular point is called a *fixation*.

Vision is the result of mapping your environment based on the aggregated information your eyes obtain from multiple fixations. But the eyes don't fix on random sections of the landscape. They are attracted first to certain features before they move to others. They *prioritize*. In several famous experiments run in the middle of the twentieth century, Russian psychologist Alfred L. Yarbus proved that, when facing a human head, our eyes fix first on those features that can better help identify the person it belongs to and his or her emotional state. **Figure 5.5** is one of the pictures included in Yarbus's papers. Notice how fixations tend to cluster around the eyes and the mouth.

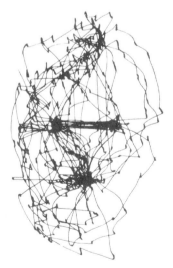

Figure 5.5 Alfred L. Yarbus studied what parts of the face attract our attention the most. This is an example of the kind of diagrams he developed. From Alfred L. Yarbus's 1967 "Eye Movements and Vision." (Reproduced with permission of Springer Publishing.)

It is the brain that merges all of the pieces of the saccadic puzzle together into an illusory, coherent mental picture. An example: Let's say I am in front of the place where I used to live when I was a professor at the University of North Carolina (**Figure 5.6**). My brain will tell me I am seeing a beautiful spring scene bathed in shades of green, brown, and blue. But what my eyes are actually sending to my brain are small snapshots from that scene within a tiny, high-resolution area—the area of my foveal vision range—set against a much blurrier surrounding.

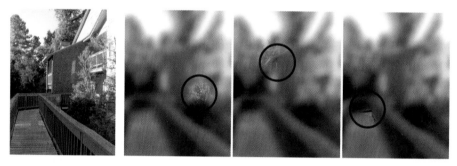

Figure 5.6 On the left, you see what your brain thinks you are seeing. On the right, you see what your eyes are really getting: tons of quick, narrow fixations, such as these views.

You've finally reached the payoff: Why is all of this relevant to information graphics and visualization? Saccadic movements and fixations are unconscious, but *they are not random*. Our species has evolved up to this day in part because it was able to efficiently identify predators, food, and receptivity in members of the opposite sex. We are designed, so to speak, to be attracted by moving creatures and objects, bright colored patches in front of us, and uncommonly shaped items, even if they are in our peripheral vision range.

Figure 5.7 represents this fact. At first, that *thing* in the corner of your eyes will not be identified because your foveas are focused elsewhere; but, as long as it is moving, it could be a potential threat, so your eyes will fix on it as soon as possible.

Here, then, is how to **translate a perceptual principle into a design principle**, (something communicators should do more often). Suppose that you are working on an animated infographic on the Mars Exploration Rovers. You are planning to include a step-by-step explanation of how the rovers get to Mars and how they unfold their wheels and solar panels.

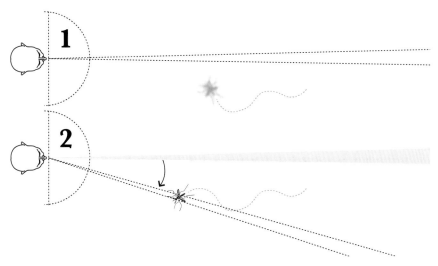

Figure 5.7 Moving objects tend to attract our eyes more than static ones.

Based on what we have just covered about the eye-brain system's attraction to moving objects and uncommon shapes, **you should never simultaneously show an animation of the robot on the right side of the screen and a text box on the left**. If you do, readers won't know what they should focus on. The text is an uncommon shape, and the robot is moving.

As shown in **Figure 5.8**, it is better to show the rover unfolding and, *only when the action has stopped*, make the text appear.

The same can be said of color. The best way to disorient your readers is to fill your graphic with objects colored in pure accent tones. Pure colors are uncommon in nature, so limit them to highlight whatever is important in your graphics, and use subdued hues—grays, light blues, and greens—for everything else. In other words: **If you know that the brain prioritizes what it pays attention to, prioritize** *beforehand*.

The Lying Brain

Your brain lies, although with good purpose. We are victims of illusions not because the brain malfunctions, but because perceiving illusions can be advantageous in some circumstances.

Quick. Go to **Figure 5.9** and tell me what you see.

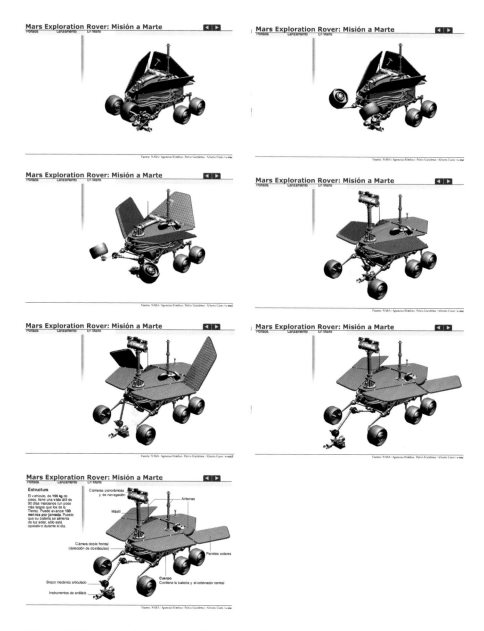

Figure 5.8 If you don't want to confuse your readers, don't show a moving object and a piece of text on opposite sides of the screen in an animated infographic. Instead, when the action stops, then let the text appear, as shown here.

Figure 5.9 Can you see two squares, a white square over four circles, and a white triangle?

I am sure you have answered: a) two overlapping squares, b) a white square partially covering four circles, and c) a white triangle pointing down, atop a black triangle that points up.

But those shapes are not there. The gray square behind the black one is not a square at all. It is an inverted L-shape. And I didn't use any ink to paint the white square and triangle. In fact, if you erase the four little Pac-Men that define the white square, the square itself will vanish. And there's no white triangle there: just three black dots.

Another striking illusion—one of my favorites—is shown in **Figure 5.10**. Hold the book you are reading in front of you with your right hand. Move the book away from you, extending your arm outward as far as you can. Cover your right eye with your left hand and focus your left eye on the cross. Now, with your left eye fixed on the cross, move the book very slowly closer to your face.

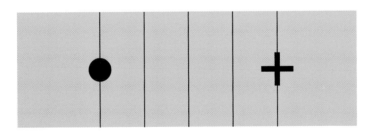

Figure 5.10 Follow the instructions in the text to view this figure, and the circle will disappear. But what shows up when it vanishes?

Tell me what happens to the circle.

Has it disappeared?

It *must* disappear. If it doesn't, try again. The circle has to vanish. Otherwise, I'd recommend you introduce yourself to the NASA SETI program—and don't forget to credit me as the discoverer of the first alien visitor to earth.

What is going on? Have your eyes stopped working? Not really, except for a small region on the retina called the *blind spot*. Go back to Figure 5.3, and notice the point where the optic nerve enters the eyeball. At that point, the retina has no photosensitive cells whatsoever. No rods, no cones.

When both your eyes are open, this is not an issue. What the brain sees is a composite image based on the information coming from the two eyes. At any time, some rays of light bouncing off of the objects in front of you may hit the blind spot of your left eye, but your right eye still notices them. That's why you still see them.

But when one of your eyes is closed or doesn't work properly, there is a small portion of the landscape that your remaining eye won't notice, because the light emanating from it is not stimulating any rod or cone. It hits your blind spot.

This is fascinating enough, but it gets better. Try the exercise again and tell me what happens when the circle vanishes. What shows up?

A line, and a surrounding patch of orange, I'll bet. But isn't that impossible? There are no light rays reflecting from the area where the circle was to stimulate your retina. You should not see anything, other than a void.

The answer to the riddle is that your brain knows that there are no voids in the world we live in. Sure, if you were to travel far enough through space and time, you might cross paths with black holes, but not on Earth. Your brain is making an assumption based on what it knows about how its environment works. It reasons: Empty areas don't exist; therefore, if my eye sees nothing, the area that I am missing is likely filled with the same colors and patterns that surround it.

The Efficient Brain

Why are we victims of visual illusions? Why doesn't the brain just see what is out there, as if it really were a video camera? **The reasons may be efficiency and response speed.**

See the three pictures in **Figure 5.11**. (I am a journalist, which explains why the image manipulation is a bit sloppy.) The picture was taken by my friend Rich Beckman. Imagine that you are a hominid walking through the savannah hundreds of thousands of years ago, and you see something that looks like random patches of brownish fur behind the grass. Would you need to stop and consciously figure out what is hiding there?

Figure 5.11 I f you were out walking on the savannah, I am sure you would not stop to figure out what your eyes were seeing before you fe;t the urge to flee. (Photograph by Rich Beckman.)

Of course not. Your brain would immediately visualize the second picture, and suggest that you are facing something that can eat you alive. It would be *completing* what your retinas receive. And it would probably prompt the release of a plentiful shot of adrenaline through your arteries, which will be useful whether you fight or flee.

In other words, **what your retina gets is not what your brain perceives**. In fact, what we commonly call *seeing* is not a single phenomenon, but a group of at least three operations: sight, perception, and cognition. Not all of what stimulates the cells in your retina is processed with the same level of detail in the brain, and not all of what the brain perceives reaches a conscious level and becomes rational understanding. Working like this makes sense. Life would be impossible if we had to think about everything that stimulates our eyes at every instant.

Scientists have proven that seeing is not exactly the same as perceiving, as people with severe brain damage reveal. For instance, V.S. Ramachandran in his illuminating *The Tell-Tale Brain: A Neuroscientist's Quest for What Makes Us Human* (2011) describes *blindsight*, a bizarre condition that leads you to see without knowing that you see. During experiments, a supposedly blind subject was seated in front of a source of light and asked to reach it with his hand. The man complained he couldn't do that because he was blind. But when he finally agreed to try, his hand grabbed the source with no hesitation. He was seeing, although his brain was not consciously aware of that sight.

In the case of *agnosia*, a term meaning "no knowledge" coined by Sigmund Freud, damage to certain parts of the brain leaves patients incapable of identifying things. They can navigate the world, and grab and release objects with high accuracy, but they cannot tell what those objects are. Paradoxically, if you ask them to describe what a chair, a glass, or a bottle is—the very same items they cannot identify—they show no major problems.

A New Diagram For Vision

Let's recap. Remember Figure 5.1, the diagram that opens this chapter, with my friend Mike screaming at the camera. As we discussed, that is not a good representation of what really happens in the brain. **Figure 5.12** offers a more accurate alternative.

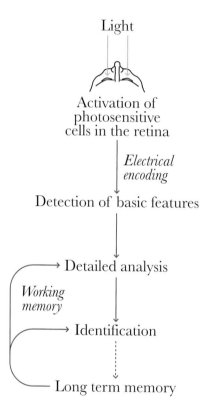

Figure 5.12 How perception really works.

Once the retina has encoded the patterns of light into electrical signals, the brain proceeds to discriminate basic object features, such as gross shapes, patches of color, and others I'll explain in the next two chapters. Only after this happens does the brain proceed to a much deeper analysis of what is being seen and to consciously identify it, based on a great deal of content that is retrieved from our memories.

But I am putting the cart in front of the horse. **Now that I've explained how the eye, the brain, light, and memory work together, I can explain how important all this is to our jobs as designers.**

6

Visualizing for the Mind

Perception is a fantasy that coincides with reality.

—Christ Firth, from *Making Up the Mind:*
How the Brain Creates Our Mental World

If you know what tricks and shortcuts the brain uses to make sense of the information gathered from the senses, you can use that knowledge to your advantage. In this chapter, I will focus on the mechanisms of detecting basic features, also called **preattentive features**. The ability to anticipate what the brain wants to do can greatly improve your information graphics and visualizations.[1]

The Brain Loves a Difference

When you open your eyes to the world, one of the first things your brain does is discriminate between background and foreground. That is, it identifies the boundaries of the objects and creatures in your vision field: where the lion ends and the grass begins, and where the grass ends and the sky begins. Evolution has

---

1 If you want to dig deeper into the contents of this chapter, take a look at the work of Ware (2004), Malamed (2009), Few (2004), and Maceachren (2004), all listed in the bibliography at the end of this book.

fine-tuned our vision to be quite good at accomplishing this feat, but it has also given other organisms the ability to impede it by using such tricks as camouflage.

The detection of object boundaries is based on variations of light intensity and color, and on how well the edges of the things you see are defined. The higher the contrast between two adjacent patches of color, the more likely they will be identified as belonging to different entities. The lower the contrast (or the blurrier the edges), the harder the brain must work to distinguish between them.

Compare the illustrations in **Figure 6.1**. The first has a high contrast, so we immediately perceive something *different* (identifying the wolf takes just an extra fraction of a second). We experience the second picture similarly, except that here the contrast is due less to light intensity than to hue. In the third illustration, the threat is more difficult to make out unless you invest considerable cognitive energy figuring out the scene and identifying the creature by its shape.

Figure 6.1 How quickly can you see the wolf in the trees in each of these illustrations?

In the first two illustrations, the differences between object (foreground) and background are sensed before attention and reason come into play. You don't know it's a wolf. You see something that may be relevant for your survival and unconsciously fix your gaze on it.

The brain is much better at quickly detecting *shade variations* than *shape differences.* Take a look at **Figure 6.2**, inspired by a picture made by Stephen Few. Suppose you are creating a table whose goal is to allow readers to quickly estimate the number of sixes in that sequence. It's hard to see the number 6 in the table on the left, but much easier in the one on the right. Assuming this is a visualization with a *function*—facilitate the identification of the number 6—the second picture is a better *tool* than the first because it was designed for what the brain is good at doing.

```
43679812551156115813415915    43679812551156115813415915
15345115251319251218914116    15345115251319251218914116
52161161241816158241415191    52161161241816158241415191
14181951281911511516182612    14181951281911511516182612
26191512214118214124411912    26191512214118214124411912
31251161531821381181413161    31251161531821381181413161
```

Figure 6.2 It is easier to spot the numeral 6 in the number sequences when we highlight it with a different shade.

Transforming a perceptual feature into a design principle is not hard in this case. If you are creating a map locating two different kinds of factories in the United States (**Figure 6.3**), you could certainly identify them with pictograms. But if you want your readers to *preattentively* detect the factories and estimate their numbers, using two different colors is a much better way to accomplish your goal.

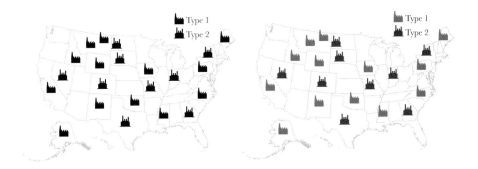

Figure 6.3 On which of these maps is it easier to identify the number of factories of each kind?

The Gestalt School of Thought and Pattern Recognition

At its core, **the visual brain is a device that evolved to detect patterns**: regions in the vision field that share a nature or that belong to different entities. In **Figure 6.4**, you will find several factors the brain uses effortlessly to discriminate between objects. With the goal of saving processing time, the brain groups similar objects (the rectangles of same size and tone) and separates them from those that look different. Then, it focuses on the different shapes. This preattentive detection feature—the instant sorting of differences and similarities—is one of the most powerful weapons in the designer's arsenal.

Figure 6.4 Some features that the brain is able to detect preattentively.

Originating in Germany at the beginning of the twentieth century, the Gestalt school of thought studied these mechanisms in depth. The main principle behind Gestalt theory is that brains don't see patches of color and shapes as individual entities, but as aggregates. In fact, the word *gestalt* means *pattern*. Striving for efficiency in how it invests its energy, the brain follows certain principles of perceptual organization. Let's take a look at some of them and learn how they can be applied to information graphics.

Proximity

This principle notes that objects that are close to each other tend to be perceived as natural groups.

Notice how hard it is not to see groups in **Figure 6.5**. It's almost impossible not to. That's because your brain is telling you that the disposition of those bars and numbers, however different they may appear in shape and size, *is not random*. They have an underlying logic, a pattern.

Applying this perception principle to an information graphic is easy: Objects that are related should be near one another in your composition, and aligned on the vertical or horizontal axis. Look at the first infographic in **Figure 6.6**. (The data is fabricated.) White strips help separate the different sections and portions. The

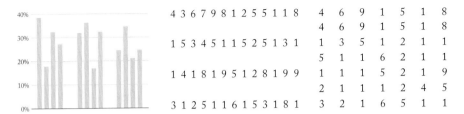

Figure 6.5 Objects close to each other will be perceived as belonging to a group.

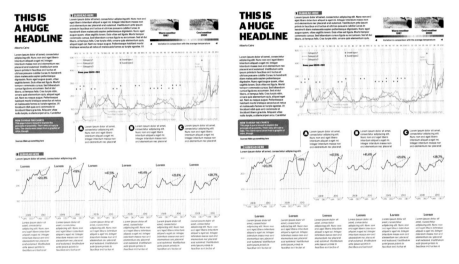

Figure 6.6 If you have several sections in your infographic, make sure that the objects that belong to them are near one another. The graphic on the left looks neat and organized, as you can clearly see the separation between its different sections. The graphic on the right does not.

second graphic appears chaotic because it wasn't designed with attention to the proximity principle. Your brain must make an effort to tell what goes with what.

Similarity

Identical objects will be perceived as belonging to a group. You can see this principle at work in **Figure 6.7**. In the case of the bar chart, you can also see the principles of Similarity and Proximity combined. These principles help the brain identify two different levels of grouping: one by the common nature of the objects, and the other based on how close the bars are.

Figure 6.7 Objects that look alike will be identified as parts of a group.

Connectedness

Objects linked by means of a graphic artifice, such as a line, will be perceived as members of a natural group. Take a look at **Figure 6.8**. When you present only the geometric shapes, the brain groups them by shade and shape. But when you add a thick black line behind some of them, connectedness overrules the previous clues for grouping. A much more powerful pattern appears.

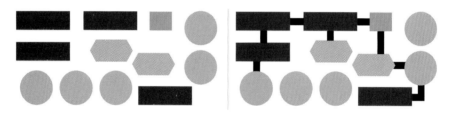

Figure 6.8 Lines are powerful clues the brain can use to perceive whether objects are related.

Continuity

The continuity principle holds that it is easier to perceive the gross shape of an object as a coherent whole when its contours are smooth and rounded than when they are angular and sharp. See **Figure 6.9**, where two node diagrams represent the connections between the mid-level managers within a company. The brain sees the connections better in the diagram on top. In the second visualization, as the straight, right-angled lines cross one another, it is much harder to complete the task.

Closure

Objects inside an area with crisp, clear boundaries will be perceived as belonging to a group. In **Figure 6.10**, even if the distance between the bars is constant among the three charts, and all are the same shade, the brain sees them as different sections of a single set of data when they are enclosed.

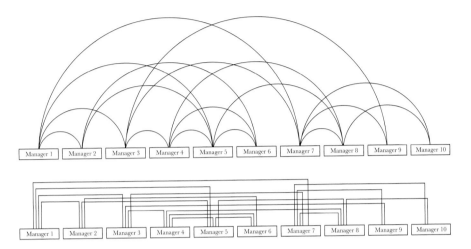

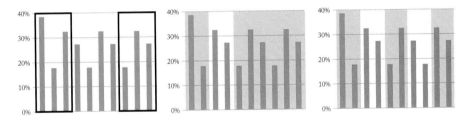

Figure 6.9 Continuity is better perceived in curves than in lines with sharp angles.

Figure 6.10 Boxing bars helps readers identify groups.

The principle of Closure is helpful when you create a multisectioned infographic, but only if applied with common sense and combined with the principle of Proximity. See the two examples in **Figure 6.11**. The one on the left looks sloppy because it's overloaded with boxes. Although the boxes are meant to aid your eye in distinguishing the parts of the composition, they are redundant. In the example on the right, I used Proximity to separate the background data (the sections at the bottom) and white spaces to define the shapes of the other portions.

So far we've looked at principles that can help us make our information graphics more functional through their organization, composition, and layout. But can a slight knowledge of visual perception also help us decide what graphical form is best suited to the tasks our graphic must help readers with? Yes, it can.

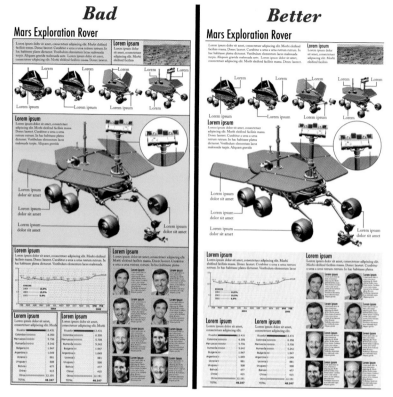

Figure 6.11 Don't overuse background boxes. Doing so will make your graphic look cluttered. If you need to differentiate between different sections, use white space.

Choosing Graphic Forms Based on How Vision Works

In 1984, William S. Cleveland and Robert McGill, statisticians working for AT&T Bell Labs, published a groundbreaking paper in the *Journal of the American Statistical Association*. It was titled "Graphical perception: theory, experimentation, and application to the development of graphical methods." Thirty years after publication, many of its contents are still relevant to a rational understanding of information graphics and visualization.

Sadly, Cleveland's and McGill's work is not widely known among journalists and graphic designers.[2] It is revered in other circles, particularly those related

---

2 Today, William S. Cleveland is a professor of statistics at Purdue University. His books *The Elements of Graphing Data* (1985) and *Visualizing Data* (1993) are must-reads for anyone interested in statistical charts.

to business and scientific visualization. Authors such as Stephen Few and Naomi Robbins have followed Cleveland's steps and delivered superb books partially inspired by them.[3]

What is important about Cleveland's and McGill's paper is that it proposes basic guidelines for choosing the best graphic form to encode data depending on the function of the display. The authors designed a list of **10 elementary perceptual tasks**, each one a method to represent data, and ranked them according to how accurately the human brain can detect differences and make comparisons between them.

Figure 6.12 shows the elementary perceptual tasks from highest to lowest accuracy. The tasks are grouped according to how well you can perceive differences in the data by using them. In other words, if two tasks are in the same bullet point, the accuracy is equivalent. The tasks include:

- Position along a common scale
- Position along nonaligned scales
- Length, direction, angle
- Area
- Volume, curvature
- Shading, color saturation

The authors based their ranking not on personal preferences or tastes, but on experiments and a careful reading of academic literature about human visual perception. They pointed out:

> A graphical form that involves elementary perceptual tasks that lead to more accurate judgments than another graphical form (with the same quantitative information) will result in a better organization and increase the chances of a correct perception of patterns and behavior.

In other words, the more accurate the judgment readers must make about the data, the higher on the scale the graphical form must be. A bar chart is *always* superior to a bubble chart or a heat map *if the goal of the graphic is to facilitate precise comparisons*, as shown in **Figure 6.13**. Here, identical quantities are encoded using three techniques: bars, areas, and color saturation. Notice that we underestimate differences when forced to compare areas. The second bar is almost double the

---

3   Robbins's *Creating More Effective Graphs* (2004) is excellent and as Clevelandesque a manual as it gets.

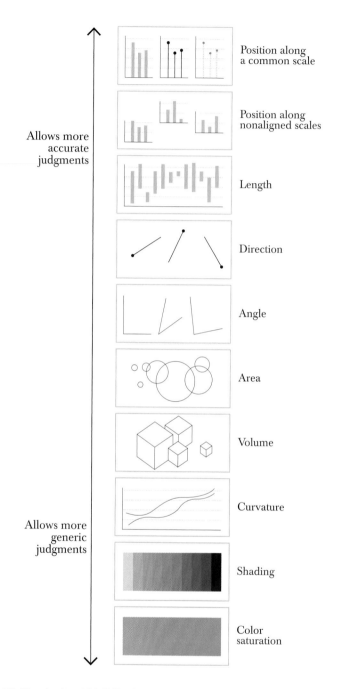

Figure 6.12 Cleveland and McGill's elementary perceptual tasks. The higher an encoding method on the scale, the more accurate the comparisons it facilitates.

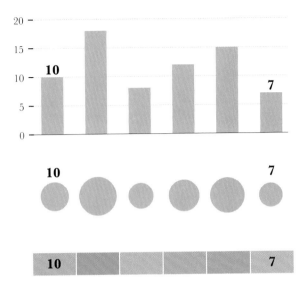

Figure 6.13 When the goal is to allow readers to make accurate comparisons, a chart based on bars or lines sitting on a single horizontal or vertical axis beats other forms of representation.

height of the first one, but the second bubble does not *preattentively* appear to be double the size of the first one.

Another example, inspired by one included in Cleveland's and McGill's paper: Suppose that you want to plot the exports between two countries. If the goal of your chart is to allow readers to see how much each nation exports to the other, a chart with two lines will be fine.

But if the goal is to display the trade balance between the two nations, the line chart is not the best way. Why? Because the human brain has difficulty comparing angles, directions, and curvatures. Better to do some subtractions, calculate the balance in favor of one of the nations, and plot the derived variable instead. You can see both examples in **Figure 6.14**. (If you don't know where Tomainia and Osterlich are, watch Charlie Chaplin's *The Great Dictator*.)

To summarize what we've discovered so far: The higher you move on Cleveland's and McGill's scale, the more accurate the judgments your readers will be able to make based on your charts. But there's another side to the story. Sometimes your goal is not to allow precise comparisons or to rank values, but to facilitate the perception of larger patterns, or the relationship of a variable with its geographical location.

In that case, it may be fine to pull from the bottom of the list and encode lots of values as shades of color on a map, or dozens of bubbles on top of the same

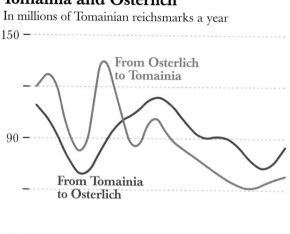

Exports between Tomainia and Osterlich

In millions of Tomainian reichsmarks a year

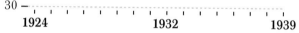

From Osterlich to Tomainia

From Tomainia to Osterlich

150 —

90 —

30 —

1924   1932   1939

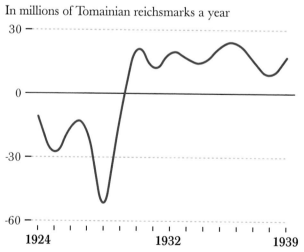

Trade balance in favor of Tomainia

In millions of Tomainian reichsmarks a year

30 —

0 —

-30 —

-60 —

1924   1932   1939

Figure 6.14 Trade balance between Tomainia and Osterlich, two of the imaginary countries in Charlie Chaplin's *The Great Dictator*. Of course, the data I used for the charts is also imaginary.

map. Cleveland's and McGill's perceptual task ranking is an invaluable tool for grounding decisions in fact and reason, rather than aesthetic taste alone, but like all conceptual tools, there are nuances and exceptions depending on the context and circumstances.

As an aside, William Cleveland expanded his ideas about charts in several more articles and books. I offer one of his insights in *The Elements of Graphing Data* especially for journalists and marketing and PR managers to keep in mind when designing infographics:

> While there is a place for rapidly understood graphs, it is too limiting to make speed a requirement in science and technology, where the use of graphs ranges from detailed in-depth data analysis to quick presentation (...). The important criterion for a graph is not simply how fast we can see a result; rather it is whether through the use of the graph we can see something that would have been harder to see otherwise or that could not have been seen at all.[4]

I would not limit that rule to science and technology. It can be applied to any infographic created to enlighten.

The Perceptual Tasks Scale as a Guide for Graphics

Rather than limit our discussion to abstractions, let me come down to Earth and show you how to use Cleveland and McGill's scale to orient your design decisions in a flexible manner.

Not long ago I read a news story about the connection between education and obesity. It highlighted several studies that found, on average, that better educated people are less likely to be obese. The problem with the story was that it didn't include a chart to prove its main point. As you saw in Chapter 1, assertions like this one tempt me to do a graphic myself. And so I did.

First, I gathered numbers: the percentage of people holding BA degrees (or higher) per state, and the percentage of people who are obese. I culled the numbers from the U.S. Census Bureau and Centers for Disease Control and Prevention. The figures may be dated—for a real infographic I would double-check them—but this is an exercise, after all.

You can see my Excel spreadsheet in **Figure 6.15**. After I entered the figures in it, I calculated the correlation between the two data series: –0.67. The *correlation coefficient*, also called *Pearson product-moment correlation coefficient*, or "r," is a

---

4 From Chapter 2 of William Cleveland's *The Elements of Graphing Data*.

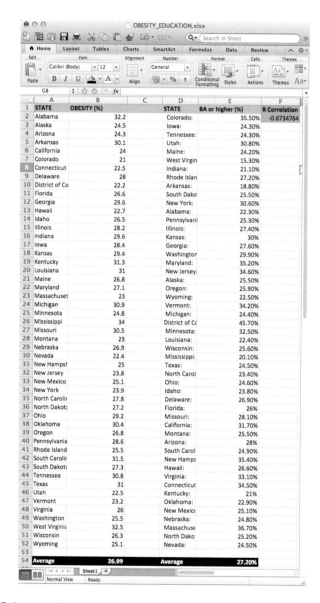

Figure 6.15 A screenshot of the spreadsheet used for this exercise.

measure of how related two variables are. If r is close to 1, the two variables are *directly* proportional: the higher the first is, the higher the second will be. If r's value is close to –1, the variables are *inversely* proportional: the higher one is, the smaller the other.

Based on this, a result of –0.67 indicates a solid negative correlation. I thought I had something interesting on my hands.

How would you encode the data so readers can see the relationship, or lack thereof, between your two variables? A table is not an efficient way to help them understand. Nor is telling them, "Hey, r is –0.67! That helps prove my point!" After all, how many newspaper readers do you suppose know what r is? We need to display the evidence visually.

How do designers proceed when they see data linked to geographical locations? Most don't bother to stop for a minute. They rush to produce a map. After all, a nice map looks good, and bubbles are trendy, so let's give them a try in a *proportional symbol map*. The results are in **Figure 6.16**. Bubble size is proportional to the encoded numbers.

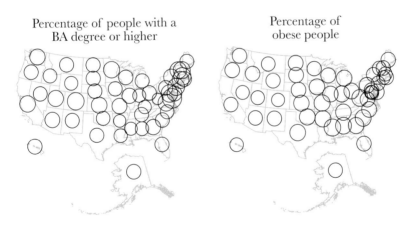

Figure 6.16 Proportional symbol maps are not the best way to represent these data sets.

It doesn't convey much, does it? The reason is that the task of area comparison is low on the Cleveland-McGill scale, and areas tend to minimize differences between values. Since the value range was not that wide in the first place, the United States looks like an ocean of almost equal-sized circles.

Proportional symbol maps can also be misleading if the regions displayed vary too much in size. Notice the dense cluster of bubbles in the northeast United States, indirectly suggesting a high concentration of people with college degrees *and* obesity in the region.

Would a *choropleth map* be more effective? A choropleth map encodes values by means of shades and colors. I tried that, too, in **Figure 6.17**. It doesn't work very

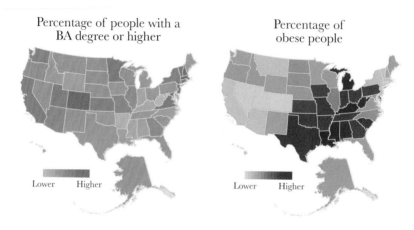

Figure 6.17 My second choice was a choropleth map. I was not very fond of it.

well either. Shading is low on our scale, indicating that it's not that great for comparisons, although it might be appropriate if you just want to offer an overview of the data. Can you tell how much higher the obesity rate is in Texas than in California? Not likely.

If I wish readers to be able to rank and compare, a bar chart or *dot chart* would be good options. You can see the data encoded as a dot chart in **Figure 6.18**. I'm sure you'll notice the big differences between states.

Are there other kinds of charts that would rank high in Cleveland and McGill's scale and, besides allowing comparisons between the values, also facilitate the visualization of the relationship between them? Yes. The first is the *scatter-plot*, shown in **Figure 6.19**. The other, a favorite of mine, is the *slopegraph* (**Figure 6.20**). Although the examples would need to be tweaked and refined to be publishable in a newspaper or magazine, they accomplish both the goals of comparing values and seeing relationships.

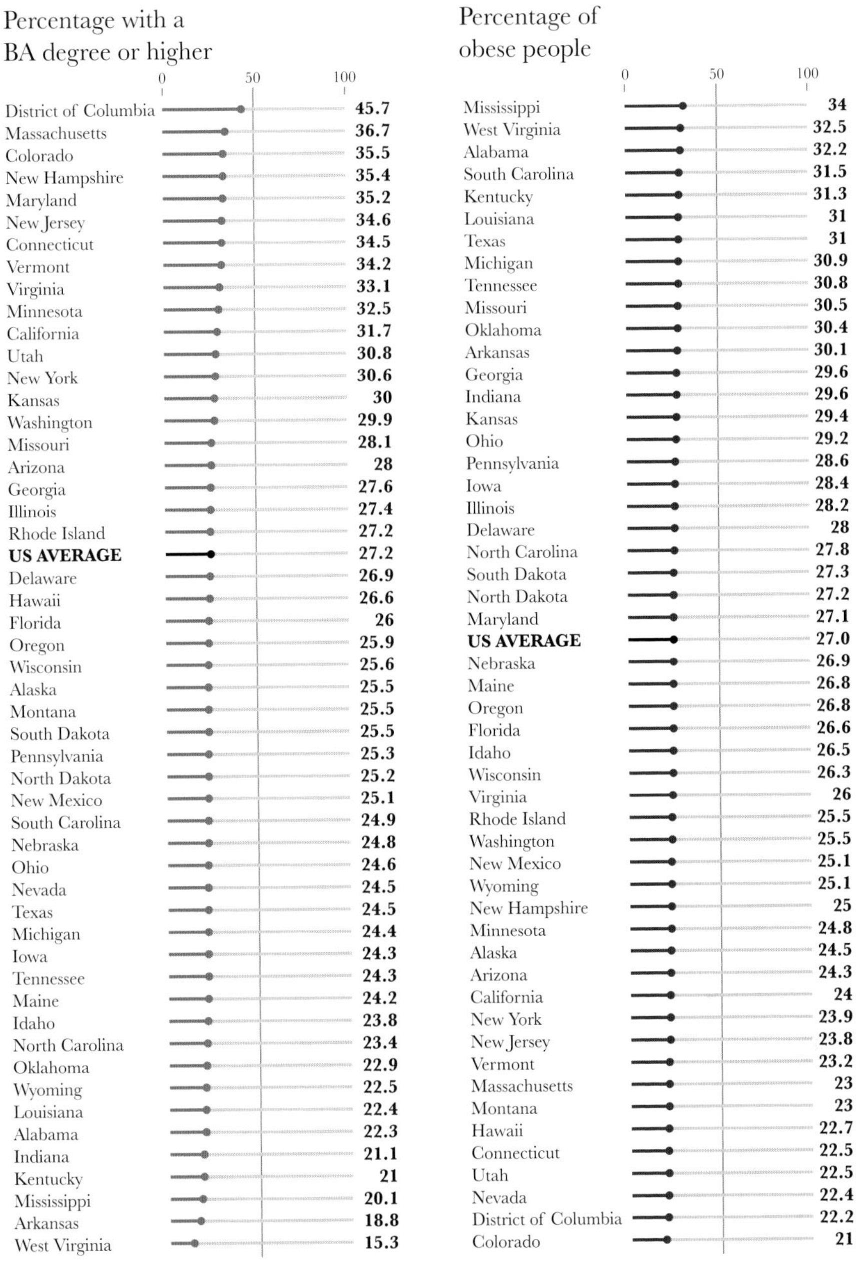

Percentage with a BA degree or higher

State	0 — 50 — 100	Value
District of Columbia		45.7
Massachusetts		36.7
Colorado		35.5
New Hampshire		35.4
Maryland		35.2
New Jersey		34.6
Connecticut		34.5
Vermont		34.2
Virginia		33.1
Minnesota		32.5
California		31.7
Utah		30.8
New York		30.6
Kansas		30
Washington		29.9
Missouri		28.1
Arizona		28
Georgia		27.6
Illinois		27.4
Rhode Island		27.2
US AVERAGE		27.2
Delaware		26.9
Hawaii		26.6
Florida		26
Oregon		25.9
Wisconsin		25.6
Alaska		25.5
Montana		25.5
South Dakota		25.5
Pennsylvania		25.3
North Dakota		25.2
New Mexico		25.1
South Carolina		24.9
Nebraska		24.8
Ohio		24.6
Nevada		24.5
Texas		24.5
Michigan		24.4
Iowa		24.3
Tennessee		24.3
Maine		24.2
Idaho		23.8
North Carolina		23.4
Oklahoma		22.9
Wyoming		22.5
Louisiana		22.4
Alabama		22.3
Indiana		21.1
Kentucky		21
Mississippi		20.1
Arkansas		18.8
West Virginia		15.3

Percentage of obese people

State	0 — 50 — 100	Value
Mississippi		34
West Virginia		32.5
Alabama		32.2
South Carolina		31.5
Kentucky		31.3
Louisiana		31
Texas		31
Michigan		30.9
Tennessee		30.8
Missouri		30.5
Oklahoma		30.4
Arkansas		30.1
Georgia		29.6
Indiana		29.6
Kansas		29.4
Ohio		29.2
Pennsylvania		28.6
Iowa		28.4
Illinois		28.2
Delaware		28
North Carolina		27.8
South Dakota		27.3
North Dakota		27.2
Maryland		27.1
US AVERAGE		27.0
Nebraska		26.9
Maine		26.8
Oregon		26.8
Florida		26.6
Idaho		26.5
Wisconsin		26.3
Virginia		26
Rhode Island		25.5
Washington		25.5
New Mexico		25.1
Wyoming		25.1
New Hampshire		25
Minnesota		24.8
Alaska		24.5
Arizona		24.3
California		24
New York		23.9
New Jersey		23.8
Vermont		23.2
Massachusetts		23
Montana		23
Hawaii		22.7
Connecticut		22.5
Utah		22.5
Nevada		22.4
District of Columbia		22.2
Colorado		21

Figure 6.18 A dot chart is equal to a bar chart when it comes to estimating proportions.

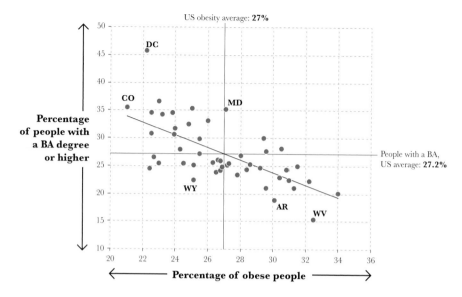

Figure 6.19 A scatter-plot.

Other Preattentive Features: Seeing in Depth

There are other features our brain detects preattentively and with ease. Consider three-dimensional vision. Why are we able to see in depth when visual perception starts with the stimulation of cells attached to a flat surface, the retina? How do we translate 2D into 3D?

We see in 3D, first, because we have two eyes. What your right eye sees is not exactly what your left eye does. You can test this easily if you put a pencil a few inches in front of your head. If you close your right eye, the pencil will appear to move slightly to the right; if you close your left eye, the pencil will move to the left. The image of the world your brain generates is a composite of the slightly different inputs it receives from both eyes.

This phenomenon, called *stereoscopic depth perception*, is not the only way to see in 3D. If it were, we would be in serious trouble when closing (or losing) one eye. Fortunately, the brain also receives tons of still images per second from each eye, thanks to the fact that it constantly scans the scene. Remember saccades, that rapid, intermittent movements of the eye as it takes in any scene? I explained those in Chapter 5.

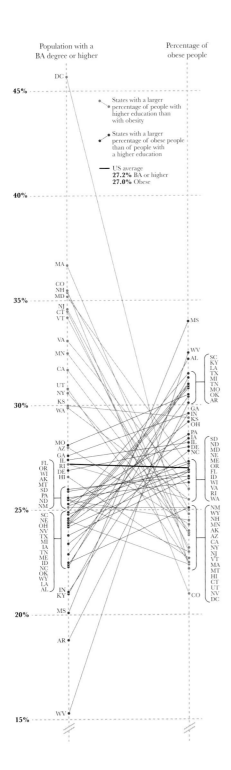

Figure 6.20 A slopegraph.

The brain uses other tricks to build the illusion of depth. Interestingly, the hints our mind extracts from our surroundings to accomplish this task are very similar to the techniques traditional artists use to simulate perspective in works of art.

For instance, the brain assumes that light comes from above. In the natural world, circumstances in which the light comes from below an object are extremely rare. Therefore, as a timesaving strategy, the brain learned to infer that if an object looks more or less like the first circle in **Figure 6.21**, it is probably concave, and if it looks like the second circle, it is convex. The illusion remains even if we simplify the circles and their shades. Keep it in mind when you design buttons for your interactive graphics. As we'll see in Chapter 9, it is important that readers are able to recognize interface elements at a glance.

Fig 6.21 Our brains define concave and convex objects by how light hits them.

The relative sizes of objects in a scene and their interposition are also powerful clues for depth perception. Notice how hard it is not to perceive objects closer to us and in front of each other in **Figure 6.22**.

Figure 6.22 Interposition is a powerful tool for building the illusion of depth.

Finally, if you remember the beginning of this chapter—I love circular structures when I write—I began with the assertion that one of the first steps in visual perception is to discriminate foreground from background; that is, to identify the edges of objects and creatures in order to know their boundaries. This feature is enlisted for depth perception as well. In **Figure 6.23**, the brain perceives *lines* that recede toward the horizon until they converge in a vanishing point, even if no real lines are present, just blurry edges. The illusion persists when we substitute the photograph with more abstract representations of the same landscape. Making the edges sharper, in fact, only strengthens this illusion.

Figure 6.23 Seeing in perspective.

So far, we've covered what it is known as *low-level visual perception*, including the most basic tasks of foreground-background differentiation, the estimation of the relative sizes of things, the extraction of simple patterns from our surroundings, and so on. I hope I've convinced you that learning about how the brain performs these tasks will help you design better information graphics and visualizations.

We are about to enter an even more fascinating territory, that of *high-level perception*, which involves the identification of what we see. These perceptual tasks answer the intriguing question suggested by renowned neurologist Oliver Sacks back in 1985:

How the hell do I know that this moving and talkative object standing in front of me is my wife, and not a hat?[5]

---

5 Fron the book, *The Man Who Mistook His Wife for a Hat and Other Clinical Tales*, by Oliver Sacks, (1985). The book's title is based on the case of a patient who suffered from visual agnosia.

7

Images in the Head

In order to understand perception, you need first to get rid of the notion that the image at the back of your eye simply gets "relayed" back to your brain to be displayed on a screen. Instead, you must understand that as soon as the rays of light are converted into neural impulses at the back of your eye, it no longer makes sense to think of the visual information as being an image. We must think, instead, of symbolic descriptions that represent the scenes and objects that had been in the image.

—V.S. Ramachandran, from *The Tell-Tale Brain:*
A Neuroscientist's Quest for What Makes Us Human

Evolution influences us to be attracted to what increases our chances of survival and reproduction and to be repelled by what harms us. If bananas were poisonous, their smell would be as repulsive to us as the stench of fresh excrement. Likewise, if feces were not a source for infections and our digestive system had evolved to extract nutrients from them, we would perceive their smell as a mouth-watering fragrance. What a dung beetle would consider a delicacy is for us the epitome of revulsion.

In other words, sensory properties are not intrinsic to objects, plants, and animals, but attributes our brains assign to them depending on how they relate to us as organisms. As I've said in previous chapters, perception is an active process. So is cognition, the ensemble of processes that identifies our environment and figures out how we can take advantage of it. Memory and certain innate skills play a crucial role in this.

How to Open an Airplane Door

One of my most shameful habits is to sometimes take the aircraft safety card with me when I leave an airplane. I know you're not supposed to do it, but I am an educator, and my act of mischief is in the service of an academic research project on visual displays of information—at least, so I like to think.

Nor am I the only one who's a bit obsessed with safety cards. Eric Ericson and Johan Phil wrote a very fine book about them a decade ago, titled *Design for Impact* (2003), and I'm sure they didn't build their personal collections by politely explaining their nerdy fascinations to the flight attendant.

Lame excuses for misbehavior aside, the old American Airlines safety card holds a special place in my heart (**Figure 7.1**). One reason is the guy with the moustache who jumps onto the ramp, arms out, an expression of fear and surprise on his face. Another reason is that this card is relevant to this book: it tells us a bit about how human visual perception works.

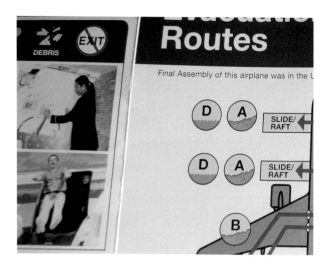

Figure 7.1 American Airlines safety card and a very surprised and mustached inhabitant (lower left). (Photograph by Photoedit.)

Back in 2006, I used this design project as the topic for a class exercise. I invited several graphic designers and journalists to a workshop to focus on the card, particularly on the section where a woman shows how to open the airplane door.

You can see a portion of it on the left side of Figure 7.1. I asked my students to tell me what they thought about the card and to propose improvements.

Their answers made sense. They responded that it takes a while to figure out what people are doing in the safety card's photographs, regardless of whether they are inflating the yellow floating vest, opening the airplane doors, or jumping down the ramp. We get it, they said, but with a different kind of display, those operations could be understood almost effortlessly. **A photograph includes too much information that's irrelevant for understanding what's going on.**

I observed that the designer of the card seemed more interested in showing *how things are*, rather than in *how things work*. A photograph is one of the most realistic of visual representations available for designers, but **perhaps what is needed here is not realism**.

Then I asked the students to propose redesigns. Many of their proposals were similar to those shown in **Figure 7.2**. All are abstractions, in which the human character in the original design is stripped of individual attributes such as skin color and clothing, and is reduced to a silhouette.

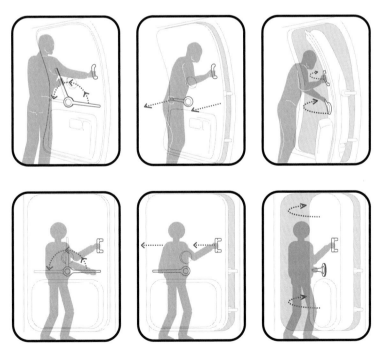

Figure 7.2 Two step-by-step explanations of how to open an airplane door in case of an emergency.

This kind of presentation follows certain rules outlined in the previous chapter. It anticipates what the human brain will try to do—find out what is relevant and what is secondary—and creates a hierarchy of elements in the display before the brain attempts that same operation. To accomplish this goal, the illustrations use red to focus the user's eyes on what is important: what you need to grab, pull, and push, and how you should do it (arrows). Everything else is gray.

What is more interesting to me, however, is that, by comparing the photographs with the line art examples, we could ask:

How is it possible that we are able to infer that a bunch of strokes and shades of gray represent a person opening a door?

The answer to this question is not obvious. The illustrated examples are very abstract, with only a vague resemblance to the original sequence. In fact, those figures *don't look like real people*. They don't have eyes, mouths, or hair, and their limbs are barely distinguishable.

Let's go a step further. See **Figure 7.3**. That is me almost a decade ago. I don't look exactly like that anymore (I wish I did). Notice that it doesn't matter how much I simplify my own image, going from a photograph to a simple set of circles and straight lines, *you still see faces* in those images. How is that possible? The answer to that question can lead to interesting insights about how to make better explanatory infographics. Let's investigate.

Figure 7.3 My face, represented with different levels of abstraction.

Recognizing by Remembering

In **Figure 7.4**, I've reproduced the diagram that opened Chapter 5. The explanation is correct until we get to the brain. What happens inside our heads is that electrical and chemical impulses are interpreted as patterns with which we associate meaning. Here's what happens when I am in front of my friend Mike's photograph:

First, I see a human face. Then I recognize that the face belongs to my friend, Mike Schimdt. Next, my brain notes that he is screaming and frowning with his eyebrows, and finally I may become concerned about why all of this is happening.

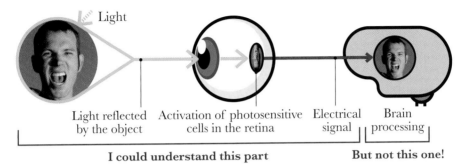

Figure 7.4 This simplistic explanation of visual perception is correct only until we get to the brain.

Cognitive psychologists find that during visual perception, information runs in two opposite and convergent pathways. The first pathway brings impulses from the retina to the brain; the other retrieves contents from our memory and brings them to the visual processing areas.

The first pathway is called **bottom-up processing**, and the second is called **top-down processing**. You can see them represented in **Figure 7.5**, along with three different kinds of memory. We have already explored several features of bottom-up processing, such as perceiving preattentive features like shapes, edges, relative sizes, and patches of color. Now it's time to explain how all that information is put together to make sense of the world.

When the cells in your retina are stimulated by light, they send impulses to the brain. The information these impulses carry is first stored and processed in **iconic memory**, a very short-term storage for visual information. The role of iconic memory in perception and cognition is to keep a coherent picture of the world that can later be interpreted by the brain. For the purposes of this book, it doesn't really matter where this iconic memory resides. Just remember that this is where preattentive features are first extracted and processed, albeit in a very rough manner.

From iconic memory, information encoded in neural impulses is transmitted to visual working memory. This, too, is a form of short-term storage, one with a quite limited capacity. To give you an idea of how small this mental warehouse

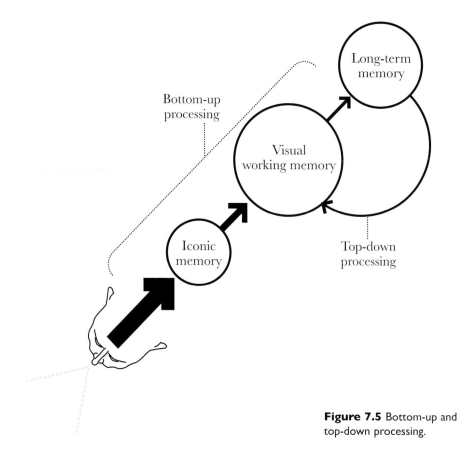

Figure 7.5 Bottom-up and top-down processing.

is, see how long you can remember the title of the most famous academic paper written about it: "The magical number seven, plus or minus two: some limits on our capacity for processing information," written by Princeton University psychologist George A. Miller in 1956[1]. The limited capacity of our visual working memory helps explain why it's not advisable to use more than four or five colors or pictograms to identify different phenomena on maps and charts. Most readers are not likely to remember what they represent.

Finally, **long-term memory** is our (almost) permanent storehouse for information that can be retrieved later on for our survival.

---

1   Recent academic papers claim that the number of items that can be handled in working memory is even smaller—four or less—and that the number depends on circumstances such as the kind of information being processed. Jeanne Farrington's (2011) "Seven plus or minus two" in *Performance Improvement Quarterly* 23 (4): 113-6 is one example.

The relationship between working memory and long-term memory can be compared to the one that exists between RAM memory and a hard drive in a computer. It is true that I've written that the brain is not a hard-drive, but its dynamics can be better understood if we make some analogies.

What happens when you click twice on a file on your desktop? The desired file was previously stored in the hard drive, which is slow, big, and more or less reliable. By opening the file with the corresponding software tool, you're transferring data to RAM memory. Like working memory in the brain, RAM memory is fast but has a limited capacity: If you keep opening files, you will soon run out of it, and the computer will ask you to start closing programs.

You can also retrieve items from your long-term memory. Visualize a red truck carrying recently cut trees. That's it. You've just asked your long-term memory (hard drive) to load materials to your working memory (RAM), which is where that mental image arises.

This is interesting enough, but it gets better: When your brain transfers visual information from the retina to working memory, it also keeps loading contents from long-term memory. It is in the confluence between impulses that come from the eyes (bottom-up processing), and impulses that come from memory (top-down processing) that object recognition occurs.

The Comparing Brain

Roughly speaking, **the brain identifies objects by comparing what you see with what you know and remember.** When it finds a match, it (figuratively) shouts "Eureka!" **Figure 7.6** builds on what you saw in Figure 7.5. Read on for an explanation of the steps.

1. An external entity (my friend Mike's face) reflects light that reaches your retinas. Photoreceptor cells are stimulated by photons and encode the patterns of light into electrochemical signals that are sent to iconic memory.

2. In iconic memory, the brain extracts the main features of what's in front of us, beginning with its gross shape over the background, followed by some interesting inside features (in this case, eyes, mouth, etc.). The extracted information is sent to working memory.

3. The brain keeps loading information from long-term to working memory. The information is not necessarily visual. It can also be propositional: for instance, if we have memorized the textual description of a very uncommon

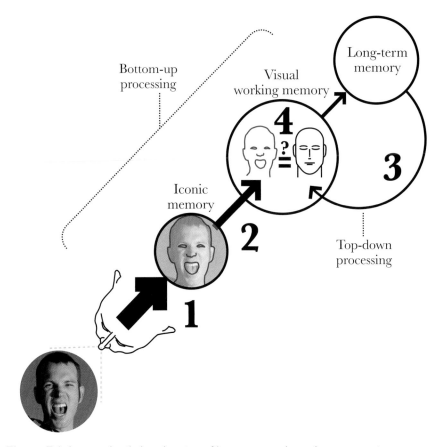

Figure 7.6 A more detailed explanation of bottom-up and top-down processing.

musical instrument, the description of it will help us identify it when we see it later on.

4. In working memory, the brain compares the patterns coming from the eyes with the patterns loaded from long-term memory. When it finds a match, it proceeds to identify an object. Have you ever wondered why you see faces and other familiar objects and creatures in clouds? Here's your answer: It's your brain making you see them.

But things are never simple when it comes to the brain. The explanation I've just given you isn't wrong, but it doesn't suffice. Some key questions need to be answered if we want to take advantage of the way the brain recognizes objects for our purposes as designers.

The Mental Imagery Debate

Discussions of visual working memory inevitably lead to the debate on the existence of mental images and our skill to generate and manipulate them. Eminent scientists have famously asserted that their thinking processes are not based on the mind speaking to itself using words, but on giving visual mental shape to concepts and ideas to facilitate their combination in some sort of imaginary space.

Here's a widely cited quote from Albert Einstein, taken from a letter to the mathematician Jacques Hadamard:

> The words of language, as they are written or spoken, do not seem to play any role in my mechanism of thought. The physical entities which seem to serve as elements in thought are certain signs and more or less clear images (...) Conventional words or other signs have to be sought for laboriously only in a second stage, where the associative play already referred to is sufficiently established and can be reproduced at will.

To understand mental images and their role in perception and cognition, imagine you've just bought a condo and that you are going to a store to buy curtains for the windows. As you arrive, you realize that you've forgotten to bring the notes you took while measuring and recording the position of each window. If you don't want to drive home again, you will try to recall the floor plan of your new place by summoning remembered images of the walls and scanning them to locate the windows.

In a famous nineteenth century experiment, Sir Francis Galton, a cousin of Charles Darwin's, asked a group of subjects what they had eaten for breakfast. He learned that most, but not all, visualized the table where they had sat that morning in order to facilitate the remembrance of the foods that were on it.

Modern scientists specializing in visual mental imagery, such as Stephen Kosslyn, ask you to imagine a capital N. Now, rotate it ninety degrees clockwise and tell me if you see a different letter. Many people say that they see a Z with their "mind's eye.[2]"

The fact that so many people say that they feel like they are seeing a Z in their minds when asked to rotate an N could be based on an illusion, say critics such as philosophers Daniel Dennet and Zenon W. Pylyshyn. It should also be noted that not all people are capable of forming visual mental images. But these objections do

2 Kosslyn has written several books on visual mental images, including *Image and Brain: the Resolution of the Imagery Debate* (1996), and *The Case for Mental Imagery* (2009). He has also written extensively about the perception of statistical charts. See the bibliography.

not explain why roughly the same neuron patterns in the working memory of the brain are activated when we *see* an object and when we *imagine* that same object.

A strong objection to the hypothesis that the brain uses visual working memory to compare information from the retinas with information from long-term memory is that it is not possible for the mental representation of an object to be based solely on picture-like mental patterns. If things were so simple, the brain would have to store an impossible number of unique *templates,* not only of every object it is possible to see, but also of all possible angles and positions that object can adopt. As in **Figure 7.7**, the brain doesn't have enough room to keep so many views of common items, such as hands and heads. So a mental image must be much more than a simple image.

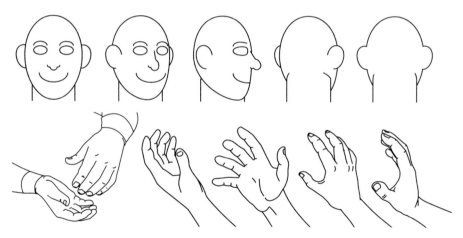

Figure 7.7 It would be impossible to store a mental visual image for every possible variation of an object.

How Do We Really Know that a Face is a Face?

Imagery theorists have their own arguments to make. For instance, in some experiments, people were presented with an object rotated varying degrees, as in **Figure 7.8**. The researchers found that the farther the object was rotated from its most common orientation, the longer it took to recognize it. Evidence suggests that, when faced with the task of identifying such pictures, we mentally rotate them until they adopt a more natural pose.

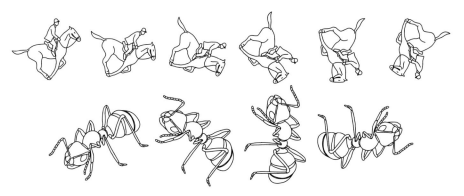

Figure 7.8 The more you rotate an object, the more difficult it is to tell what it is.

Visual object recognition theory is much more sophisticated and nuanced than its critics like to admit. Smith and Kosslyn (2007)[3] explain that there are at least three models that explain how the brain recognizes objects and creatures. The models are not mutually exclusive, but work complementarily. Depending on the circumstances, we rely more on one than on the others. An object can be identified based on its main features, on its components, and on its configuration.

Recognition based on *features* explains why we still see a face in the most abstract drawing in Figure 7.3 at the beginning of this chapter. It is not necessary for the brain to perceive every single detail of a face to be able to recognize it as a face. It is enough to identify several *nonaccidental properties* of it. A nonaccidental property is a feature that usually belongs to a particular kind of entity. For example, if the brain preattentively extracts shapes that look like eyes, a mouth, and a nose, it is likely to identify a face.

Dehaene (2009) suggests that junctures and corners are an important component of feature-based recognition. The points where the main lines of an object converge or sharply change orientation are critical to identifying it. The brain has neurons that are specialized in detecting these features.

See **Figure 7.9** to understand this idea. The first shape is almost unrecognizable, whereas in the second example we can perceive a stool. What is more interesting is that I have removed the same amount of ink in both drawings, but one of them is more identifiable because it preserves corners, angles, and edges that are particular to a stool (or something very similar to it).

3 *Cognitive Psychology: Mind and Brain* is a wonderful, comprehensive and deep introduction to cognitive psychology. It is written for undergraduates, so should be understandable to most readers with minimum effort.

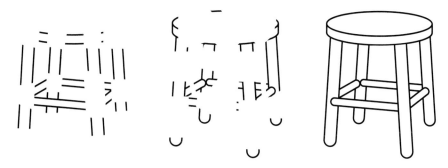

Figure 7.9 It is easier to identify an object when we can see its corners and junctures.

The second strategy the brain uses to identify objects is to pay attention to their *components*. It is likely that the brain memorizes structural descriptions of what it perceives, meaning that you are able to recognize a cell phone regardless of the angle at which you see it, and regardless of its size and screen height, because you see little numbered buttons, a screen, and other distinctive features that pertain to a generic object category called "cell phones."

Lastly, we have *configuration-based* object recognition. This strategy involves a more holistic approach than the identification of nonaccidental features and parts of an object. In this case, the brain pays attention to how the components of an object are spatially arranged, and to how they relate to one another, in order to identify it.

This model has been used in several studies of facial recognition with interesting results. Research suggests that when trying to recognize a specific person, the brain first identifies the object as a generic face, and then focuses on those features farthest away from a prototypical, generic face.

This may explain why we are so quick to identify the character portrayed in a good caricature: because cartoonists *anticipate what the brain will try to do* and exaggerate precisely the features that most noticeably deviate from the norm. For an example, see **Figure 7.10**, created by my friend, the multitalented artist Ricardo Martínez. Can you tell who those folks are? I bet you can in the blink of an eye.

Applying Object Recognition to Information Graphics

What we know today about how the brain recognizes objects solves a mystery posed in 1956 by the psychologists T.A. Ryan and C.B. Schwartz, in their paper, "Speed of perception as a function of mode of presentation," published in the *American*

Figure 7.10 Illustrations by Ricardo Martínez (*El Mundo*).

Journal of Psychology. Ryan and Schwartz showed participants in a study several images based on the same scene: a photograph, a shaded illustration, and a line art drawing. See **Figure 7.11**, which I created using my stepson's hand.

When they measured the speed at which the participants were able to identify the components of the scene, the psychologists were surprised to find that the most abstract depiction was the most efficient at this goal. As irrelevant or redundant

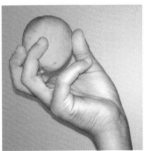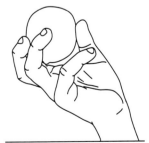

Figure 7.11 The content of the line art drawing is more easily recognizable, on average.

information was removed from the illustration, its main features became more pronounced, facilitating its identification, because the brain had to work less to extract them.

V.S. Ramachandran, a professor of neuroscience at the University of California, San Diego, explains the advantages of using sketches and line art in certain cases in his book *The Tell-Tale Brain* (2011):

> A sketch can be more effective because there is an attentional bottleneck in your brain. You can pay attention to only one aspect of an image or one entity at a time (...). In the dynamics of perception, one stable percept (perceives image) automatically excludes others (...). Neural networks in your brain constantly compete for limited attentional resources. Thus when you look at a full-color picture, your attention is distracted by the clutter of texture and other details in the image. But a sketch of the same object allows you to allocate all your attentional resources to the outline, where the action is.[4]

So, how is all this related to information graphics?

See **Figure 7.12**, an infographic on ice hotels made by my team at *Época* magazine. Each year in winter, a few companies build these structures of ice and steel in Canada, Sweden, Norway, Finland, Romania, and Switzerland. And they are real hotels. You can book a room and stay there, and even enjoy some ice cream.

If you pay attention to the graphic, you will see that there are two very different kinds of illustrations: The one at the center is hyper-realistic, extremely detailed and beautiful. The others, surrounding the first one, are simplified and abstract. Why the difference? Because of the functions of each illustration, which complement one another. **One illustration shows how the hotel *looks*, while the others show how something *works*.**

The drawing styles are matched to their goals. If the goal is to explain machines, mechanisms, and processes, a very realistic style is not appropriate because, as Ramachandran points out above, "Your attention is distracted by the clutter of texture and other details." Better to use a sketch-like display, so attention is focused on what really matters.

Looking Ahead

In Chapters 5, 6, and 7, I have given you a glimpse of what you can learn by exploring the psychology of perception and cognition. It would be presumptuous,

---

4 If you read only one general introduction to how the mind works, and want it to relate tangentially to information graphics and visualization, it should be Ramachandran's *The Tell-Tale Brain* (2011).

though, to pretend that I have covered everything that needs to be known to adapt our designs to what the brain can and cannot do. That's beyond my reach not only because I am no neuroscientist, but also because new discoveries are made every month. I would recommend you keep an eye on the field.

The key idea to remember is that **vision is an active process. Our mind actively maps our surroundings, and uses rules and tricks to do it.** Antonio Damasio explains it beautifully:

> Consciousness allows us to experience maps as images, to manipulate those images, and to apply reasoning to them (...) action and maps, movements and mind, are part of an unending cycle (...) The construction of maps never stops even in our sleep (...) The human brain is a mimic of the irrepressible variety. Whatever sits outside the brain (...) is mimicked inside the brain's networks. In other words, the brain has the ability to represent aspects of the structure of nonbrain things and events (...) It is not a mere copy, a passive transfer from the outside of the brain toward its inside. The assembly conjured by the senses involves an active contribution offered from inside the brain.[5]

The better we understand the shortcuts the mind uses to make sense of the world, the better we will be able to anticipate them and to take advantage of them for our purposes. As Robert Spence has pointed out (2007) **visualization is not something that happens on a page or on a screen; it happens in the mind.** The representation on the page or screen is merely an aid to facilitate that insight.

5　Antonio Damasio, *Self Comes to Mind: Constructing the Conscious Brain* (New York: Pantheon, 2010).

Diagram
NEWS IN PERSPECTIVE

Kiruna **Jukkasjärv**
Torne Rive
Sea of
Norway   Polar Arctic Circle
SUÉCIA

Atlantic
Ocean

FINLAND
NORWAY   **150 mi**

a - Hotel Glace - Canada
b - Iglu-Dorf - Switzerland
c - Ice Lodge - Norway
d - Icehotel - Sweden
e - Alta Igloo Hotel - Norway
f - Lumi Hotelli - Finland
g - Ice Hotel Bâlea Lac - Romania

Jukkasjärvi is close to the city
of Kiruna, which is 1,000 feet
above sea level. The ice used
build the Ice Hotel comes
from the Torne River, which fl
through the region.

The Biggest Igloo

How to build a 60,000 square foot
hotel made of ice and snow

Rodrigo Cunha, Gerson Mora

ONCE the winter starts in the Northern Hemisphere, a team of architects, designers and artists
meets in **Jukkasjärvi**, a Swedish town in the
Arctic Circle, to put up another edition of **Icehotel,**
the most traditional hotel made of ice, first
conceived in 1989 for an exhibition near the Torne
River. Since then, the ritual is repeated annually.
The construction of the complex opens in November and ends on December 30 every year. It stays
open until April, when it begins to melt with the
arrival of spring. In total, the hotel has **60 rooms
and 20 suites that can house thousands of
guests per season**. But plan to stay there only if
you like cold: the internal temperature ranges
from 15.8ºF to 24.8ºF. At least six other
networks have already built similar hotels
elsewhere in the world.

Engineers
soften edges
and smooth the
surface of the building.

HOW THE ICE HOTEL IS BUILT

Extraction of ice blocks
After a group of snow tractors
flattens the snow on the Torne
River **(1)**, the extraction of
blocks of ice begins **(2)**. More
than 1,000 tons of ice are
removed and stored **(3)**. They
will be used in the construction
of walls and pillars.

Snow production
Specialized machinery drains
water from the river **(4)** and
throws it into the air, where it is
transformed into dense
snowflakes. The snow produced
in this way is transported **(5)**
and sprayed onto the iron
structure **(6)**.

A chainsaw
cuts the ice

Water drainage
400 ounces
per minute

Water
becomes snow

Cold air

Sources: Icehotel Art&Design Group, National Geographic and BBC

Figure 7.12 An ice hotel, an interesting place to stay for your Christmas holidays.

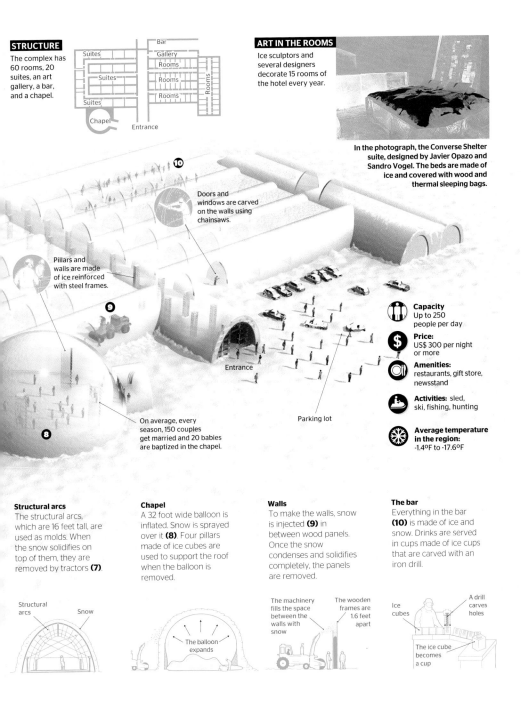

STRUCTURE

The complex has 60 rooms, 20 suites, an art gallery, a bar, and a chapel.

Suites

Suites

Suites

Bar

Gallery

Rooms

Rooms

Rooms

Rooms

Chapel   Entrance

ART IN THE ROOMS

Ice sculptors and several designers decorate 15 rooms of the hotel every year.

In the photograph, the Converse Shelter suite, designed by Javier Opazo and Sandro Vogel. The beds are made of ice and covered with wood and thermal sleeping bags.

Doors and windows are carved on the walls using chainsaws.

Pillars and walls are made of ice reinforced with steel frames.

Entrance

On average, every season, 150 couples get married and 20 babies are baptized in the chapel.

Parking lot

Capacity
Up to 250 people per day

Price:
US$ 300 per night or more

Amenities:
restaurants, gift store, newsstand

Activities: sled, ski, fishing, hunting

Average temperature in the region:
-1.4ºF to -17.6ºF

Structural arcs
The structural arcs, which are 16 feet tall, are used as molds. When the snow solidifies on top of them, they are removed by tractors **(7)**.

Chapel
A 32 foot wide balloon is inflated. Snow is sprayed over it **(8)**. Four pillars made of ice cubes are used to support the roof when the balloon is removed.

Walls
To make the walls, snow is injected **(9)** in between wood panels. Once the snow condenses and solidifies completely, the panels are removed.

The bar
Everything in the bar **(10)** is made of ice and snow. Drinks are served in cups made of ice cups that are carved with an iron drill.

Structural arcs   Snow

The balloon expands

The machinery fills the space between the walls with snow

The wooden frames are 1.6 feet apart

Ice cubes

A drill carves holes

The ice cube becomes a cup

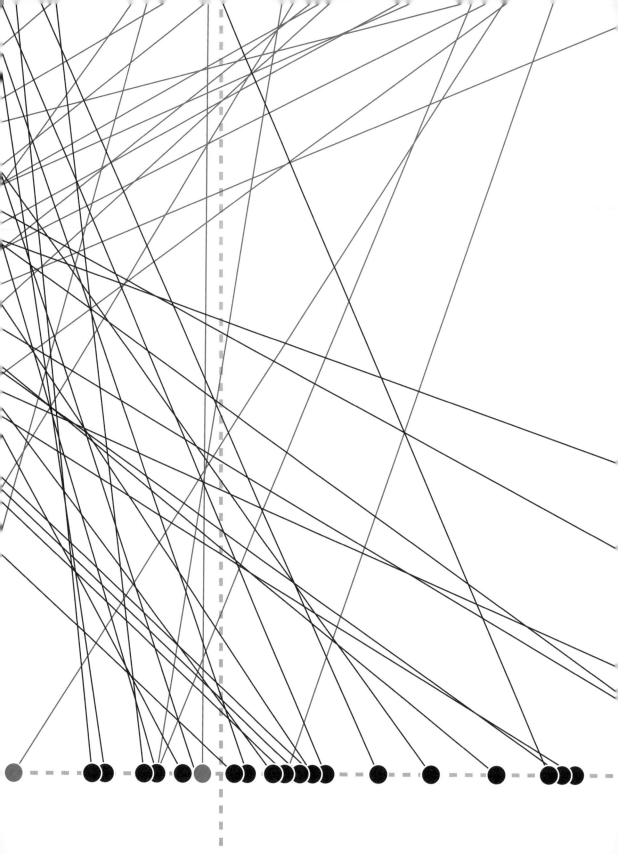

practice

8

Creating Information Graphics

A large part of the infographic's intrinsic appeal seems to lie in its visual reductionism of complex information. Reductionism itself is not inherently bad—in fact, it's an essential part of any kind of synthesis, be it mapmaking, journalism, particle physics, or statistical analysis. The problem arises when the act of reduction—in this case rendering data into an aesthetically elegant graphic—actually begins to unintentionally oversimplify, obscure, or warp the author's intended narrative, instead of bringing it into focus.

—Reif Larsen, from "This Chart Is a Lonely Hunter:
The Narrative Eros of the Infographic"

Good content reasoners and presenters are rare, designers are not.

—Edward Tufte, from an *AdAgeStat* blog

I'm often asked in workshops and seminars how I develop my own projects. Specifically, people want to know if I have a particular method for designing graphics that inform and attract readers. As a journalist, my approach is infused with lessons learned in the newsroom:

Start with a strong focus, do as much research as you can, organize, summarize, and then deliver your conclusions in a structured and visually appealing manner.

At first glance, there's nothing strikingly original about this. The real lessons come as the graphic is created, in the problems that must be solved and the decisions made along the way. My goal in this chapter is to walk you through my thought process for several projects developed with my team at Brazil's *Época* magazine (see the Acknowledgments to learn more about Marco Vergotti, Gerson Mora, Rodrigo Cunha, Luiz Salomão, Gerardo Rodríguez, Erik Scaranello, and Pedro Schimidt), where I worked as infographics director between 2010 and 2011. As you'll see, the following cases share a common creative methodology:

1. Define the focus of the graphic, what story you want to tell, and the key points to be made. Have a clear idea of how the infographic will be useful to your readers, and what they will be able to accomplish with it.

2. Gather as much information as you can about the topic you are covering. Interview sources, look for datasets, and write or storyboard ideas in quick form.

3. Choose the best graphic form. What shapes should your data adopt? What kind of charts, maps, and diagrams will best fit the goals you set in the first step?

4. Complete your research. Flesh out your sketches and storyboards.

5. Think about the visual style. Choose typefaces, color palettes, etc.

6. If you've been sketching offline, move the design to the computer. Complete the graphic using the appropriate software tools.

Many designers I know skip the preliminaries and jump directly to steps 5 and 6. Big mistake. **Before you think about style, you must think about structure.** Let me show you how.

Brazilian Saints

Brazil is a land of sometimes shocking paradoxes, a reality that Brazilians face with a sense of humor as well as concern. These paradoxes make the country a paradise for journalists.

For example, Brazil has the largest number of Catholics in the world. Yet, among the many hundreds of saints that the Catholic Church has canonized, **only two are of Brazilian origin**. Meanwhile, almost 70 people are on the church's waiting list to be considered for sainthood.

Now, review the paragraph I just wrote in the context of the infographics production process I outlined, and you will see that we've completed step 1: Define the focus. The idea for this focus came from a former intern at *Época*, Eliseu Barreira Júnior, who was a journalism student at Universidade de São Paulo (USP). He became curious about Catholic saints after talking to a couple of sources and thought it would make an interesting visual story. It did indeed: Not many people in Brazil are aware of the sanctity paradox.

The story was approved in an editorial meeting. The next step was to gather all the data, a big challenge, because the Catholic Church has no centralized, online database of all candidates for canonization. Eliseu first had to phone several local dioceses to ask if they had proposed anyone for sanctification in the past. He learned that all candidates were funneled through a retired Brazilian nun who is in charge of reviewing the proposals and sending them to the Vatican. Eliseu used her as a source as well. It took him four days to compile a list of Brazilian candidates for canonization and to gather portraits of 36 of them. That was more than half of the time we invested in completing the entire project!

While Eliseu was doing his research, the rest of the department and I were collecting background information. We wanted to show how many saints were named by each Pope in the past two centuries, explain how someone becomes a saint, and highlight the fact that, despite Latin America's standing as the most deeply Catholic region in the world, it has pushed a relatively small number of people through canonization. In fact, most of the saints made during John Paul II's and Benedict XVI's papacies come from Europe and Asia, apparently in an effort to promote Catholicism in those regions.

Figure 8.1 shows one of our first sketches for the project. I designed the layout in Adobe Illustrator. If you compare it to the final project in **Figure 8.2**, you will notice that the structure survived, but the look is entirely different.

This illustrates the point I made at the outset: You need to build a solid backbone for your information, a reading path, an order, and a hierarchy, before you lock yourself into a style for your display. The structure is the skeleton and muscles of your graphic; the visual style is the skin. With no bones to support it, the skin of your project will collapse.

SAINTS OF BRAZIL

INTRO

THE CANONIZATION PROCESS

1

Lorem ipsum dolor sit amet, consectetur adipiscing elit. Suspendisse hendrerit volutpat sem, et convallis lectus pharetra at. Integer congue felis quis diam tincidunt viverra. Cras at ligula turpis, consectetur ultrices velit. Fusce sagittis justo et orci luctus laoreet. Aliquam non nisl purus, ut porttitor lorem.

2

Lorem ipsum dolor sit amet, consectetur adipiscing elit. Suspendisse hendrerit volutpat sem, et convallis lectus pharetra at. Integer congue felis quis diam tincidunt viverra. Cras at ligula turpis, consectetur ultrices velit. Fusce sagittis justo et orci luctus laoreet. Aliquam non nisl purus, ut porttitor lorem.

WHO THE BRAZILIAN SAINTS ARE

Lorem ipsum dolor sit amet, consectetur adipiscing elit. Suspendisse hendrerit volutpat sem, et convallis lectus.

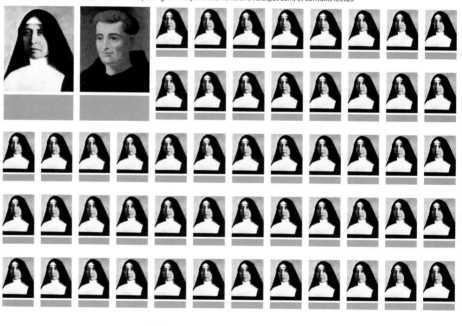

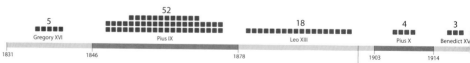

Figure 8.1 First layout for the Brazilian Saints project.

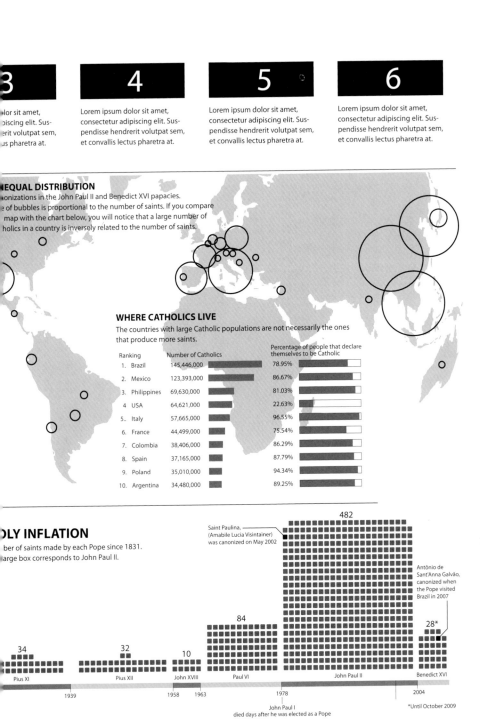

3

lor sit amet,
oiscing elit. Sus-
erit volutpat sem,
us pharetra at.

4

Lorem ipsum dolor sit amet,
consectetur adipiscing elit. Suspendisse hendrerit volutpat sem,
et convallis lectus pharetra at.

5

Lorem ipsum dolor sit amet,
consectetur adipiscing elit. Suspendisse hendrerit volutpat sem,
et convallis lectus pharetra at.

6

Lorem ipsum dolor sit amet,
consectetur adipiscing elit. Suspendisse hendrerit volutpat sem,
et convallis lectus pharetra at.

EQUAL DISTRIBUTION

onizations in the John Paul II and Benedict XVI papacies.
e of bubbles is proportional to the number of saints. If you compare
map with the chart below, you will notice that a large number of
holics in a country is inversely related to the number of saints.

WHERE CATHOLICS LIVE

The countries with large Catholic populations are not necessarily the ones
that produce more saints.

Ranking		Number of Catholics	Percentage of people that declare themselves to be Catholic
1.	Brazil	145,446,000	78.95%
2.	Mexico	123,393,000	86.67%
3.	Philippines	69,630,000	81.03%
4	USA	64,621,000	22.63%
5..	Italy	57,665,000	96.55%
6.	France	44,499,000	75.54%
7.	Colombia	38,406,000	86.29%
8.	Spain	37,165,000	87.79%
9.	Poland	35,010,000	94.34%
10.	Argentina	34,480,000	89.25%

OLY INFLATION

ber of saints made by each Pope since 1831.
large box corresponds to John Paul II.

482

Saint Paulina,
(Amabile Lucia Visintainer)
was canonized on May 2002

Antônio de
Sant'Anna Galvão,
canonized when
the Pope visited
Brazil in 2007

84

28*

34

32

10

| Pius XI | Pius XII | John XVIII | Paul VI | John Paul II | Benedict XVI |

1939   1958   1963   1978   2004

John Paul I
died days after he was elected as a Pope

*Until October 2009

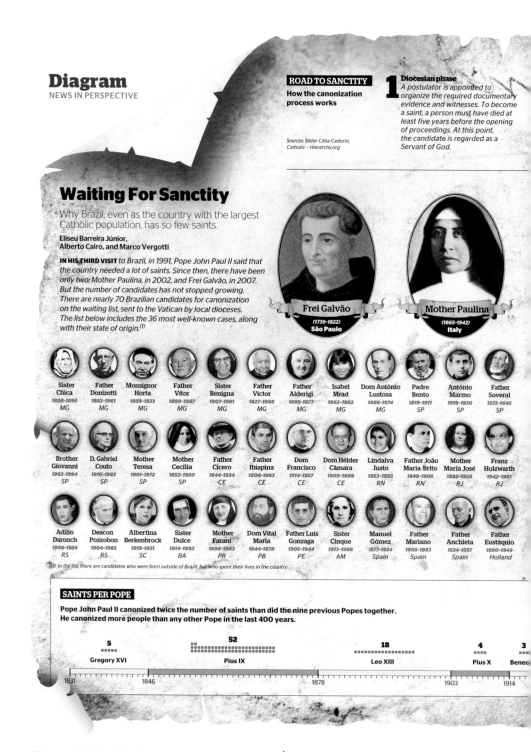

Diagram
NEWS IN PERSPECTIVE

ROAD TO SANCTITY
How the canonization
process works

Sources: Sister Célia Cadorin,
Catholic – Hierarchy.org

1 **Diocesian phase**
A postulator is appointed to
organize the required documentary
evidence and witnesses. To become
a saint, a person must have died at
least five years before the opening
of proceedings. At this point,
the candidate is regarded as a
Servant of God.

Waiting For Sanctity
Why Brazil, even as the country with the largest
Catholic population, has so few saints.

Eliseu Barreira Júnior,
Alberto Cairo, and Marco Vergotti

IN HIS THIRD VISIT to Brazil, in 1991, Pope John Paul II said that
the country needed a lot of saints. Since then, there have been
only two: Mother Paulina, in 2002, and Frei Galvão, in 2007.
But the number of candidates has not stopped growing.
There are nearly 70 Brazilian candidates for canonization
on the waiting list, sent to the Vatican by local dioceses.
The list below includes the 36 most well-known cases, along
with their state of origin.[1]

Frei Galvão
(1739-1822)
São Paulo

Mother Paulina
(1865-1942)
Italy

Sister Chica *1808-1895* MG	Father Donizetti *1882-1961* MG	Monsignor Horta *1859-1933* MG	Father Vitor *1899-1987* MG
Sister Benigna *1907-1981* MG	Father Victor *1827-1905* MG	Father Alderigi *1895-1977* MG	Isabel Mrad *1962-1982* MG
Dom Antônio Lustosa *1886-1974* MG	Padre Bento *1819-1911* SP	Antônio Marmo *1918-1930* SP	Father Soveral *1572-1645* SP

Brother Giovanni *1903-1994* SP	D. Gabriel Couto *1910-1982* SP	Mother Teresa *1901-1972* SP	Mother Cecília *1852-1950* SP
Father Cícero *1844-1934* CE	Father Ibiapina *1806-1883* CE	Dom Francisco *1914-1957* CE	Dom Hélder Câmara *1909-1999* CE
Lindalva Justo *1953-1993* RN	Father João Maria Brito *1848-1905* RN	Mother Maria José *1882-1959* RJ	Franz Holzwarth *1942-1981* RJ

Adílio Daronch *1908-1924* RS	Deacon Pozzobon *1904-1985* RS	Albertina Berkenbrock *1919-1931* SC	Sister Dulce *1914-1963* BA
Mother Farani *1906-1963* PR	Dom Vital Maria *1844-1878* PB	Father Luís Gonzaga *1905-1944* PE	Sister Cinque *1913-1988* AM
Manuel Gómez *1877-1924* Spain	Father Mariano *1905-1983* Spain	Father Anchieta *1534-1597* Spain	Father Eustáquio *1890-1943* Holland

(1) In the list, there are candidates who were born outside of Brazil, but who spent their lives in the country.

SAINTS PER POPE

Pope John Paul II canonized twice the number of saints than did the nine previous Popes together.
He canonized more people than any other Pope in the last 400 years.

5	52	18	4	3
Gregory XVI	Pius IX	Leo XIII	Pius X	Bened

1831   1846   1878   1903   1914

Figure 8.2 Brazilian Saints project, as published by *Época*, São Paulo, Brazil. Translated
from Portuguese.

At this stage testimonies of those who witnessed the life, virtues, and reputation of holiness are collected. The material is delivered to the **Congregation for the Causes of Saints** at the Vatican.

2 **Roman Phase**
A commission of cardinals and bishops analyze the documents. If approved, the candidate is declared Venerable by the Pope.

To become a **beatus** (someone worshiped by a particular group of believers), a venerable must have a miraculous cure proven. A martyr doesn't need to have a proven miracle to be beatified. It is just necessary to demonstrate that he or she died in the name of the faith.

The **canonization** occurs when a second miracle is proven. It must happen after beatification. The Pope issues a decree that the candidate must be worshiped by the entire Catholic Church.

UNEQUAL DISTRIBUTION

The size of the circles is proportional to the number of people canonized since 1978, during the papacies of John Paul II and Benedict XVI. Comparing the map with the graphics below, it is possible to see that having a large number of Catholics doesn't guarantee that a country will have a proportional number of saints. According to experts consulted by Época, this can be due to the lack of people trained to present canonization cases to the Vatican in Brazil.

103 Korean martyrs

BRAZIL 2 saints

In the past 32 years, more than 300 Asian candidates have been canonized, mainly in China, North and South Korea, Vietnam, and Japan. It is a way for the Catholic Church to promote itself in that region of the world.

FIGURES

US$400,000
Average cost of a canonization process. The team responsible for the process has 25 people: 7 judges, 8 theologians, 5 cardinals, and 5 bishops.

378 years
is the time that it took to have Father Anchieta beatified.

10,000
is the number of documents that led to the canonization of Frei Galvão.

3,000
canonization and beatification processes are currently under review in the Vatican.

Countries with largest Catholic populations (Millions of adherents).

BRAZIL	145
Mexico	123
Philippines	70
USA	65
Italy	58
France	44
Colombia	38
Spain	37
Poland	35
Argentina	34

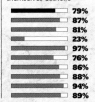

Percentage that declare themselves Catholic

	79%
	87%
	81%
	23%
	97%
	76%
	86%
	88%
	94%
	89%

79%

of Brazilians say they are Catholics. In the world, there are 50 nations whose populations are at least 50% Catholic.

Number of priests per country. (Thousands of people).

Italy	50
USA	45
Poland	28
Spain	25
France	22
India	20
Germany	18
Brazil	17
Mexico	15
Canada	8

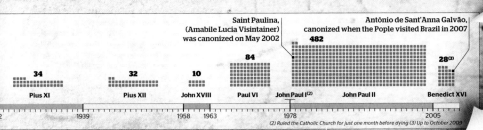

Saint Paulina, (Amabile Lucia Visintainer) was canonized on May 2002

Antônio de Sant'Anna Galvão, canonized when the Pople visited Brazil in 2007

482

84

28[3]

34   **32**   **10**

Pius XI   **Pius XII**   **John XVIII**   **Paul VI**   **John Paul I**[2]   **John Paul II**   **Benedict XVI**

2   1939   1958   1963   1978   2005

(2) Ruled the Catholic Church for just one month before dying (3) Up to October 2009

The Changing Face of Brazil's Population

Sometimes it is not the story that leads you to search for a particular kind of data. Sometimes, it is data that leads you to a story.

Maybe you remember the example on fertility that opened Chapter 1. I made that graphic while working on a real project for *Época* about how Brazilian population trends have changed in the past half-century.

In November 2010, the Brazilian Institute of Geography and Statistics (IBGE) was about to release the data for the latest census, conducted every 10 years. *Época* is a weekly magazine, so it cannot limit itself to summarizing what daily publications have already published during the week. One of my responsibilities as infographics director was to think up unexpected angles for stories that newspapers cover in detail. The fertility graphic was one of those. We knew that all kinds of media would echo IBGE's press releases. Would it be possible to go beyond what we predicted our competitors would do? It was no easy task. Brazilian media, particularly infographics desks, are extremely creative.

I was feeling a bit desperate when I remembered that a few days before, I had seen a story citing preliminary figures disclosed by the IBGE that indicated that the **Brazilian fertility rate** (the average number of children per woman) **was already below 1.9**. The statistic was counterintuitive. I was intrigued. In the minds of many foreigners—and I was one of them, having been there only a few months—Brazil is still an underdeveloped country where women tend to nurture huge families with four or five children, at least.

But **experience tells you not to trust intuition when you can rely on data**. I went to the World Bank databases and downloaded the fertility figures from all countries. Then, I plotted them in a line chart and highlighted Brazil. **Figure 8.3** might look familiar. It's very similar to one of the charts I designed for Chapter 1 when I was trying to find out if the hypotheses in Matt Riddley's *The Rational Optimist* made sense.

Impressive, isn't it? On average, in 1950, Brazilian women had more than six children. But that number has dropped below the replacement rate of 2.1—the minimum number of children couples must have to keep the population stable in the long term. Any country that scores below that will either face an older and

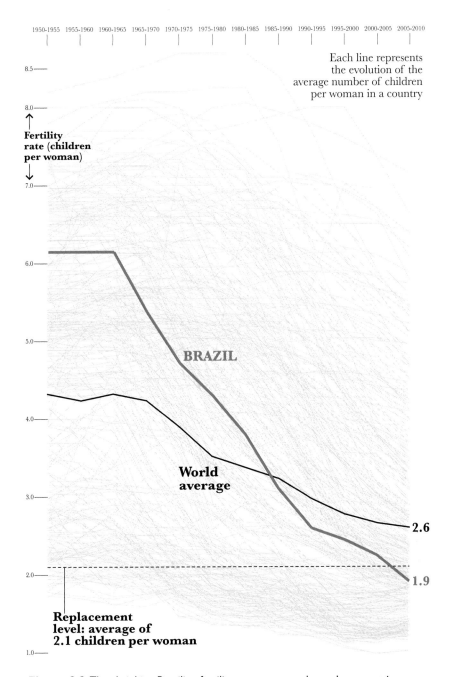

Figure 8.3 The shrinking Brazilian fertility rate, compared to other countries.

smaller population in the future, or will have to open its borders to more young immigrants hungry for opportunities.

All of this was pretty interesting, but it was not enough to be considered a proper journalistic story. I needed a narrative that tied the data together and was compelling enough to be read. Fortunately for me, *Época's* managing editor, Helio Gurovitz, holds a B.A. in computer science, which he got years before he decided to become a journalist, so he knows numbers. He proposed a headline for the double-page infographic we were planning: *"Brazil's Demographic Opportunity."* Then he outlined a possible narrative:

1. Start with the news: the data from the new Brazilian census. We already knew it would show that Brazil experienced healthy population growth between 2000 and 2010.

2. At the same time, the fertility rate is down compared with other countries and regions.

3. The dramatic loss of fertility will eventually lead to a smaller and older population.

4. In spite of how dire that sounds, Brazil can take advantage of the situation by investing in education now.

I liked Helio's idea so much that I rushed back to my computer and started putting together a layout. I wanted to publish the story as soon as possible. The only catch was that the IBGE had not officially released the census data. But, digging into its website, I had seen that it had published a shaded map with the new numbers. So they did have the figures, although they had not yet told the press.

I phoned the IBGE press department and requested access to the organization's database. I wanted to use it with a software program I had recently become acquainted with, called Estatcart, which was developed by the IBGE itself.

Estatcart is a Geographic Information System, or *GIS tool*. Simply speaking, in any GIS tool, you start with an empty map such as the one in **Figure 8.4** (that is Estatcart's interface). Then, you link the map to a Microsoft Excel spreadsheet or to a database. The colors of the regions change depending on the numbers in the dataset. You can imagine that if you are faced with the task of mapping the variation in population in the more than 5,000 municipalities of Brazil, such a tool is invaluable. If you don't have access to one, you will have to painstakingly color those regions *one by one*.

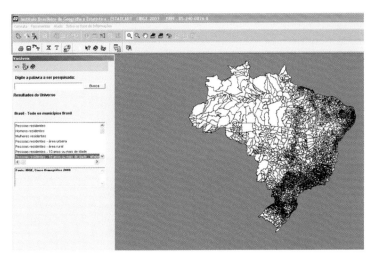

Figure 8.4 Estatcart's interface.

Unfortunately, the IBGE decided to make me wait until it released the data to all newspapers and magazines, my urgency notwithstanding. I still wanted our story to run before they released the official numbers, so I copied the figures from the interactive map. You could call it manual hacking.

I then formatted the data to Estatcart's requirements, which resulted in the map you see in **Figure 8.5**. The green regions had the higher increase in population between 2000 and 2010, while the regions in orange and red suffered declines.

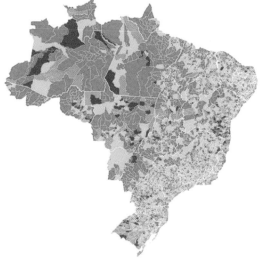

Figure 8.5 A map designed with Estatcart and then styled in Adobe Illustrator.

Brazil's Demographic Oportunity

How Brazil can take advantage
of a future with fewer children per couple.

Alberto Cairo and Francine Lima

Data provided by the Brazilian Institute of Geography and Statistics (IBGE) offer
a mixed portrait of the Brazilian population. On one side, the population of the country
has increased by 10% in the last decade, but the fertility rate has dropped below
the critical average of 2.1 children per woman. Demographers have pointed out
that this poses challenges to public officials: how to sustain Social Security, above
all. Nonetheless, those same demographers say that Brazil can transform this
situation into an opportunity if it starts investing heavily on education now.

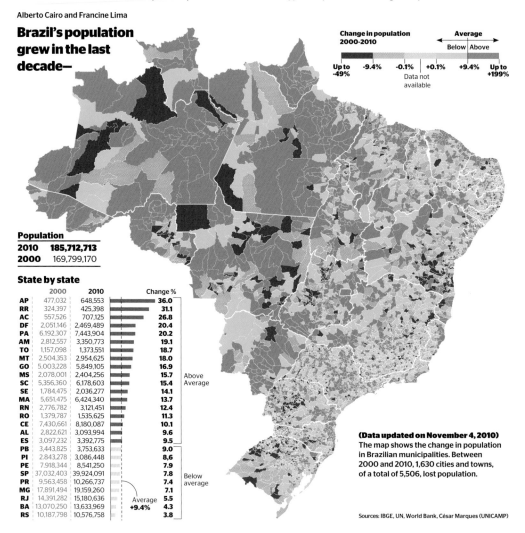

Brazil's population grew in the last decade—

Change in population 2000-2010

Average — Below | Above

Up to -49% | -9.4% | -0.1% | +0.1% | +9.4% | Up to +199%

Data not available

Population

2010	185,712,713
2000	169,799,170

State by state

	2000	2010	Change %	
AP	477,032	648,553	36.0	
RR	324,397	425,398	31.1	
AC	557,526	707,125	26.8	
DF	2,051,146	2,469,489	20.4	
PA	6,192,307	7,443,904	20.2	
AM	2,812,557	3,350,773	19.1	
TO	1,157,098	1,373,551	18.7	
MT	2,504,353	2,954,625	18.0	
GO	5,003,228	5,849,105	16.9	
MS	2,078,001	2,404,256	15.7	Above Average
SC	5,356,360	6,178,603	15.4	
SE	1,784,475	2,036,277	14.1	
MA	5,651,475	6,424,340	13.7	
RN	2,776,782	3,121,451	12.4	
RO	1,379,787	1,535,625	11.3	
CE	7,430,661	8,180,087	10.1	
AL	2,822,621	3,093,994	9.6	
ES	3,097,232	3,392,775	9.5	
PB	3,443,825	3,753,633	9.0	
PI	2,843,278	3,086,448	8.6	
PE	7,918,344	8,541,250	7.9	
SP	37,032,403	39,924,091	7.8	Below average
PR	9,563,458	10,266,737	7.4	
MG	17,891,494	19,159,260	7.1	
RJ	14,391,282	15,180,636	5.5	Average +9.4%
BA	13,070,250	13,633,969	4.3	
RS	10,187,798	10,576,758	3.8	

(Data updated on November 4, 2010)
The map shows the change in population
in Brazilian municipalities. Between
2000 and 2010, 1,630 cities and towns,
of a total of 5,506, lost population.

Sources: IBGE, UN, World Bank, César Marques (UNICAMP)

Figure 8.6 One of the first drafts for the Brazilian population infographic.
Translated from Portuguese.

—but fertility rate is below what was expected—

A study in 2004 estimated that in 2010, the fertility rate would be 2.4 children per woman, on average. But new data collected by the IBGE prove that the fertility rate is already 1.9, below the threshold called "replacement rate." When the fertility rate drops below this number, the population of a country will eventually start to shrink and grow older.

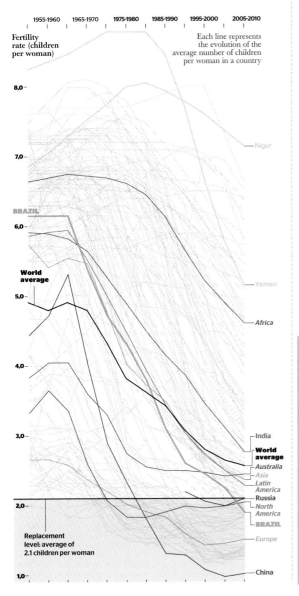

—and population will be smaller—

Forecasts made in 2004 anticipated that Brazil's population would stop growing in 2040. But the most recent data from the IBGE suggests that this could happen much earlier, in 2030.

Millions of people

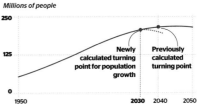

—and older—

Comparing the current population pyramid with the one predicted for 2050

Number of people per age group (millions)   2050   2005

How Brazil can transform the population challenge into an opportunity

As the population ages, the proportion of people of working age increases. The country will therefore have more people producing wealth (if the labor market can absorb them) and fewer children to consume investments. It is a window of opportunity, because in some cases the number of people of working age tends to decline when older people are leaving the market.

The population under 15 years of age is falling today. A smaller number of students in public schools will facilitate the quality of teaching, if the amount invested in education stays the same.

Educational policy focused on low-income youth favors the formation of a more skilled workforce and greater social mobility. In the future, Brazil will reach the stage of Europe and Japan, which struggle to support their elders. This is why it's so important to prepare a more balanced retirement system.

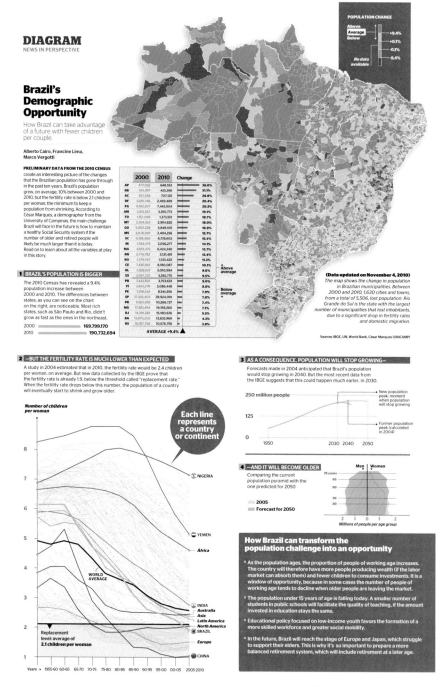

Figure 8.7 Brazil's Demographic Opportunity. Published by *Época*, São Paulo, Brazil. Translated from Portuguese.

While I was taking care of the nerdy stuff, one of our reporters, Francine Lima, interviewed a well-known demographer to give context to the data and provide insights into how a challenge can be transformed into an opportunity. In brief: Brazil could support an older population in the future if it starts preparing right now. The next 20 years will see a swell in numbers of people between 16 and 60 years old. They will be eager to work. If Brazil manages to give them the right education in the present, they will transform the country's economy for the better. They will generate not only more taxes, but also more internal and foreign investment. We decided to make those points in the last part of the graphic.

With all the material in hand, I put together the layout you see in **Figure 8.6**.

As my layout was quite rough (I am not a good designer, lacking an eye for color and font choices), Marco Vergotti, the head of *Época's* print infographics, transformed it into the gorgeous display that was finally published in the magazine (**Figure 8.7**). You could say that this project is an example of low-tech data journalism and highly effective teamwork.

Inequality and the Economy

I am not ashamed to admit that I copy from the people I admire. You should not be either. As Austin Kleon reminds us in his inspiring *Steal Like an Artist* (2012), "Every new idea is just a mashup or a remix of one or more previous ideas." The thin red line between elegant theft and plagiarism is defined by how much you can pay homage to someone else's ideas by adding something that is truly yours.

In May 2010, *The New York Times* published a chart titled "Driving Shifts Into Reverse," made by Hannah Fairfield. It was a most uncommon kind of scatter-plot (**Figure 8.8**). You will learn more about Hannah in the Profiles section.

Remember that a scatter-plot allows you to see the relationship between two variables, one on the horizontal axis and the other on the vertical axis. What was surprising about Hannah's graphic was that the points on the line were years, so her scatter-plot had to be read as if you were following a path marked by years instead of miles. The position of each dot-year depends on the average miles driven per capita (horizontal axis) and the price of a gallon of gasoline (vertical axis). In other words, the farther to the right a dot is, the more miles Americans drove, and the higher the dot on the vertical scale, the more expensive gasoline was.

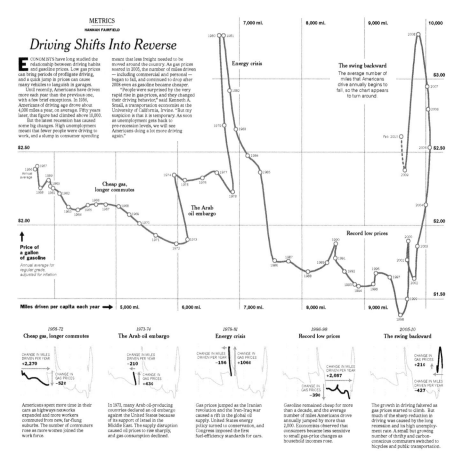

Figure 8.8 "Driving Shifts Into Reverse," a graphic by Hannah Fairfield for *The New York Times.*

The chart is not intuitive at first, but, once you understand how it works, it's illuminating. See, for instance, the Arab oil embargo between 1973 and 1974: Oil prices spiked, and the line turns backward (left to right), meaning that the miles driven per capita that year went from around 6,150 to nearly 5,900. During the energy crisis at the beginning of the 1980s, oil prices soared, and Americans tended to keep their driving to a minimum. If you go back in time to the period from 1956 to 1972, you will notice that oil prices were stable, and the population tended to increase commutes. I considered this graphic a masterpiece at the time, and still do.

I was so inspired by Hannah's project that I used it as a template for a graphic I was working on at the time, mentioned in the introduction to this book.

In February 2011, Letícia Sorg, a reporter for *Época*, recommended I read *The Spirit Level: Why Greater Equality Makes Societies Stronger* (2009), by Richard Wilkinson and Kate Pickett. Letícia was planning to interview Wilkinson, a professor at the University of Nottingham. She wanted to enrich the interview with some graphics.

The Spirit Level itself includes plenty of charts. The book uncovers the tight connection between inequality (measured with an index called GINI, developed by Italian sociologist Corrado Gini) and several negative social indicators, such as the number of people in prison, the rate of teenage pregnancy, the prevalence of obesity, and the impact of mental diseases. But we wanted to go a bit beyond the book, and discuss the problem of inequality in Brazil.

Historically, Brazil has been one of the most unbalanced countries in the world. After democracy was reinstated in the 1980s, Brazil experienced spurts of rapid economic development, interspersed with periods of stagnation and hyperinflation. The chronic economic instability was accompanied by unpredictable variations in inequality. In good times, most of the benefits of growth accrued to the rich portion of the population. In bad times, it was the poor who suffered the most, as the rich were able to shelter their money from crisis and inflation using varied investment tricks.

Brazil stabilized during Fernando Henrique Cardoso's (FHC) tenures, first as finance minister (1993-1994), and later as president of the Republic (1995-2002). Cardoso got inflation under control, transformed Brazil's economy, and laid the groundwork for Luiz Inácio "Lula" da Silva's presidency (2003-2011), who was the most successful in raising the quality of life for millions of Brazil's poor people. Under Lula, continued economic growth was accompanied by a steady drop in income inequality, thanks in part to many income distribution and social advancement programs.

For this project, inspired by Fairfield's scatter-plot, I put my data in an Excel spreadsheet (**Figure 8.9**). Note the columns highlighted in yellow. The first is GDP in billions of dollars; the second is inequality, measured with the GINI Index. The higher the score, the higher the inequality.

Next, I selected the two columns and told Excel to create a scatter-plot. I also told it to connect the dots (which, remember, represent years) with a line. **Figure 8.10** shows the result. Notice the slow economic growth between 1981 (first dot) and 1993 (twelfth dot); they are not that far apart in the horizontal axis. Also note the huge vertical variations of the line in between those years, visual evidence of the wild changes in inequality.

GDP and GINI comparison								
	A	B	C	D	E	F	G	H	I
1			GDP Change		GDP index	GINI math		GDP FINAL	GINI FINAL
2	1980				100				
3	1981		-4,4		95,6	57,5		463.767	57,5
4	82		0,6		96,1736	58,2		494.988	58,2
5	83		-3,4		92,9037	58,4		497.067	58,4
6	84		5,3		97,82759	58,4		543.113	58,4
7	85		8		105,6538	59		603.761	59
8	86		8		114,1061	58,1		663.664	58,1
9	87		3,6		118,2139	59,3		707.519	59,3
10	88		-0,1		118,0957	61		733.756	61
11	89		3,3		121,9929	63		785.830	63
12	1990		-4,3		116,7472	60,6		782.132	60,6
13	91		1,5		118,4984	59		818.213	59
14	92		-0,5		117,9059	57,4		833.052	57,4
15	93		4,7		123,4475	59,7		893.402	59,7
16	94		5,3		129,9902	59,5		965.612	59,5
17	95		4,4		135,7098	59,2		1.027.327	59,2
18	96		2,2		138,6954	59,2		1.069.400	59,2
19	97		3,4		143,411	59,3		1.125.009	59,3
20	98		0		143,411	59,2		1.138.123	59,2
21	99		0,3		143,8412	58,6		1.157.791	58,6
22	2000		4,3		150,0264	58,6		1.233.817	58,6
23	1		1,3		151,9768	58,7		1.278.254	58,7
24	2		2,7		156,0801	58,2		1.333.480	58,2
25	3		1,1		157,797	57,6		1.377.810	57,6
26	4		5,7		166,7914	57		1.494.694	57
27	5		3,2		172,1288	56,4		1.584.604	56,4

Figure 8.9 A screenshot of the Excel spreadsheet I used to compare GDP growth with income inequality.

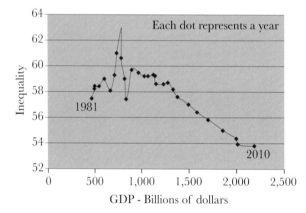

Figure 8.10 Excel's default options could be improved. I am not very fond of blue lines over gray backgrounds.

The chart made in Excel didn't look very good. By default, Excel creates graphics with strange-looking gray backgrounds and seemingly random color choices. So I switched to Adobe Illustrator, refining the style and adding the copy and explainers (**Figure 8.11**). To those familiar with Brazil's recent history, the visual impression is shocking: Prior to 1993-1994, the line goes up and down. Once you get to Itamar Franco's and FHC's presidencies, the line stabilizes and stretches out. **The pace of economic growth increases, and inequality plunges non-stop.**

When the Brazilian Economy Improves, Inequality Doesn't Drop

The graphic below shows the correlation between Brazilian GDP (horizontal axis) and inequality (vertical axis) between 1981 and 2010. The position of the points, each representing a year, depends on how high GDP and inequality were. You can notice, for instance, that the economy grew between 1986 and 1989 because the line tends to move to the right, but inequality also grew, as the point representing 1989 is much higher than the ones before. You can also see that, during Lula da Silva's government, the economy expanded almost as much as during the terms of the other presidents who preceded him combined.

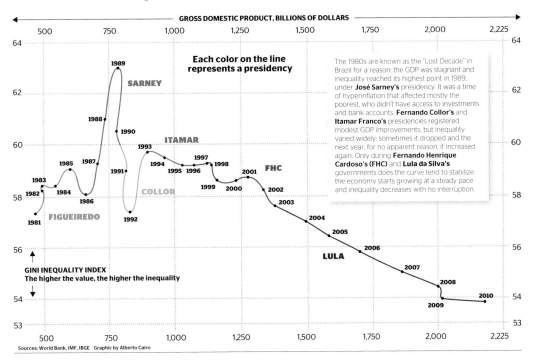

Figure 8.11 Income inequality and GDP in Brazil.

A Word on Structure, Color, and Type

To end this chapter, I would like to show you some infographics that illustrate two lessons I've learned through the years on how to design effective information graphics:

Keep type and color under control, and

Create a solid layout by imagining your graphics as if they were groups of rectangles.

In July 2010, *Science* magazine published an article on "genetic signatures of exceptional human longevity" written by researchers from Boston University. The scientists identified certain combinations of genes that are extremely common in people who live beyond 100 years.

Época magazine published a long story on the article. As a key part of it, during the planning meeting, my colleague Gerson Mora—arguably the best 3D news artist in Brazil—and I decided that we needed a big information graphic that

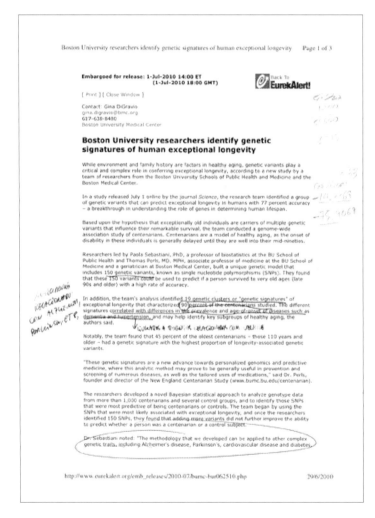

Figure 8.12 Notes on a press release.

answered three interrelated questions: **why we get old**, **why and how cells stop reproducing**, and **what factors make those processes faster or slower**. That's the first step for any project: defining its goals and scope.

The second step is to gather your information. Obviously, we needed to read *Science*'s article. You can see a printout of the press release in **Figure 8.12**. It's filled with notes and underlines scribbled in English, Spanish, and Portuguese made as I was trying to understand it. At the same time, on another piece of paper, I was drawing a very rough node chart (**Figure 8.13**). I learned to do such organizational trees from my father, who taught me to use them as study aids for my high school exams.

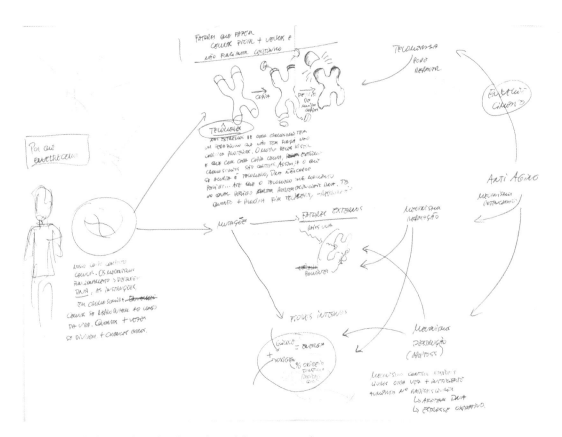

Figure 8.13 Get used to sketching ideas while you research a project.

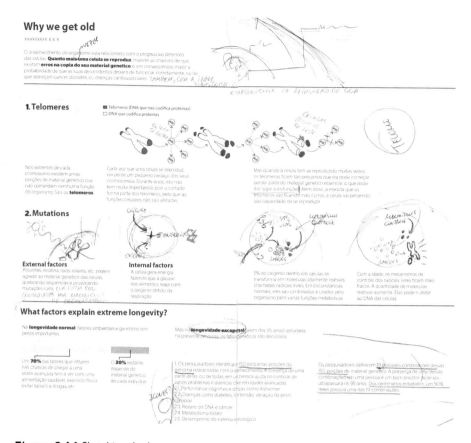

Figure 8.14 Sketching the layout.

We used other sources for this project. I am a fan of popular science books, so I retrieved some volumes from my shelves, including Matt Ridley's *Genome: The Autobiography of a Species in 23 Chapters*, and Mel Greaves' *Cancer: The Evolutionary Legacy*.

With my notes in front of me on my desk, I created a sketch of the layout, shown in **Figure 8.14**. (I've translated the headlines into English so you can understand its structure.) That's the narrative backbone I mentioned earlier. You should not proceed to developing a graphic on the computer before you've devised something like this—a precise outline of the graphic's elements and how they relate to one other. If you compare the sketch with the actual infographic we published (**Figure 8.15**), you will see that we followed it quite closely. Planning your content in advance saves a lot of time down the road.

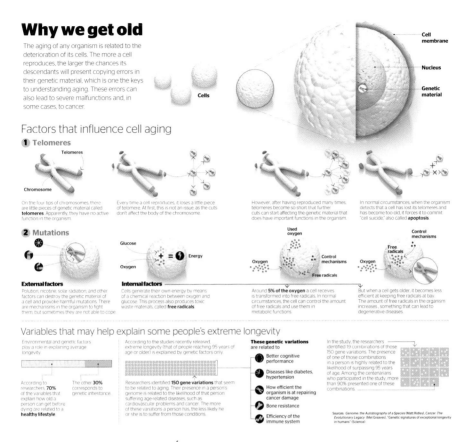

Why we get old

The aging of any organism is related to the deterioration of its cells. The more a cell reproduces, the larger the chances its descendants will present copying errors in their genetic material, which is one the keys to understanding aging. These errors can also lead to severe malfunctions and, in some cases, to cancer.

Figure 8.15 Why We Get Old. *Época*. Translated from Portuguese.

Notice something else about the sketch: the relative lack of color and sameness of the type. This is not just a minimalist aesthetic choice, but a practical one. **Limiting the amount of colors and different fonts in your graphics will help you create a sense of unity in the composition.** I usually recommend to my students at the University of Miami and the University of North Carolina at Chapel Hill to **stick to just two or three colors** and **play with their shades**. You may pick a neutral tone for the background elements (bluish gray in this case), and an accent color to highlight the most relevant stuff (yellow). **Do the same with fonts. Choose just one or two**: a solid, thick one for headlines, and a readable one for body copy.

Regarding the structure, notice that almost all parts of the graphic fit into rectangles (**Figure 8.16**). This is because I tend to be a bit conservative in my layouts. Visualizing my projects as sets of rectangles of different sizes before I even start designing charts, maps, and illustrations helps me come up with a clear hierarchy and to guide readers through a logical reading path.

You can see this organizational principle at work in many of the projects I've designed alone or with colleagues and friends since I started doing infographics back in 1997. **Figure 8.17** and **Figure 8.18** contain two examples, one an infographic on giant waves and another on new telescopes that are being built in South America. In **Figure 8.19**, you can see the invisible rectangles that enclose the different sections and how they compare to the rough layouts we created to organize their contents.

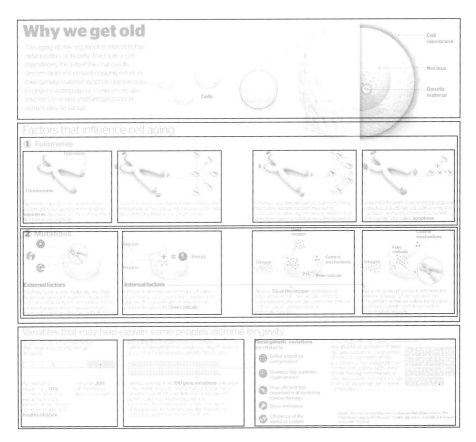

Figure 8.16 Organizing your composition as if it were a set of rectangles of different sizes helps you design a structure and a hierarchy.

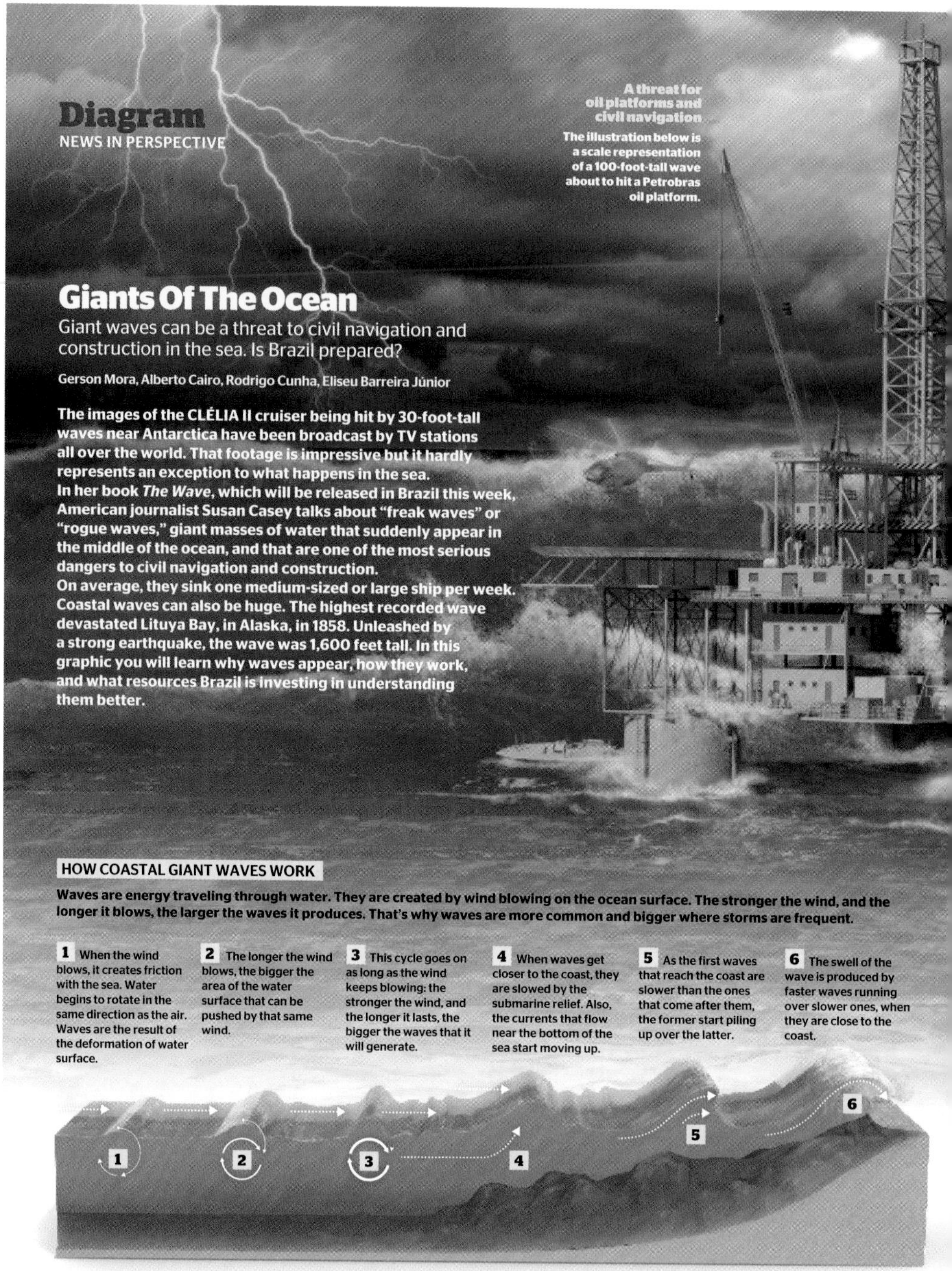
Diagram
NEWS IN PERSPECTIVE
A threat for oil platforms and civil navigation
The illustration below is a scale representation of a 100-foot-tall wave about to hit a Petrobras oil platform.
Giants Of The Ocean
Giant waves can be a threat to civil navigation and construction in the sea. Is Brazil prepared?
Gerson Mora, Alberto Cairo, Rodrigo Cunha, Eliseu Barreira Júnior
The images of the CLÉLIA II cruiser being hit by 30-foot-tall waves near Antarctica have been broadcast by TV stations all over the world. That footage is impressive but it hardly represents an exception to what happens in the sea.
In her book The Wave, which will be released in Brazil this week, American journalist Susan Casey talks about "freak waves" or "rogue waves," giant masses of water that suddenly appear in the middle of the ocean, and that are one of the most serious dangers to civil navigation and construction.
On average, they sink one medium-sized or large ship per week. Coastal waves can also be huge. The highest recorded wave devastated Lituya Bay, in Alaska, in 1858. Unleashed by a strong earthquake, the wave was 1,600 feet tall. In this graphic you will learn why waves appear, how they work, and what resources Brazil is investing in understanding them better.
HOW COASTAL GIANT WAVES WORK
Waves are energy traveling through water. They are created by wind blowing on the ocean surface. The stronger the wind, and the longer it blows, the larger the waves it produces. That's why waves are more common and bigger where storms are frequent.
1 When the wind blows, it creates friction with the sea. Water begins to rotate in the same direction as the air. Waves are the result of the deformation of water surface.
2 The longer the wind blows, the bigger the area of the water surface that can be pushed by that same wind.
3 This cycle goes on as long as the wind keeps blowing: the stronger the wind, and the longer it lasts, the bigger the waves that it will generate.
4 When waves get closer to the coast, they are slowed by the submarine relief. Also, the currents that flow near the bottom of the sea start moving up.
5 As the first waves that reach the coast are slower than the ones that come after them, the former start piling up over the latter.
6 The swell of the wave is produced by faster waves running over slower ones, when they are close to the coast.
1
2
3
4
5
6

Figure 8.17 Giant Waves, for *Época*. Translated from Portuguese. The illustration in the center is not mere decoration, but a proportional representation of how big a 100-foot wave is, compared to an average oil platform.

GIANT WAVES IN BRAZIL

Brazil doesn't keep a centralized record of giant waves in national waters. But Petrobras, the public oil company, takes them into consideration when it builds extraction platforms.

Campos Basin

Santos Basin

Mathematical models have predicted that waves during a storm can reach an average of 26 feet with a maximum of 48 feet.

Simulations developed in 2010 have predicted that the maximum height of a wave in Santos (never observed) is 67 feet.

WAVE SIMULATOR

The Polytechnic School of the University of São Paulo (Poli-USP), using funding from Petrobras, opened a lab to study giant waves in December 2009. The main element in the laboratory is a 36-foot-wide and 13-foot-deep pool for simulating giant wave patterns . The waves are generated by 148 rubber flaps, attached to small engines and controlled by a computer.

SOURCES: The Wave (Susan Casey), Poli-USP, BBC Science and Nature

HOW FREAK WAVES WORK

"Freak" or "rogue" waves are giant waves that appear in the middle of the sea. They are very dangerous due to their unpredictability. Recent research has identified three different factors that influence their likelihood.

A   **B**   **C**

Cold water   Warm water

A Regions where storms are common, such as the North Atlantic, are also the ones where freak waves appear with higher frequency. The strong winds that stir those waters are a key factor.

B Submarine relief is another factor. Shallow waters in the North Sea, between the UK and Scandinavia, are prone to freak waves for the same reason that big waves appear in coastal areas.

C The confluence of warm and cold currents (see map on the right) creates dynamics that make giant waves more likely.

Frequency and height of freak waves

←····Lower   Higher····→

Freak waves are more common in regions near the Poles. They are also frequent in South African national waters. In that area, the Agulhas Current meets cold water that is pushed from the South Pole by strong winds.

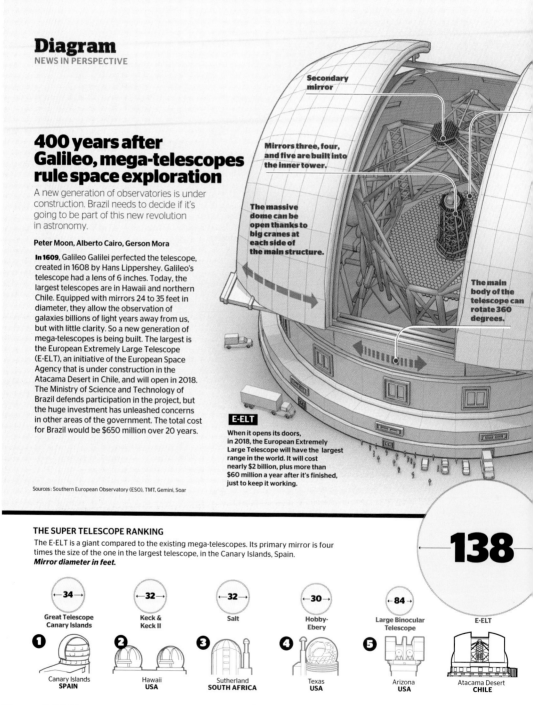

Diagram
NEWS IN PERSPECTIVE

Secondary mirror

Mirrors three, four, and five are built into the inner tower.

400 years after Galileo, mega-telescopes rule space exploration

A new generation of observatories is under construction. Brazil needs to decide if it's going to be part of this new revolution in astronomy.

Peter Moon, Alberto Cairo, Gerson Mora

In 1609, Galileo Galilei perfected the telescope, created in 1608 by Hans Lippershey. Galileo's telescope had a lens of 6 inches. Today, the largest telescopes are in Hawaii and northern Chile. Equipped with mirrors 24 to 35 feet in diameter, they allow the observation of galaxies billions of light years away from us, but with little clarity. So a new generation of mega-telescopes is being built. The largest is the European Extremely Large Telescope (E-ELT), an initiative of the European Space Agency that is under construction in the Atacama Desert in Chile, and will open in 2018. The Ministry of Science and Technology of Brazil defends participation in the project, but the huge investment has unleashed concerns in other areas of the government. The total cost for Brazil would be $650 million over 20 years.

The massive dome can be open thanks to big cranes at each side of the main structure.

The main body of the telescope can rotate 360 degrees.

E-ELT

When it opens its doors, in 2018, the European Extremely Large Telescope will have the largest range in the world. It will cost nearly $2 billion, plus more than $60 million a year after it's finished, just to keep it working.

Sources: Southern European Observatory (ESO), TMT, Gemini, Soar

THE SUPER TELESCOPE RANKING

The E-ELT is a giant compared to the existing mega-telescopes. Its primary mirror is four times the size of the one in the largest telescope, in the Canary Islands, Spain.
Mirror diameter in feet.

138

← 34 →
Great Telescope Canary Islands
❶
Canary Islands
SPAIN

← 32 →
Keck & Keck II
❷
Hawaii
USA

← 32 →
Salt
❸
Sutherland
SOUTH AFRICA

← 30 →
Hobby-Ebery
❹
Texas
USA

← 84 →
Large Binocular Telescope
❺
Arizona
USA

E-ELT
Atacama Desert
CHILE

Figure 8.18 New Telescopes in South America, for *Época*. Translated from Portuguese.

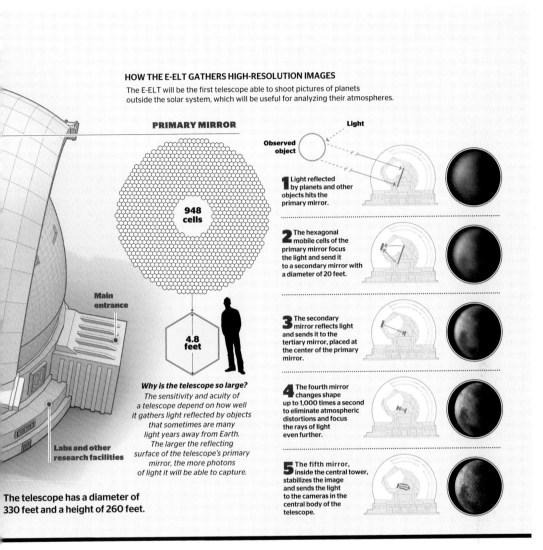

HOW THE E-ELT GATHERS HIGH-RESOLUTION IMAGES

The E-ELT will be the first telescope able to shoot pictures of planets outside the solar system, which will be useful for analyzing their atmospheres.

PRIMARY MIRROR

Light

Observed object

948 cells

Main entrance

4.8 feet

Labs and other research facilities

Why is the telescope so large?
The sensitivity and acuity of a telescope depend on how well it gathers light reflected by objects that sometimes are many light years away from Earth. The larger the reflecting surface of the telescope's primary mirror, the more photons of light it will be able to capture.

1 Light reflected by planets and other objects hits the primary mirror.

2 The hexagonal mobile cells of the primary mirror focus the light and send it to a secondary mirror with a diameter of 20 feet.

3 The secondary mirror reflects light and sends it to the tertiary mirror, placed at the center of the primary mirror.

4 The fourth mirror changes shape up to 1,000 times a second to eliminate atmospheric distortions and focus the rays of light even further.

5 The fifth mirror, inside the central tower, stabilizes the image and sends the light to the cameras in the central body of the telescope.

The telescope has a diameter of 330 feet and a height of 260 feet.

TELESCOPES WITH BRAZILIAN INVOLVEMENT
Brazil participates on just two of the largest telescopes.

OTHER LARGE TELESCOPES UNDER CONSTRUCTION
Besides the E-ELT, there are other projects in development.

Radio telescope 66 antennas

Gemini

Built in Cerro Pachón, Chile, and the Mauna Kea volcano, Hawaii, these twin telescopes have mirrors with a diameter of 26.5 feet. Brazil participates by covering 2.4% of the total cost in exchange for the right of using them for observations.

Soar

Built in Cerro Pachón, Chile, the Southern Astro Physical Research Telescope has a mirror with a diameter of 13.5 feet. The Brazilian National Scientific Development Council covers a great portion of its costs.

Thirty Meters Telescope (TMT)

Opening: 2018
Cost: $1 billion
Mirror: 98 feet
Place: Hawaii
Built by: USA, Canada, China, India

Telescópio Gigante Magalhães (GMT)

Opening: 2018
Cost: $600 million
Mirror: 80.4 feet
Place: Chilean Andes
Built by: USA, Australia, South Korea

Atacama Large Millimeter Array (Alma)

Opening: 2012
Cost: $1.3 billion
Place: Atacama, Chile
Built by: European Union, USA, Canada, Japan, Taiwan, Chile

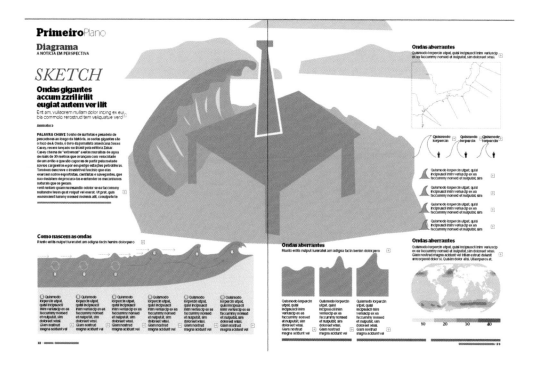

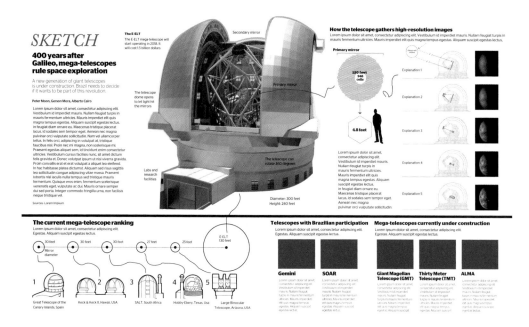

Figure 8.19 Sketches and structures for the Giant Waves and Telescopes projects.

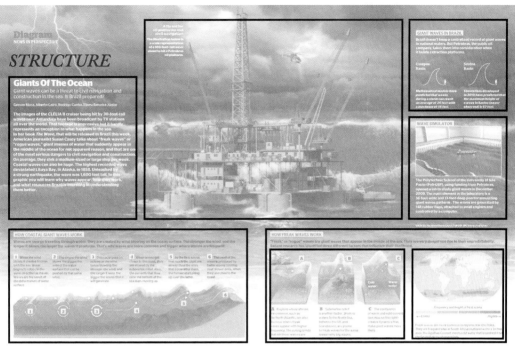

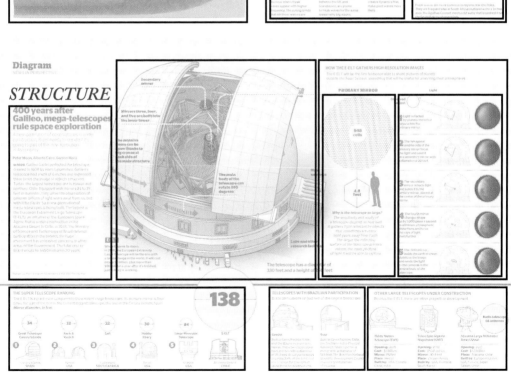

9

The Rise of Interactive Graphics

What makes something simple or complex? It's not the number of dials or controls or how many features it has: It is whether the person using the device has a good conceptual model of how it operates.

—Donald A. Norman, from *Living With Complexity*

In the summer of 1996, Don Wittekind, a visual journalist who picked up some programming skills in a technical position at the *Atlanta Journal-Constitution*, got a phone call from Leavett Biles, the graphics director at the *South Florida Sun-Sentinel*, one of the major newspapers in the state. Biles was spearheading a major transformation in the newsroom, which involved the production of more video, audio, and motion graphics content.

He told Wittekind, "I know about you. I want you to come down here and produce multimedia informational graphics."

"But, Mr. Biles," Don replied, puzzled, "I have no idea how to make multimedia informational graphics."

"Nobody does," said Biles. "We're gonna invent them."

So they did. In the next decade, thanks to a multimedia gallery called *The Edge*, the *Sun-Sentinel* would become one of the pioneers in producing interactive visualizations and motion graphics, first using technologies such as Adobe Director, and later, Macromedia Flash (Adobe bought Macromedia in 2005). As primitive as they appear to us today, some of their early interactive graphics, such as the one on fire ants in **Figure 9.1**, were eye-openers for many professionals.

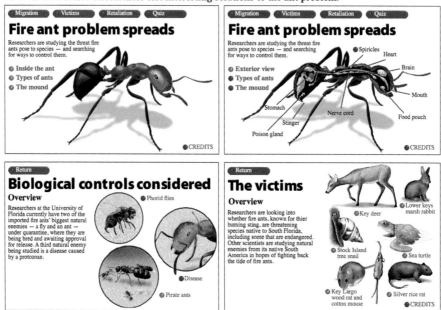

Figure 9.1 Fire Ant Attack. The *South Florida Sun-Sentinel*, published in 1996. One of the earliest examples of news interactive graphics (http://www.sun-sentinel.com/broadband/theedge/sfl-edge-t-fire-ant,0,324587.flash).

Similar moves were made by other media organizations, such as the *Chicago Tribune*, which used rising stars like Andrew DeVigal and Steve Duenes (both at *The New York Times* at this writing) to develop online news graphics. What all of them remember very clearly is the excitement of entering uncharted territory of play buttons and moving arrows rather than plain old ink, paper, and still pictures.

I cherish those early days myself. In the beginning of 2000, I was hired by *El Mundo*, a Spanish national newspaper, to produce interactive graphics. Like Don

Wittekind, I was clueless about interaction or animation. All I had was a short career in print visual journalism. I accepted the offer anyway. One reason was that the director of *El Mundo's* online operation was Mario Tascón, someone I had admired since my college days. Mario had been infographics director of *El Mundo* between 1991 and 1998. The quality of the work his department put out had inspired publications worldwide. Mario also hired Rafael Höhr, a talented designer who has recently became the graphics director at London's *Sunday Times*.

Compared to the infographics and visualization wonders you see nowadays in news websites such as *The New York Times*, *The Washington Post*, MSNBC, and *The Guardian*, our efforts at the beginning of the century look crude and naïve. But at the time, they were breakthrough. We were devising new ways of telling stories. I still remember the blast I felt when I learned how to program a very simple calculator of the Body Mass Index for an infographic on stomach-reduction surgery (**Figure 9.2**), and when I first used audio in a very rough 3D animation (**Figure 9.3**). Those were good times, indeed.

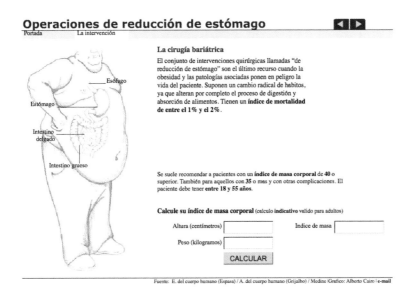

Figure 9.2 Stomach-reduction surgery and Body Mass Index calculator (http://www.elmundo.es/elmundosalud/documentos/2004/02/estomago.html).

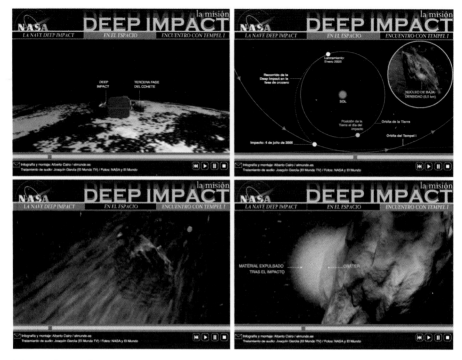

Figure 9.3 NASA's Deep Impact mission. Crashing a probe against a meteorite (http://www.elmundo.es/elmundo/2004/graficos/dic/s4/deepimpact/index.html).

Early Lessons on Interaction Design

Before 2000, those of us who got into interactive news infographics learned by trial and error. Many of us had little idea of the rich tradition of research in related areas such as human-computer interaction and software engineering. As I would later discover, interaction design is not limited to the digital world: Some of the classics in the literature focus on the functionality of physical devices. Learning the basics from them can save you a lot of headaches, so let me take you on a quick tour of the concepts.

The Design of Everyday Things by Donald A. Norman, originally published in 1988, is a perfect starting point. It's not a book about interactive graphics, but about how we deal with common stuff such as door handles and coffee makers. Donald Norman is an advocate of putting the user's needs ahead of the designer's aesthetic concerns. The principles he proposed are directly translatable into guidelines for infographics.

Visibility

The more visible the functionality of an object, the easier it will be for users to create a mental model of what they can obtain from it. Norman encourages designers to take advantage of "natural mappings" or physical analogies to the real world. If something is important in your graphic, **highlight it in such a way that readers can *sense* its relevance and how it operates**.

For instance, **if you are designing buttons, make them mimic physical buttons**. The first couple of buttons in **Figure 9.4** don't look like buttons, do they? The second pair is better because it simulates the patterns of highlights and shades of objects in relief. But its functionality is not obvious at first glance. We have to read the words "next" and "previous" to understand what will happen if we click them. An arrow is more effective if what we want someone to intuitively understand what will happen if he clicks on it.

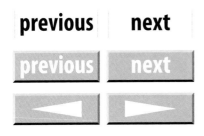

Figure 9.4 If you want your readers to be able to identify buttons in your graphics, make them look like buttons.

The principle of visibility is related to what Norman calls *perceived affordances*. **The shape of an object must visually suggest what it "affords."** You can understand this by taking a look at the controls of my bike in **Figure 9.5**. Its brakes are activated by handles that, due to their curved shape, adapt to my hands, inviting me to pull them. The overall design of the device gives me further clues about how to make it work: sit, put your feet on the pedals, and push them to make that metal serrated wheel rotate. The consequences of this are clear: **If you want readers to press, pull, push, or spin virtual objects on a computer screen, design those objects so as to suggest that they are pressable, pullable, pushable, and spinnable**.

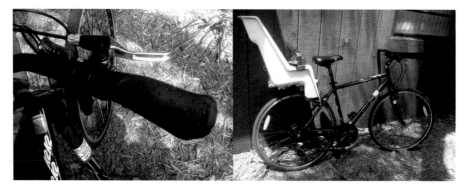

Figure 9.5 Most of the controls on my bike are intuitively understandable, even the baby seat that I am never able to install without hurting my fingers.

The principle of visibility is relevant not only for the design of interfaces, but also for the organization of visual elements in graphic design. Imagine that you are working on a piece on the killing of Osama bin Laden in Abbottabad, Pakistan. You wish to create a step-by-step explanation and include a 3D illustration[1] of the compound where he lived.

Then you add rollover buttons that readers can use to explore the steps of the operation, as the first two pictures show in **Figure 9.6**. The buttons are visible. But does this approach make sense? Of course not. **If a piece of information is indispensable to understand the whole story, it should always be visible**, not hidden behind a layer of interactivity. Unfortunately, this is what happens in many interactive visualizations: **Readers are forced to keep clicking to reveal data that should be visible at all times**.

Feedback

For every action, readers should perceive a reaction, a response that indicates that the operation they were trying to achieve has been successful (**Figure 9.7**). This reaction could be a visual cue, a subtle sound (so long as it's not repetitive and annoying), or a response that appears instantly on screen. If a reader clicks a button and nothing happens immediately, it will seem that the button is not working correctly.

1   I made this 3D illustration with Autodesk Maya 2010.

Bin Laden's Compound in Abbottabad, Pakistan

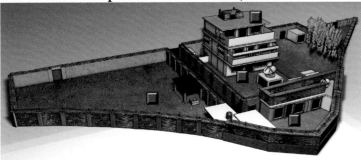

Bin Laden's Compound in Abbottabad, Pakistan

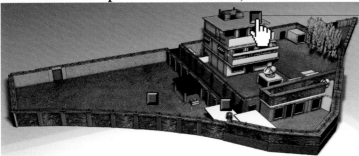

Step 3
Osama bin Laden is killed on the third floor of the compound.

Bin Laden's Compound in Abbottabad, Pakistan

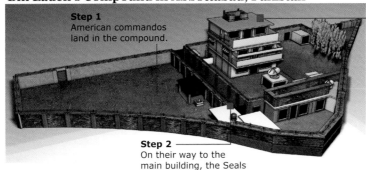

Step 1
American commandos land in the compound.

Step 3
Osama bin Laden is killed on the third floor of the compound.

Step 2
On their way to the main building, the Seals engaged Bin Laden's aids.

Figure 9.6 Two takes on a hypothetical graphic about Bin Laden's death. Does it make sense to force readers to click or roll over the buttons to get important information? Wouldn't it be better to make those steps visible all the time, or make them show up in order, as this is a step-by-step explanation?

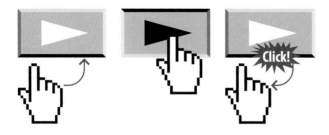

Figure 9.7 Make sure that readers receive clues when they interact with your graphic.

Constraints

Think of an interface as a mediator between users and a goal. As such, interactive graphics designers must think not only about what they will offer their readers, but also how they will orient their navigation. Any infographic can offer just a small amount of interactive possibilities, depending on what we want users to achieve with the graphic or extract from it. **To avoid confusion, the designer consciously imposes limits**.

Think about a scroll bar, for instance. You can only manipulate it up to a point and in one direction, vertical or horizontal. In **Figure 9.8**, in one of the infographics included in a big multimedia documentary project made by students of mine at UNC-Chapel Hill, the reader can rotate 3D illustrations of whales to see them from different angles, but only horizontally.

Another example of constraint happens when we disable buttons so readers won't be able to click on them by mistake and miss important information. In **Figure 9.9**, in an animation that belongs to the same project, the "next" button disappears when it is not needed, suggesting that you have reached the end of a scene.

Consistency

A rule in traditional graphic design states that **entities of similar nature should look alike**. That is, elements of the same kind—whether they are headlines, body copy, footnotes, or whatever—should always be designed with the same typefaces, size, and style. The same can be said of the design of interfaces.

It is also advisable to **place your buttons in the same screen position,** because learning how even the most simple interface works takes time. You don't want to force readers to hunt for the "zoom" button because you've moved it to a different location.

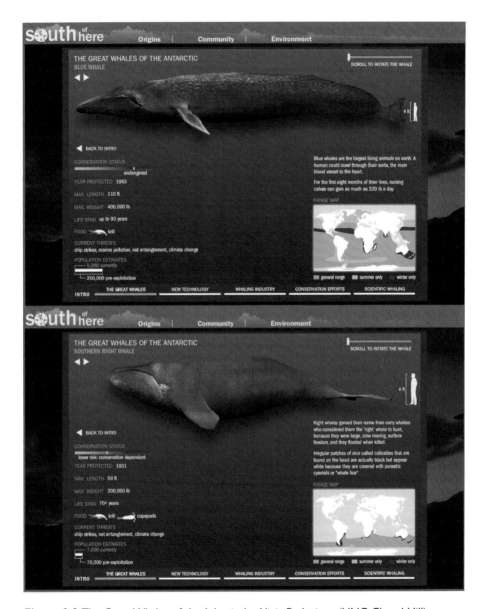

Figure 9.8 The Great Whales of the Atlantic, by Alicia Parlapiano (UNC-Chapel Hill). This graphic is part of the multimedia documentary *South of Here*, about the Patagonia region, in South America (http://www.southofhere.org).

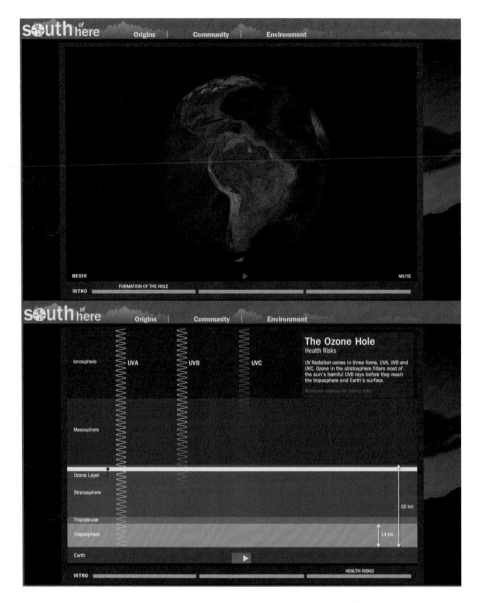

Figure 9.9 The Ozone Hole, by Wilson Andrews (UNC-Chapel Hill). This graphic is also part of the multimedia documentary *South of Here* (http://www.southofhere.org).

Interface consistency can also be sustained throughout a series of graphics. For instance, if I put screenshots of some of my old projects for *El Mundo* side by side, as in **Figure 9.10**, you will see that their interfaces are pretty similar. Once a reader learns to navigate one of those graphics, he or she will be able to navigate others with no effort.

Structuring Interactive and Animated Infographics

In 1996, Ben Shneiderman, a professor of computer science at University of Maryland, defined what he called the **Visual Information-Seeking Mantra: "Overview first, zoom and filter, then details on demand."**[2] This deceptively simple organizational principle was originally conceived to be used in the visualization of data for analysis, but, taking its meaning in the broad sense, it can be applied to any kind of graphical presentation of facts and phenomena: **First, present the most important figures or the most relevant points. Then, allow readers to dig into the information, explore, and come up with their own stories**.

Some of your infographics will necessarily be **linear**; that is, each step of the presentation will depend on understanding the previous one. Think about the visual reconstruction of a terrorist attack or an explanation on some new scientific device. Other graphics will be **non-linear**, giving readers choices for navigating the information using buttons, scroll bars, and other means. In either case, as shown in **Figure 9.11**, you would introduce the topic using a clear headline and a short intro. Don't throw tons of data at readers if you don't explain first what it means.

Interaction designer and consultant Jenifer Tidwell identifies several **techniques for navigating and browsing information graphics**:[3]

- Scroll and pan.
- Zoom.
- Open and close.
- Sort and rearrange.
- Search and filter.

---

2 Shneiderman, Ben. "The Eyes Have It: A Task by Data Type Taxonomy for Information Visualizations." Proc. IEEE Visual Languages, 1996, pp. 336-343.

3 Tidwell, Jenifer (2005) *Designing Interfaces*. O'Reilly Media.

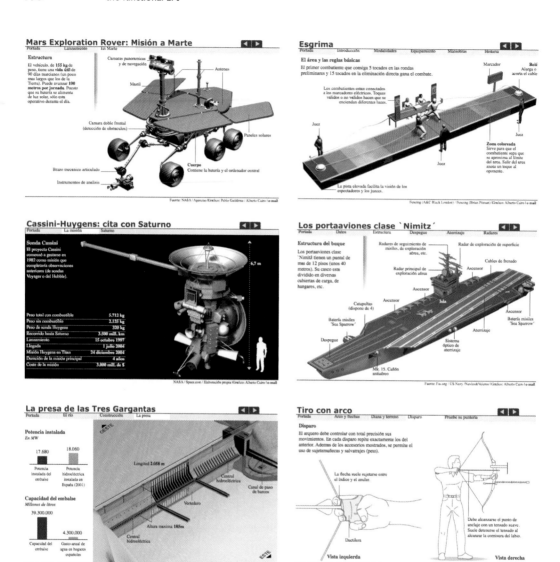

Figure 9.10 Assorted screenshots of infographics I made for *El Mundo*, between 2001 and 2005. Because I used a very similar interface for each, readers can navigate each new graphic easily.

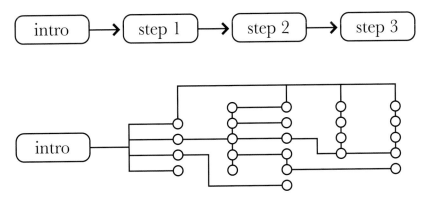

Figure 9.11 Examples of linear and non-linear structure.

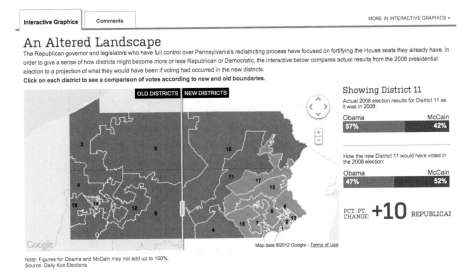

Figure 9.12 An Altered Landscape. Reprinted with permission of *The Wall Street Journal*. Copyright © 2012 Dow Jones & Company, Inc. All Rights Reserved Worldwide (http://online.wsj.com/article/SB10001424052702304444604577338403379964394.html).

You can see almost all of these at work in the interactive graphics in **Figures 9.12, 9.13, and 9.14**, all published by *The Wall Street Journal*.

The most common use of the **scroll and pan** technique is the vertical scroll on a website that allows you to see the part of the page that doesn't fit on the screen. On an interactive map, the pan tool allows you to move around until you find the area of interest. But you can use this simple tool in more creative ways. In **Figure 9.12**, for instance, the horizontal scroll lets you compare a map of Pennsylvania before and after its districts were redrawn by Republican legislators. The graphic is built on Google Maps, so you can pan around and **zoom** in and out, in case you are interested in seeing the neighboring states.

Figure 9.13 shows other techniques at work, including the open and close technique. The graphic is a database of 100 counties in the United States with the greatest numbers of veterans of the Afghanistan and Iraq wars. The data is presented on a map and in a table. Focus on the table first. By default, it is organized by veteran population, starting with the largest concentration.

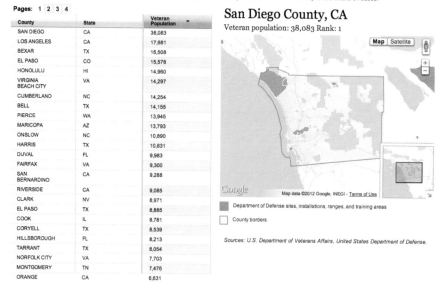

Figure 9.13 Where Are the Veterans of Iraq and Afghanistan? Reprinted with permission of *The Wall Street Journal*, Copyright © 2012 Dow Jones & Company, Inc. All Rights Reserved Worldwide (http://online.wsj.com/article/ SB10001424052702304636404577300272621321602.html).

What if you want to see only the veterans in one state? You would have to **sort and rearrange** the table by clicking on the top tabs. You can reorganize by county, by alphabetical order, by state, or by veteran population. You cannot **search** for specific counties, though. That would have been very nice, as some readers may be interested in comparing two or more different areas. Although it can be done with the current interface, it would take some work.

In Figure 9.13, you can also **open and close** new windows. If you click on the counties on the table or on the map, a text box will appear containing the veterans' base names, the military branch they belonged to, and other details.

Figure 9.14 is an interesting case. It is a huge infographic showing how different companies compare in areas such as revenue per employee, net income, and cash. You can add and erase companies from the mix, rearrange them, sort them by industry, and search for one of them. Every time that you complete one of these operations, the line charts on top change their scales to fit the newcomer.

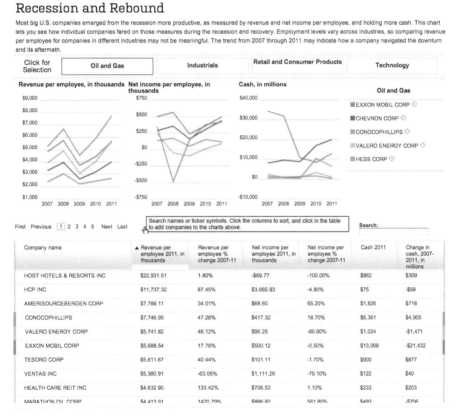

Figure 9.14 Recession and Rebound. Reprinted with permission of *The Wall Street Journal*, Copyright © 2012 Dow Jones & Company, Inc. All Rights Reserved Worldwide (http://online.wsj.com/article/SB10001424052702303772904577332493399116320.html).

Different Kinds of Interaction

When I started doing online information graphics, I spent quite a bit of time trying to conceptualize the different kinds of interactive experiences my team and I were offering to our readers. We were allowing them to click, scroll, open and close new windows, and move around the scene in some cases. Would it be possible, I wondered, to categorize those techniques based on how the user might experience the interface's capabilities?

Professors Yvonne Rogers, Helen Sharp, and Jennifer Preece provided an answer.[4] They proposed four broad **styles of interaction** that can coexist in a single website or, in our case, an information graphic or visualization.

Instruction

In the most basic and common kind of interaction, **the user tells the infographic to do something** by means of pressing buttons, typing commands, or double-clicking the mouse. Even using this simple style of interaction, you can come up with very creative results. **Figure 9.15** offers an example, a segment of a multimedia documentary project I participated in with several of my colleagues and students from UNC-Chapel Hill; the University of Santiago de Compostela, Spain; and the University of Los Andes, Chile.

In the infographic, readers not only see how a traditional Spanish musical instrument—the zanfona—works, but *they can also play it*. The students who created the graphic interviewed an artisan who designs zanfonas, and then a folk musician who was asked to play every single note with his instrument. The students recorded the sounds and programmed the interactive presentation.

Conversation

This kind of interaction allows the user to have a dialogue with the presentation, as if he is having a conversation with another real person. It's not something that we see in information graphics and visualization very often, but I envision a future in which I can change the parameters of a calculator such as the one in **Figure 9.16** by talking to my cell phone, instead of typing and clicking.

4 Their book, *Interaction Design: Beyond Human-Computer Interaction* (3rd ed., 2011, Wiley) is a deep and comprehensive introduction to the field.

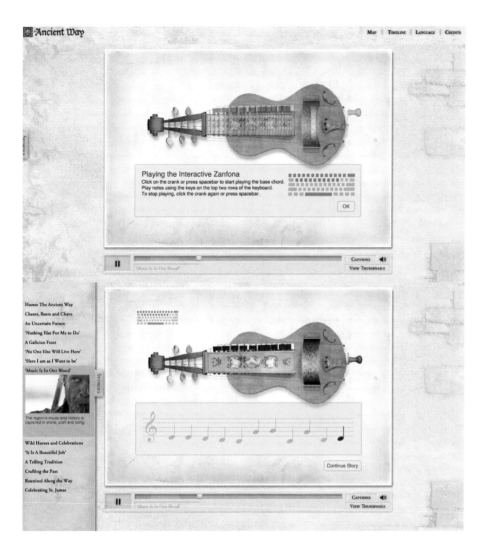

Figure 9.15 The Ancient Way, "Music is in our blood." This infographic allows the viewer to play a traditional Spanish instrument by means of his or her keyboard (http://theancientway.jomc.unc.edu/portal.htm).

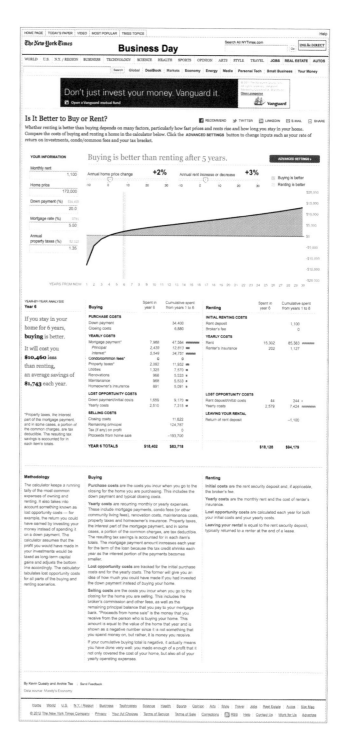

Figure 9.16 "Is It Better to Buy or Rent?" One of my all-time favorite *New York Times* interactive presentations. Try to input your own data into this simulator and have fun comparing them to other scenarios at http://www.nytimes.com/interactive/business/buy-rent-calculator.html.

Manipulation

Think of your computer's desktop: You create folders and then drag them around, place them inside other folders, choose their colors, sizes, and even appearance. Generally, **we allow manipulation when we let readers change the structure and appearance of what is presented to them so they can achieve certain goals**.

Applying this style to infographics can be fun. **Figure 9.17**, created by my team at *El Mundo*, offers an example. Back in 2005, soaring real estate prices in Spain caused such a problem that the government decided it should take action. Thousands of young working couples couldn't move out of their parents' homes because home prices were so steep.

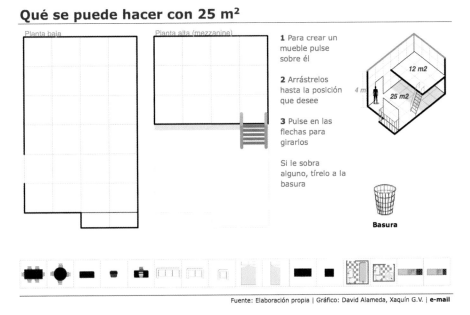

Figure 9.17 "What You Can Do in 25 Square Meters," from *El Mundo*. Furnish your apartment and see if you and your partner still fit in (http://www.elmundo.es/elmundo/2005/graficos/abr/s2/casa_25.html).

The government vetted a plan to invest in the construction of apartments that were between 270 and 390 square feet. Politicians in the opposing party called the idea a joke: It would be hard enough for a single person to live in such a small space, much less a couple, they argued. And what if that couple decides to have children? After all, low fertility is a challenge Spain has faced for the past 20 years.

My colleagues David Alameda and Xaquín González decided that we could engage readers by letting them see for themselves how difficult it is to furnish such a tiny apartment. In the graphic, you select the pieces of furniture you want to buy, and then drag them around until you find an arrangement that lets you walk between the couch and the TV set to reach the bathroom. No easy task, I assure you.

Exploration

I am not a hardcore videogame player, but I still remember the crazy amount of hours I spent playing *Wolfenstein 3D*, the 1992 videogame that created the first-person shooter genre, popularized later by blockbusters such as *Doom* and *Quake*. What made that game so addictive was the feeling that you were in charge of the action. You were not represented in the story by a cartoony hero running around on the screen. *You* were the hero. *You* held that gun and shot it at hundreds of aggressive (and, yes, cartoony) Nazi bullies.

The kind of interaction these games apply is called *exploration*, and it can be used in information graphics with interesting results. See **Figure 9.18**, an interactive graphic made by my student Vu Nguyen for a documentary project on the city of Arequipa, in Peru. Arequipa's historical buildings have a very characteristic architectural style, so Vu decided to let readers navigate inside some of them. The 3D models in the graphic can be rotated and, once you enter one of the rooms, you can spin a 360-degree picture as if you were in the middle of it.

How to Plan For Interactive Infographics

I often say that a person who admires a lot of people is fortunate, but the person who has the luck of working alongside those whom he admires is privileged. I have been privileged. Many years ago, I was hired by the newspaper I used to read as a college student (*El Mundo*) and, in the summer of 2007, I had the opportunity to participate in a project published by the newspaper to which I subscribe to today, *The New York Times*.

You will learn about *The New York Times* graphics desk in the next section, so I will skip an in-depth explanation about how this award-winning department

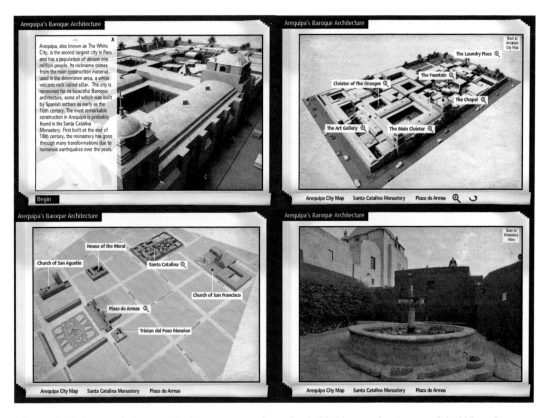

Figure 9.18 Arequipa's Baroque Architecture, an infographic by Vu Nguyen that is part of the White City Stories student documentary project (http://whitecitystories.jomc.unc.edu/).

functions. To end this chapter, I am going to focus on a specific piece that I helped develop, after having been invited to spend a couple of days in the newsroom by the head of infographics, Steve Duenes. The graphic, shown in **Figure 9.19**, is an example of what I think is the best way to approach a complex endeavor: Do research, plan, correct, execute, deliver.

My role in this project was to aid with the research, planning, sketching, and storyboarding for a couple of days. Joe Ward, Graham Roberts, Shan Carter, and John Branch designed the graphic after I left. The whole process of putting the animation together took one week.

Spanish tennis player Rafael Nadal was among the highlights of the 2007 U.S. Open. The *Times* had defined the focus for the graphic before I arrived in New York. Through the years, Nadal had been adapting his game to different kinds of

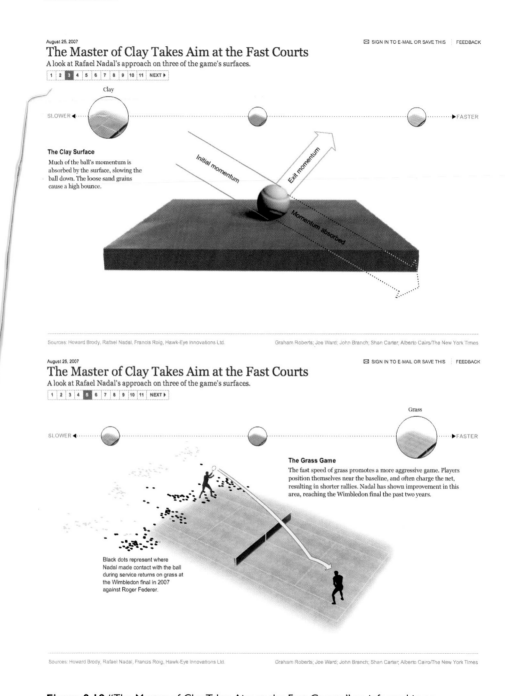

August 25, 2007

The Master of Clay Takes Aim at the Fast Courts
A look at Rafael Nadal's approach on three of the game's surfaces.

Figure 9.19 "The Master of Clay Takes Aim at the Fast Courts," an infographic on Rafael Nadal and the U.S. Open for *The New York Times* (http://www.nytimes.com/interactive/2007/08/25/sports/tennis/20070827_NADAL_GRAPHIC.html).

surfaces. In Spain, he became accustomed to clay courts, which are called "slow": When the ball hits the ground, the clay deforms and, because of friction, absorbs a considerable proportion of the ball's momentum (the energy the ball carries, so to speak). On a clay surface, balls bounce off slowly and high, so players tend to use a defensive game and stay behind the baseline.

But the surface at the U.S. Open is a "fast" surface: hard, with a concrete foundation. When the ball hits the ground, the friction is less than on a clay surface. The bounce is lower and much faster, because the amount of momentum the surface absorbs is negligible.

I find that fascinating. Personally, I couldn't care less about sports, something that my Spanish and Brazilian colleagues and basketball-crazed UNC students used to find amusing. I don't even care about soccer.[5] But I do love getting into the scientific, technical side of sports. Working on this graphic, I learned a lot when I interviewed University of Pennsylvania professor Howard Brody. After studying high-energy nuclear physics, Brody started doing research on the physics of sports. He has written three books on the science of tennis.

My phone conversation with Brody was enlightening. While talking to him, I scribbled my thoughts. You can see one of the pages in **Figure 9.20**.

The next step was to organize how the information would flow in the infographic; that is, how many steps it would take to explain everything. I drew a very rough storyboard and wrote plenty of notes underneath each frame (**Figure 9.21**). At the same time, I produced still pictures for a second storyboard, one that would help me visualize what the graphic would look like (**Figure 9.22**). For those panels, I used Illustrator and Maya, a 3D design tool.

When I saw the project published a few days after I left, I was impressed. The structure was pretty close to the one on the rough storyboard, and the look was similar to the one on the second set of sketches. But the team at the *Times* had very much improved the original ideas. That's the reward you get when you have the privilege of working alongside such a talented group of people.

---

5 Stories of my lack of sports awareness abound. Between 2010 and 2011, I lived in Brazil, where soccer is second to none in arousing public enthusiasm. One day I hailed a cab in São Paulo. Noticing my accent, the driver asked, "How is Spain doing?" I replied that the economy was pretty unstable. The driver informed me that Spain was playing North Korea in the World Cup at that very moment, and that was what he had inquired about. A few days later, Spain won the championship.

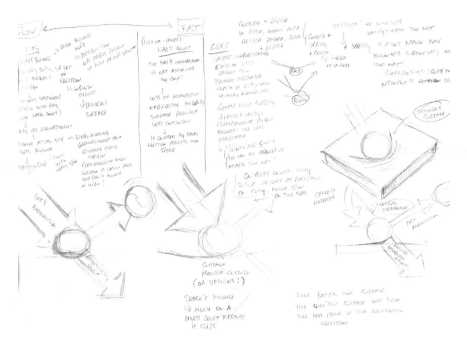

Figure 9.20 One of the many pages that I filled with notes for the project on Rafael Nadal.

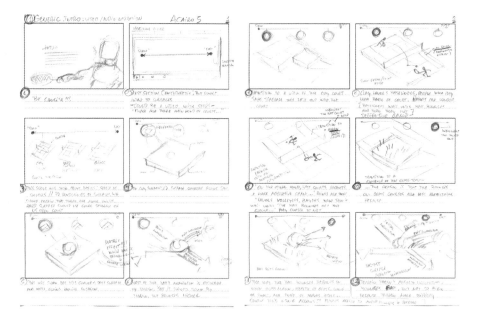

Figure 9.21 The first page of the storyboard for the Nadal project.

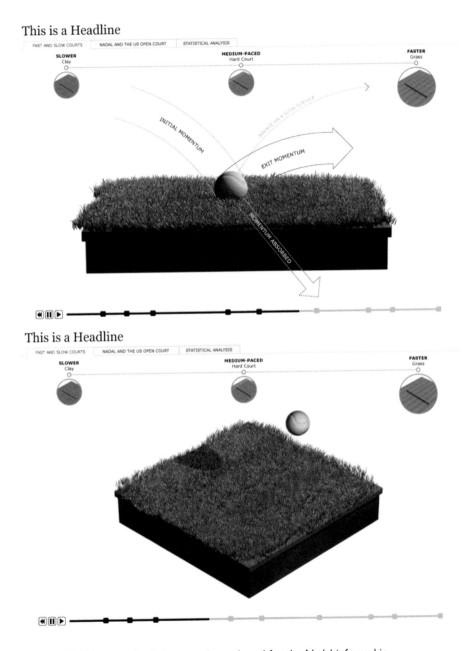

Figure 9.22 Two panels of the second storyboard for the Nadal infographic.

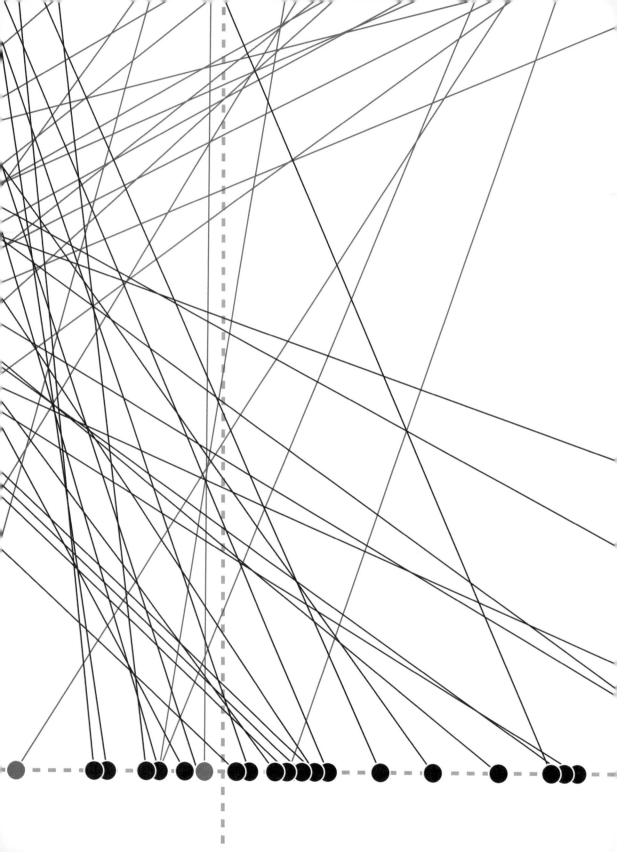

PART IV

profiles

Profile 1
John Grimwade
(*Condé Nast Traveler* magazine)

The Infographics Gentleman

John Grimwade is graphics director of *Condé Nast Traveler* magazine (based in New York) and has his own information graphics business (www.johngrimwade.com). He has produced infographics for more than 30 major magazines and several books. Before moving to the United States, he worked for 14 years in newspapers in London (including six years as head of graphics at *The Times*). He co-hosts the annual Malofiej "Show Don't Tell" infographics workshop in Pamplona, Spain, and teaches information graphics at the School of Visual Arts in Manhattan.

The first time I crossed paths with John Grimwade's work was when I was about to finish my B.A. in Journalism, in the summer of 1997. I had been offered an internship in the information graphics desk of *La Voz de Galicia*, the biggest regional newspaper in northwestern Spain. As my knowledge of the discipline was minimal, Manuela Mariño and Xoan González (father of Xaquín G.V. [González Veira], who you will meet in Profile 3), who led the department at the time, recommended that I take a look at some Malofiej publications. Malofiej[1] is the International

---

1 Visit http://www.malofiej20.com.

Infographics Summit, organized every year by the Spanish chapter of the Society for News Design. The event includes the most important competition in this field, which receives submissions from newspapers and magazines from all over the world. The winners are showcased in a series of large-format books.

While browsing several of these books, one graphic caught my eye. It was titled "The Transatlantic Superhighway," and it explained the busy flow of flights over the Northern Atlantic (**Figure 10.1**). I was enthralled by its elegance and deceptive simplicity. My colleagues told me that the piece—which had won a Silver Medal at Malofiej—had been designed by a certain British *maestro* named John Grimwade. "Along with Nigel Holmes, Grimwade is the best in this business," they added with a tone of reverence.

Years later, John and I became friends. He is a true gentleman, one of those professionals who are always willing to help rookies (as I was when I met him) with inexhaustible patience. He has also been a constant source of inspiration for me and for many others in this industry. In the current era of big data, complex programming, and information overload, his visual style—stripped down, precise, and graceful—is a reminder that good design is not about mastering technology, but about facilitating clear communication and the understanding of relevant issues.

Q Is it true that the way you produce graphics has not changed much in the 40 years that you have worked as an information graphics designer?

John Grimwade It is. I started doing information graphics many years before computers entered newsrooms. When they did, many colleagues said it was a huge change, but not for me. Maybe our methods of work have shifted a bit but the core principles are exactly the same.

Q What are those core principles?

JG Our main goal should be to tell a story clearly by achieving order and having some sort of narrative through each graphic. Any project should start by analyzing what your story is about and then finding the best way to tell it by splitting it up into easily digestible chunks, without losing depth.

When I design a graphic, I try to establish a hierarchy, too. In the planning stage, one of the first things I do is to identify the main components of the story and define how they are going to be sequenced on the page or on screen.

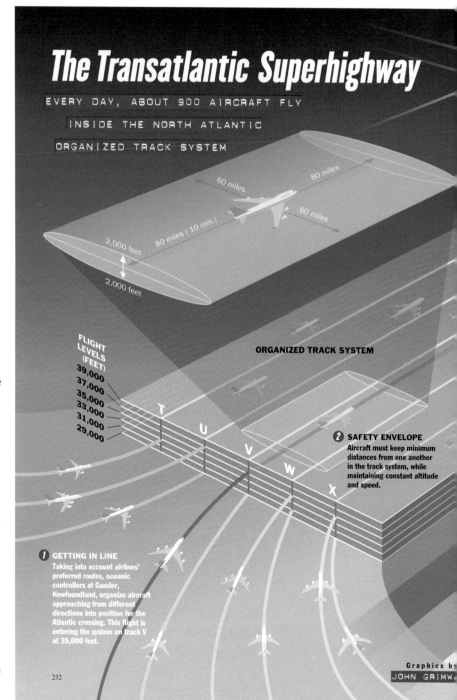

The Transatlantic Superhighway

EVERY DAY, ABOUT 900 AIRCRAFT FLY

INSIDE THE NORTH ATLANTIC

ORGANIZED TRACK SYSTEM

80 miles

60 miles

60 miles

2,000 feet

80 miles (10 min.)

2,000 feet

FLIGHT LEVELS (FEET)
39,000
37,000
35,000
33,000
31,000
29,000

ORGANIZED TRACK SYSTEM

T

U

V

W

X

2 SAFETY ENVELOPE
Aircraft must keep minimum
distances from one another
in the track system, while
maintaining constant altitude
and speed.

1 GETTING IN LINE
Taking into account airlines'
preferred routes, oceanic
controllers at Gander,
Newfoundland, organize aircraft
approaching from different
directions into position for the
Atlantic crossing. This flight is
entering the system on track V
at 35,000 feet.

Graphics by
JOHN GRIMW

232

Figure 10.1 "The Trans-atlantic Superhighway." *Condé Nast Traveler*, 1996, by John Grimwade, who explains the graphics: "This is an explanation of the system that controls flights over the Northern Atlantic. A reporter had a map of air-traffic control [see Figure 10.2], but it was difficult to read. I wanted to understand the system more thoroughly, so I made contact with the head of Oceanic Control in Gander, Newfoundland. Amazingly, there were no visualizations available of the system as a dimensional dia-gram. So I thought, why not make one? Rough versions went back and forth until we were both happy with the graphic."

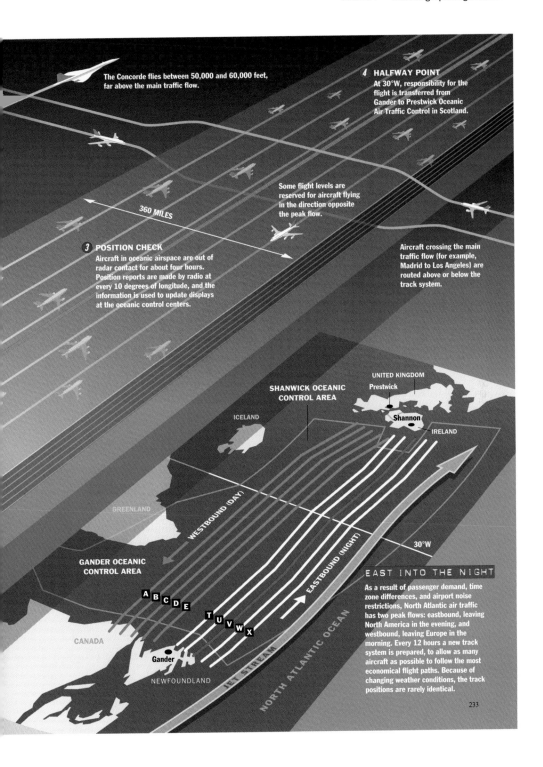

The Concorde flies between 50,000 and 60,000 feet, far above the main traffic flow.

4 HALFWAY POINT
At 30°W, responsibility for the flight is transferred from Gander to Prestwick Oceanic Air Traffic Control in Scotland.

360 MILES

Some flight levels are reserved for aircraft flying in the direction opposite the peak flow.

3 POSITION CHECK
Aircraft in oceanic airspace are out of radar contact for about four hours. Position reports are made by radio at every 10 degrees of longitude, and the information is used to update displays at the oceanic control centers.

Aircraft crossing the main traffic flow (for example, Madrid to Los Angeles) are routed above or below the track system.

UNITED KINGDOM
Prestwick

SHANWICK OCEANIC
CONTROL AREA

ICELAND

Shannon

IRELAND

WESTBOUND (DAY)

GREENLAND

EASTBOUND (NIGHT)

30°W

**GANDER OCEANIC
CONTROL AREA**

A B C D E
T U V W X

CANADA

Gander

NEWFOUNDLAND

JET STREAM

NORTH ATLANTIC OCEAN

EAST INTO THE NIGHT
As a result of passenger demand, time zone differences, and airport noise restrictions, North Atlantic air traffic has two peak flows: eastbound, leaving North America in the evening, and westbound, leaving Europe in the morning. Every 12 hours a new track system is prepared, to allow as many aircraft as possible to follow the most economical flight paths. Because of changing weather conditions, the track positions are rarely identical.

233

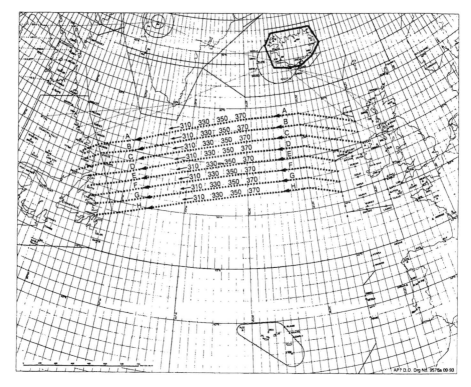

Figure 10.2 One of the source materials for the "The Transatlantic Superhighway." An air-traffic control map.

Q That sounds like Journalism 101 to me. When you write a story, the best thing to start with is a structure for your writing.

JG That's because it is! The only difference between a traditional journalist and us is the language. Journalists use words; we use pictures, charts, graphs, maps, diagrams, and illustrations.

I think one of the reasons why some people of my generation were very successful is because we were designers, but we got embedded in journalistic environments. We worked with reporters and editors. That taught us that we should strive for clarity because we are an interface between a chaotic world of information and the user who wants to understand something. If we can't bring users clarity, I think we have kind of failed, actually.

When I see a graphic I am interested in, I try to read it critically, and one question I ask over and over again is "What's the point? What's the story?" That's what you have to do when you work on a project. It's not enough to do good research

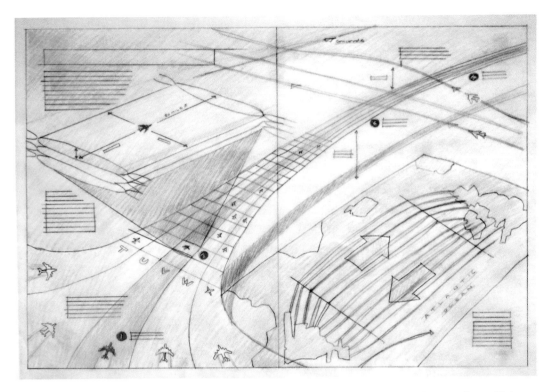

Figure 10.3 One of the sketches for "The Transatlantic Superhighway" infographic, shown in Figure 10.1.

and then present your information to your readers. You have to edit that information. We, infographics designers, must work as reporters but, above all, as editors.

Q   **Is that why you have expressed reservations about the emerging field of data visualization? Many infographics designers in newspapers and magazines seem to be embracing it with enthusiasm, but you have said that sometimes it feels that visualization designers seem to just throw data at their users, without worrying about presenting coherent stories.**

JG   Embracing a new technique or a new technology is great. Data visualization can be really powerful and useful. I can see a lot of potential in it. Nonetheless, I also feel that many visualization designers try to transform the user into an editor. They create these amazing interactive tools with tons of bubbles, lines, bars, filters, and scrubber bars, and expect readers to figure the story out by themselves, and draw conclusions from the data. That's not an approach to information graphics I like. Not all readers are data analysts!

Maybe I am old-school, but I don't believe I am alone in that concern. Think of Hans Rosling[2] and the way he interacts with his wonderful bubble visualizations. He doesn't just show stuff; he explains the main points, focusing the reader's attention on the most interesting parts of the information. After that, if readers want to navigate deeper into other possible stories, they can do it. But first, they are exposed to a traditional, linear narrative that lays out the basic facts.

Q   Is it possible to find a synthesis between what information graphics designers have been doing for the past 30 or 40 years and what data visualizers are trying to achieve nowadays?

JG I am convinced that we will see that in the future. *The New York Times*[3] is exploring that path at this point. For instance, in many of their interactive graphics, they present complex sets of data, and they let you go really deep into the figures and their connections. But beforehand, they give you some context, some pointers as to what you can do with those data. If you don't do this, if you don't include this layer of information, which the designers call the "annotation layer," you will end up with a visualization that may look really beautiful and intricate, but that will leave readers wondering, "What has this thing really told me? What is this useful for?"

It's like a visualization I saw the other day that plotted the flow of taxis in New York City, as well as their positions at every time of the day and night. It looked really cool but, after a minute, I asked myself: What is this about? What am I supposed to see here? Is it really that surprising that the flow of taxis is really heavy between La Guardia and JFK, or that there are fewer taxis during the night than during the day? That's not a very revealing insight, is it?

Or take some gorgeous recent maps that show people tweeting all over Europe in the languages of the countries they live in. All right, that's really interesting [*said tongue-in-cheek*]: The Germans are tweeting in German! The map certainly looks beautiful with all those little color dots shining here and there, but it's not that enlightening. It doesn't convey much, and that's a problem. You need to orient readers into the story before they can navigate your graphics on their own.

Q   Let's talk a bit about your own design process. How do you get started?

JG When we do a story for *Condé Nast Traveler* magazine, I try to be involved in it as early as possible. Sometimes it happens that reporters don't realize they

2 See Profile 8: Hans Rosling.
3 See Profile 3: Steve Duenes and Xaquín G.V.

will need infographics in their pieces until they get back from trips, so I prefer to meet with them before they depart. It helps me get a clear idea of what shape the story is going to take, of its focus, and it helps reporters understand how the copy and the visual elements on the pages are going to complement each other.

I bring paper and pencils to those meetings. While we talk, I keep scribbling. I do very rough sketches and take notes about the key elements. It's in these meetings when I decide what we need to show with the graphic so its content doesn't overlap too much with what the copy will tell or the photographs will show.

Q   It seems that you put a lot of work in the planning stage of your projects, judging by the detailed sketches and roughs you produce. (*See Figure 10.3 and Figure 10.5*.)

JG They are part of my thinking process. After the preliminary meetings are over, I go to my studio and work out the structure of the graphic in a rough form. I find that in pencil I can just do a rough version, arrange the elements as I wish, and throw away whatever I feel is not related to the points I want to get across. There's virtually nothing invested in those sketches.

If you try to do something like that in a computer, you will somehow feel committed to your first ideas. Sketching out using design software requires a lot of effort. Later, when you go over your plans with editors, everything may need to change for some reason, maybe because the focus of the story has switched. If you are enamored with your own computer graphics, those that took so much time to develop, you may feel resistant to change them down the road.

In other words: at first, don't just draw a box in Adobe Illustrator and start working inside it. That's a very bad way to start: You make a lot of art decisions and then trap yourself into them. I constantly see graphics that have been done like that. A big image or illustration was put in the middle first and then the designer tried to make all the other elements in the composition work around it, instead of coming up with a solid structure that would help tell the story you need to tell. This doesn't happen when you work with pen and paper before you proceed to the artwork phase.

I try to encourage my students at the School of Visual Arts to draw as many sketches as possible, due to this attachment factor that everybody experiences every now and then. Sometimes they feel intimidated by hand drawing, but I tell them that they don't need to be Leonardo da Vinci. What they need to come up with is not art; they don't need to worry about aesthetics at this point, but about the structure. In many cases, just a bunch of very simple, rough, and badly drawn sketches made with cheap pencils or crayons will suffice to help you understand

Figure 10.4 "Grand Central Terminal," 1998. *Condé Nast Traveler*, by John Grimwade. "This infographic is part of a feature that reported the completion of the Grand Central Terminal restoration. At the time, I was walking through the building every day on my way to work, so the reference was right in front of me. I used the simple approach of taking a cross-section and manually projecting it backward. John Tomanio, who worked with me at *Condé Nast Traveler*, solved my problems in getting the ceiling exactly right. He photographed it looking straight up, and then projected the image onto the inside of a cylinder using a 3-D program."

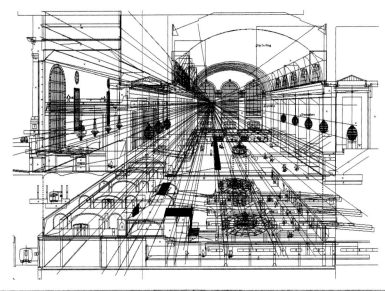

Figure 10.5 Sketches for the "Grand Central Terminal" infographic.

how to organize a story, how to create a good sequence of steps, and a good hierarchy in your layout.

Q   Speaking of students, you are well known for your openness to give advice to beginners and help them develop their own styles. What would you recommend to someone who is planning to pursue a career in information graphics and visualization? What should that person study?

JG That's very difficult question. I guess the challenge is that you are asking me to think backward. I learned to design infographics by working in a newsroom. Decades ago, I landed in a news publication and learned the craft on the job.

I would say, however, that the first skill you need to master is to look at graphics with a critical eye. Read newspapers, magazines, and textbooks; visit websites that showcase infographics and visualizations; and analyze if they help you understand important matters. If they don't, they are not good. The next thing would be to reflect on the changes that would make those presentations tell clearer messages. And, if you have the time, you can maybe even make those changes.

You also have to ponder if you have the passion to enter this field. Infographics is not the easiest task. It might look like it is but it sure as hell isn't. You need years of self-teaching and trial-and-error to master the techniques and tools. If you don't feel the drive to be absolutely meticulous about research and coming to grips with the story, you just can't produce a good information graphic. If you think you are going to skim across the top and treat it like some kind of art job, it's very unlikely that you are going to be much of a success. I don't know how to find or fuel that kind of passion, though.

Figure 10.6 One of the discarded illustrations made for the "Seven Ages of the 747" project.

Q   I would say this passion you talk about reminds me of the passion good educators nourish. It's the need to be curious, to learn, and to tell others about what you have learned. Journalists feel that kind of passion as well.

JG It's really a journalistic passion, yes. In fact, some of the best people I have worked with used to be traditional journalists until they realized the power of visual storytelling. When you think about it, infographics and visualization are really amazing tools for telling stories when used correctly, aren't they?

Column	Country	Medals	GDP (billions)	Medals/Billions
1	Ethiopia	7	$8	0.875
2	Georgia	4	$5	0.800
3	Belarus	15	$22	0.682
4	Bulgaria	12	$24	0.500
5	Romania	19	$73	0.260
6	Hungary	17	$99	0.172
7	Russia	92	$582	0.158
8	Slovakia	6	$41	0.146
9	Greece	16	$203	0.079
10	Australia	49	$631	0.078
11	Ukraine	23	$311	0.074
12	New Zealand	5	$99	0.051
13	Thailand	8	$163	0.049
14	Poland	10	$241	0.041
15	China	63	$1,649	0.038
16	Netherlands	22	$577	0.038
17	Iran	6	$162	0.037
18	Turkey	10	$301	0.033
19	Austria	7	$290	0.024
20	Norway	6	$250	0.024
21	Sweden	7	$346	0.020
22	Spain	19	$991	0.019
23	Italy	32	$1,672	0.019
24	Germany	49	$2,714	0.018
25	Brazil	10	$604	0.017
26	France	33	$2,002	0.016
27	Great Britain	30	$2,140	0.014
28	Canada	12	$979	0.012
29	US	102	$11,667	0.009
30	Japan	37	$4,623	0.008

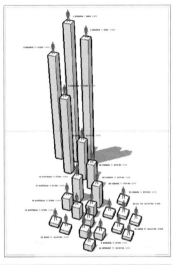

Figure 10.7
A spreadsheet and early sketches and layouts for the "Medal Exchange" infographic.

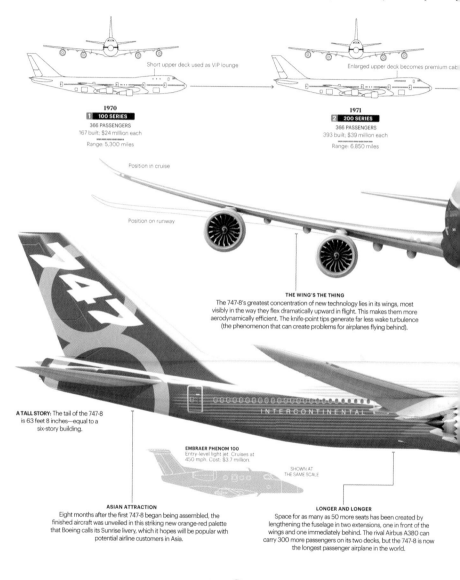

The Five Ages of the 747

Since it began flying passengers in 1970, the Boeing 747 has stayed on top of its

Short upper deck used as VIP lounge

Enlarged upper deck becomes premium cab

1970
1 100 SERIES
366 PASSENGERS
167 built; $24 million each
Range: 5,300 miles

1971
2 200 SERIES
366 PASSENGERS
393 built; $39 million each
Range: 6,850 miles

Position in cruise

Position on runway

THE WING'S THE THING
The 747-8's greatest concentration of new technology lies in its wings, most visibly in the way they flex dramatically upward in flight. This makes them more aerodynamically efficient. The knife-point tips generate far less wake turbulence (the phenomenon that can create problems for airplanes flying behind).

A TALL STORY: The tail of the 747-8 is 63 feet 8 inches—equal to a six-story building.

INTERCONTINENTAL

EMBRAER PHENOM 100
Entry-level light jet. Cruises at 450 mph. Cost: $3.7 million.

SHOWN AT THE SAME SCALE

ASIAN ATTRACTION
Eight months after the first 747-8 began being assembled, the finished aircraft was unveiled in this striking new orange-red palette that Boeing calls its Sunrise livery, which it hopes will be popular with potential airline customers in Asia.

LONGER AND LONGER
Space for as many as 50 more seats has been created by lengthening the fuselage in two extensions, one in front of the wings and one immediately behind. The rival Airbus A380 can carry 300 more passengers on its two decks, but the 747-8 is now the longest passenger airplane in the world.

LIGHTEN UP
In addition to nearly 500 passengers, a 747 can carry 20 tons of freight and 625 pieces of baggage, all of which can be unloaded in 15 minutes.

Figure 10.8 "Five Ages of the 747." *Condé Nast Traveler*, 2011, by John Grimwade. "Projects often take big shifts along the way. I was originally thinking of a fly-past of 747s to show the history, but every angle we tried did not clearly show the key features of the new 747 aircraft that had been announced. The new model is much longer than the previous ones, and it has dramatically upswept wings. So I moved to a more conventional plan-like display."

MAY 2011 • PG: **171**

adopting new technologies. The latest is the most radical step in its decades-long evolution.

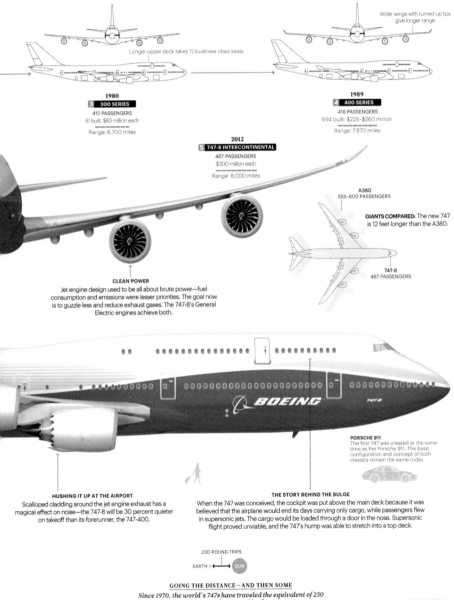

Wider wings with turned-up tips give longer range

Longer upper deck takes 12 business-class seats

1980
3 **300 SERIES**
412 PASSENGERS
81 built; $83 million each
Range: 6,700 miles

1989
4 **400 SERIES**
416 PASSENGERS
694 built; $228–$260 million
Range: 7,670 miles

2012
5 **747-8 INTERCONTINENTAL**
467 PASSENGERS
$300 million each
Range: 8,000 miles

A380
555–800 PASSENGERS

GIANTS COMPARED: The new 747 is 12 feet longer than the A380.

747-8
467 PASSENGERS

CLEAN POWER
Jet engine design used to be all about brute power—fuel consumption and emissions were lesser priorities. The goal now is to guzzle less and reduce exhaust gases. The 747-8's General Electric engines achieve both.

PORSCHE 911
The first 747 was created at the same time as the Porsche 911. The basic configuration and concept of both classics remain the same today.

HUSHING IT UP AT THE AIRPORT
Scalloped cladding around the jet engine exhaust has a magical effect on noise—the 747-8 will be 30 percent quieter on takeoff than its forerunner, the 747-400.

THE STORY BEHIND THE BULGE
When the 747 was conceived, the cockpit was put above the main deck because it was believed that the airplane would end its days carrying only cargo, while passengers flew in supersonic jets. The cargo would be loaded through a door in the nose. Supersonic flight proved unviable, and the 747's hump was able to stretch into a top deck.

230 ROUND-TRIPS
EARTH ⟷ SUN

GOING THE DISTANCE—AND THEN SOME
Since 1970, the world's 747s have traveled the equivalent of 230 trips to the sun and back.

ILLUSTRATION BY **JOHN MACNEILL**

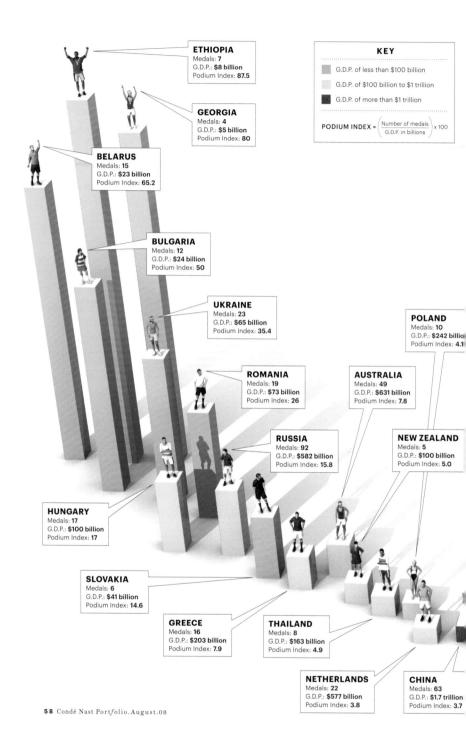

KEY

- G.D.P. of less than $100 billion
- G.D.P. of $100 billion to $1 trillion
- G.D.P. of more than $1 trillion

PODIUM INDEX = (Number of medals / G.D.P. in billions) x 100

ETHIOPIA
Medals: 7
G.D.P.: $8 billion
Podium Index: 87.5

GEORGIA
Medals: 4
G.D.P.: $5 billion
Podium Index: 80

BELARUS
Medals: 15
G.D.P.: $23 billion
Podium Index: 65.2

BULGARIA
Medals: 12
G.D.P.: $24 billion
Podium Index: 50

UKRAINE
Medals: 23
G.D.P.: $65 billion
Podium Index: 35.4

POLAND
Medals: 10
G.D.P.: $242 billio
Podium Index: 4.1

ROMANIA
Medals: 19
G.D.P.: $73 billion
Podium Index: 26

AUSTRALIA
Medals: 49
G.D.P.: $631 billion
Podium Index: 7.8

RUSSIA
Medals: 92
G.D.P.: $582 billion
Podium Index: 15.8

NEW ZEALAND
Medals: 5
G.D.P.: $100 billion
Podium Index: 5.0

HUNGARY
Medals: 17
G.D.P.: $100 billion
Podium Index: 17

SLOVAKIA
Medals: 6
G.D.P.: $41 billion
Podium Index: 14.6

GREECE
Medals: 16
G.D.P.: $203 billion
Podium Index: 7.9

THAILAND
Medals: 8
G.D.P.: $163 billion
Podium Index: 4.9

NETHERLANDS
Medals: 22
G.D.P.: $577 billion
Podium Index: 3.8

CHINA
Medals: 63
G.D.P.: $1.7 trillion
Podium Index: 3.7

Figure 10.9 "Medal Exchange." *Condé Nast Portfolio*, 2008, by John Grimwade: "This is an interesting approach to covering the Olympics in a business magazine just before the Beijing games. We're all used to the conventional medals table, but what happens if the Athens medals total is divided by the GDP of the country? Then we see who did the most with the least resources. Ethiopia is the winner. The U.S. and Japan are way down the list."

◯◯◯

demystifier

Medal Exchange

Sure, the world's economic powerhouses dominate the Olympics. Or do they?

· · ·

by Jessica Liebman

Do wealthier countries take home more Olympic medals? Conventional wisdom suggests that they would. It's no secret that having the financial resources to invest in human potential leads to success: The U.S. is the richest country in the world and has won more Olympic medals than any other nation. But if you introduce some elementary math and divide a country's medal tally by its gross domestic product, the numbers rearrange themselves dramatically. Ethiopia's track-and-field victories lift the poverty-stricken state to the top of the pile, while economic powerhouses like Japan, France, and the U.S. finish near the bottom. Here's a look at our surprising results, based on medal counts from the 2004 Summer Games in Athens and G.D.P. data from the same year.

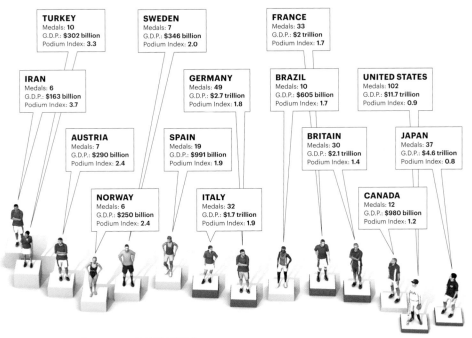

TURKEY
Medals: **10**
G.D.P.: **$302 billion**
Podium Index: **3.3**

SWEDEN
Medals: **7**
G.D.P.: **$346 billion**
Podium Index: **2.0**

FRANCE
Medals: **33**
G.D.P.: **$2 trillion**
Podium Index: **1.7**

IRAN
Medals: **6**
G.D.P.: **$163 billion**
Podium Index: **3.7**

GERMANY
Medals: **49**
G.D.P.: **$2.7 trillion**
Podium Index: **1.8**

BRAZIL
Medals: **10**
G.D.P.: **$605 billion**
Podium Index: **1.7**

UNITED STATES
Medals: **102**
G.D.P.: **$11.7 trillion**
Podium Index: **0.9**

AUSTRIA
Medals: **7**
G.D.P.: **$290 billion**
Podium Index: **2.4**

SPAIN
Medals: **19**
G.D.P.: **$991 billion**
Podium Index: **1.9**

BRITAIN
Medals: **30**
G.D.P.: **$2.1 trillion**
Podium Index: **1.4**

JAPAN
Medals: **37**
G.D.P.: **$4.6 trillion**
Podium Index: **0.8**

NORWAY
Medals: **6**
G.D.P.: **$250 billion**
Podium Index: **2.4**

ITALY
Medals: **32**
G.D.P.: **$1.7 trillion**
Podium Index: **1.9**

CANADA
Medals: **12**
G.D.P.: **$980 billion**
Podium Index: **1.2**

ILLUSTRATION *by* BRYAN CHRISTIE DESIGN

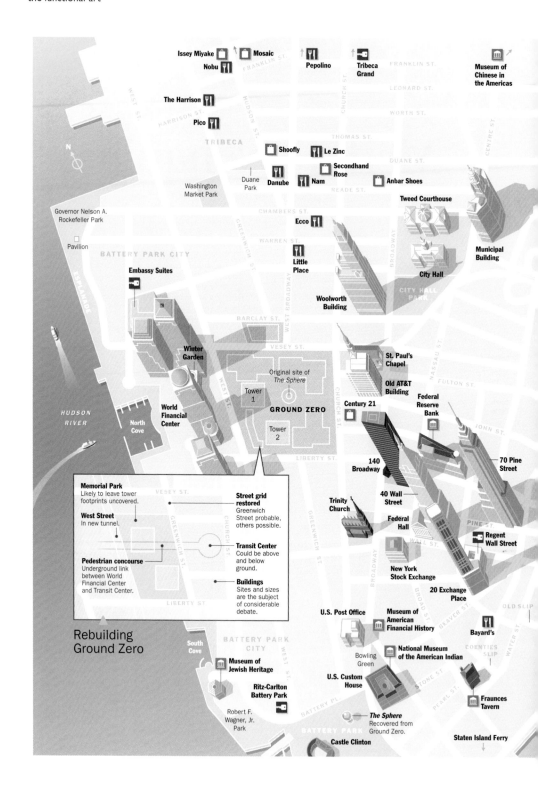

Rebuilding
Ground Zero

The
Manhattan Project

All eyes are trained, these days, on New York's
downtown—and there's no better time to be there.
From TriBeCa to Battery Park, from the Hudson
River to the East River, here are the don't-miss
classics—plus everything new and coming

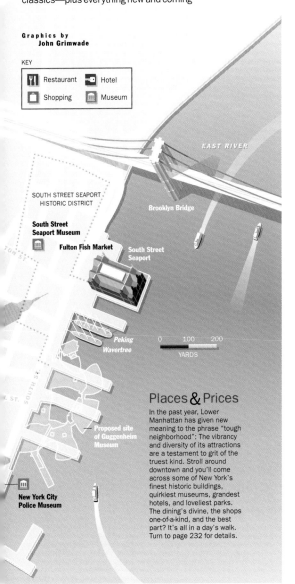

**Graphics by
John Grimwade**

KEY

| | Restaurant | | Hotel |
| | Shopping | | Museum |

EAST RIVER

SOUTH STREET SEAPORT
HISTORIC DISTRICT

**South Street
Seaport Museum**

Brooklyn Bridge

Fulton Fish Market

South Street
Seaport

Peking
Wavertree

0   100   200
YARDS

Proposed site
of Guggenheim
Museum

**New York City
Police Museum**

Places & Prices

In the past year, Lower
Manhattan has given new
meaning to the phrase "tough
neighborhood": The vibrancy
and diversity of its attractions
are a testament to grit of the
truest kind. Stroll around
downtown and you'll come
across some of New York's
finest historic buildings,
quirkiest museums, grandest
hotels, and loveliest parks.
The dining's divine, the shops
one-of-a-kind, and the best
part? It's all in a day's walk.
Turn to page 232 for details.

Figure 10.10 "The Manhattan Project,"
Condé Nast Traveler, 2002, by John Grimwade.
"One year after the September 11 attacks,
we ran a feature reminding our readers that
the downtown area of Manhattan still had a
lot to offer. It has stylized buildings, where
I tried to capture the essence of the building rather than aerial-photograph accuracy,
and a clear street grid. This is very much my
graphic approach to making maps: Remove
the unnecessary detail, and focus on the
story. In 2003, I reworked the map into a
different format for a handout at the Society
of Publication Designers conference." (See
Figure 10.11 to see the second map.)

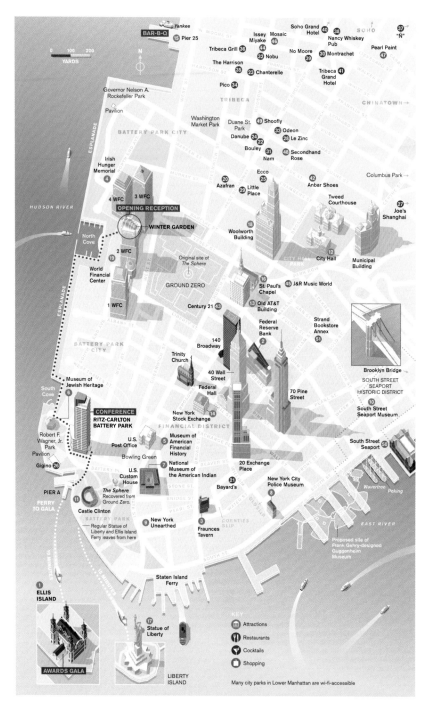

Figure 10.11 A redesign of "The Manhattan Project" for the Society of Publication Designers' conference, in 2003.

Profile 2
Juan Velasco and Fernando Baptista
(*National Geographic* magazine)

Information Art

Juan Velasco is the art director of *National Geographic* magazine. From 1998 to 2001, Juan was the graphics art director for *The New York Times*. Prior to this he was a graphics reporter for the Spanish newspaper *El Mundo* (Madrid). He is also an instructor for the Malofiej "Show, Don't Tell" infographics workshop in Pamplona (Spain), and for the University of Hong Kong's Journalism and Media Studies Centre. With his own business, 5W Infographics, Juan has done graphics redesigns for newspapers such as *Le Monde* (France) and *Tribune de Geneve* (Switzerland). He has won multiple Society of Newspaper Design awards and Malofiej awards, and he was a Pulitzer finalist in 2000 with a team of reporters from *The New York Times*.

Fernando G. Baptista is senior graphics editor of *National Geographic* magazine. He worked for *El Correo*, a local newspaper in Spain, for 14 years before moving to Washington, D.C., in 2007. Baptista made several art reconstructions for museums in Spain, and created graphics and illustrations for many books. Baptista also taught information graphics for six years at the University of Navarra, in Spain, and in the Masters of Journalism program of *El Correo*.

A friend of mine once told me that if Leonardo da Vinci lived in our era, he would probably be hired as an information graphics designer at *National Geographic* magazine. I admit that this sounds like a hyperbole, but it's exactly what I thought the first time I walked in to Fernando Baptista's office at the *NGM* headquarters, in Washington D.C. "Wow," I whispered to myself, "this looks like Leonardo's workshop!"[4] At least, it did in my imagination.

Fernando's walls are covered with beautiful sketches of works in progress. Several clay models of animals and buildings decorate a desk close to his computer. All those props are the remains of the multiple iterations every graphic goes through at the publication which I would argue takes illustration-based infographics most seriously in the world.

Fernando is one of the three senior graphics editors and two senior maps editors who help art director Juan Velasco in conceptualizing the graphics and illustrations that *National Geographic* magazine publishes every month. Juan's team also includes two junior editors and five production assistants who are in charge of designing simple charts and maps and who aid senior editors in large, long-term projects.

Juan is quick to point out that their work would not succeed if it was not for the help of one research editor and two copy editors, one for infographics and the other one for maps, who are also part of his operation. "Names of regions, rivers, and mountains change so often that we would make a lot of mistakes if we didn't double-check every map we produce," he told me. That kind of precision, as you will see in the following conversation, extends to every single detail of all drawings in the magazine.

Q   One of the myths of *National Geographic* magazine is that you spend months, and even sometimes more than a year, working on every infographic. Is that true?

Juan Velasco It is, but that statement needs a disclaimer. It's not that each of us gets stuck with a single graphic for that long. Fernando, me, and the others in the team can have six or seven ongoing projects simultaneously. Each of those projects can take, yes, several months to complete. But when you really calculate how many hours or days we spend on them, it's not usually longer than four or five weeks per infographic.

---

4 If you want to see a photograph of Fernando's office and get more details about the projects in this Profile, refer to Lesson 3 in the DVD.

I am aware that this figure is beyond what your average news publication can invest on any single project, but the level of accuracy and precision we want our graphics and illustrations to have demands that they are filtered several times, double-checked with sources, and reviewed by as many experts as possible.

Q   Can you expand on the process to create infographics at the magazine?

JV When a story is approved to be published, we gather what we call a "story team" in the newsroom. The story team is a group of five or six people who work together on the project for an extended period of time: a photo editor, a copy editor, an infographics or art editor, a cartographer, and a researcher.

After this is done, the team meets on a regular basis for several weeks or even months and thinks about the best way to approach the project. The goal is to come up with a formal proposal to be sent to the editor-in-chief. This proposal specifies how the story is going to be covered and what assets will be needed: text, photographs, maps, graphics, and illustrations.

Right after he reads the proposal, the editor-in-chief helps the team to focus the story even more, and also decides on how many pages it will use. The researcher in the team then does some pre-research for a week or two, and passes the information to the artist in charge of creating the art for the story.

Q   What does that pre-research consist of?

Fernando Baptista It's a variety of things: scientific articles, books, and even maps and drawings. For an explanatory illustration we made about Göbekli Tepe, a Neolithic temple in Turkey (**Figure 10.12**), for instance, the researcher, Patricia Healy, put together a huge map based on several sources, and she pasted pictures and drawings on it for me to figure out the position of the ruins. I took that map, which was really big, with me when I traveled to the site.

Q   Did you really go to Turkey to do your own research?

FB I did! It's not very usual for an infographics artist to travel anywhere for work, is it? But we do it all the time at *National Geographic*. The artist needs to visit whatever it is he or she is going to portray, as we want our drawings to be as accurate as possible.

Göbekli Tepe is near the border between Turkey and Syria, close to the city of Urba. I flew there and met with the chief archeologist, Klaus Schmidt, from the German Archaeological Institute, who has been working there since 1994. I spent three days with Klaus and his team.

BUILDING GÖBEKLI TEPE

People must have gathered from far-flung settlements to erect the first known temples. Using flint tools, they carved pillars and shaped blocks for walls mortared with clay. When a new temple was completed, the old one was buried. How the temples were used is unknown.

Head
Arm
Belt
Hands
Animal-skin loincloth

Carvings mark the pillars as stylized human figures, but did they represent powerful people or supernatural beings?

A pillar's shape was refined before being carved and placed.

■ Pillars
■ Excavated
■ Unexcavated
□ Area shown in illustration

Entry pillars

159 ft

Sanctuary grounds
Geomagnetic surveys of the 22-acre site suggest that at least 20 temples were built, from about 9600 to 8200 B.C. The oldest known are shown above.

Quarrying a pillar
The T-shape was incised directly into a bed of lime-stone. Pressure applied with levers then broke the rock along natural fracture lines, freeing the pillar.

Figure 10.12 "Building Göbekli Tepe," the oldest known temple in the world. (*National Geographic* stock.)

Human muscle moved the limestone pillars, weighing up to 16 tons, from quarries as far as a quarter mile away.

The inner ring had no door and may have been accessed with ladders. Animal pelts may have hung on the pillars as offerings.

Offerings

Children may have helped by hauling rainwater collected in cisterns for drinking.

A sunken U-shaped block formed the entry pillars.

Spectator access?
Earthen embankments may have given pilgrims a view of ceremonies inside the rings. Or the temple may have been roofed and exclusive.

Possible roof

FERNANDO G. BAPTISTA (ART) AND LAWSON PARKER (MAP AND DIAGRAMS), NGM STAFF; PATRICIA HEALY
SOURCES: KLAUS SCHMIDT, JENS NOTROFF, AND OLIVER DIETRICH, GERMAN ARCHAEOLOGICAL INSTITUTE; IAN KUIJT, UNIVERSITY OF NOTRE DAME

When I got there, I was carrying several rough sketches with me to explain to them what we were planning to do (**Figure 10.13**). Those sketches changed completely, of course, after I received suggestions from the archeologists.

One of the main challenges in understanding the layout of the temple is that it has been only partially excavated. There are certain portions that are not well preserved, or that have not been preserved at all. I would say that only one-third of the remains are visible today. To make a visual reconstruction of Göbekli Tepe, you have to rely not only on the on-site observations, but also on what the scientists working there think it may have looked like more than 10,000 years back. It's like putting a complex puzzle together.

Q   So you spent more than two weeks doing just research, after the story was approved by the editor-in-chief.

FB Yes, but that was only the beginning. After I got back from Turkey, I made several clay models of the temple to visualize and analyze its structure and its proportions (**Figure 10.14**).

Q   Why clay? Why didn't you use 3D software?

FB I feel more comfortable working with an actual object that I can manipulate with my hands, rather than on a computer screen. I am pretty fast at making this kind of very rough model. It's less time consuming for me to do it this way than to use a 3D software tool. It's also useful in meetings: I used to carry the clay model with me all the time when we had to discuss the graphic with editors, and we were able to decide on what angle was more appropriate for viewing the temple.

The final model I made was reviewed and corrected by Klaus Schmidt and his team. I spent two days in Berlin with them and came back to the U.S. with tons of notes that forced me to remake several portions of the sculpture. That was really exhausting, but also rewarding.

Q   The drawing of the temple in the graphic you ran in the magazine looks fantastic.

FB It's not really a drawing—it's the clay model. We shot several pictures of it, and I used Photoshop to add textures to the wall, grass, people, etc.[5] An important thing to remember is that none of those is made up. The researcher assigned to each project must also document the surroundings: vegetal species, the colors of the terrain, how people were most likely dressed at that time. All those details

---

5 Watch Lesson 3, in the DVD, to see an extended photo gallery of the Göbekli Tepe project.

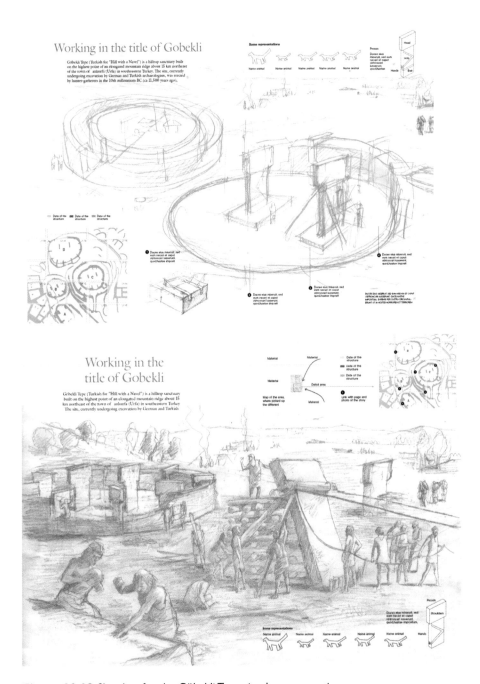

Figure 10.13 Sketches for the Göbekli Tepe visual reconstruction.

Figure 10.14 More sketches for the Göbekli Tepe visual reconstruction.

need to be as precise as possible. Everything that we show in an illustration is backed by data and reviewed by experts.

Q   This is related to something you mentioned to me a while ago, Juan. You told me that the illustrations you make at _National Geographic_ are really data visualizations. What do you mean?

JV Good illustrated graphics, in addition to being often the best way to tell a story, show enormous amount of data. They just display it differently than a quantitative data visualization. Our illustrations are not just nice-looking drawings, but accurate depictions of reality, with thousands of very precise data points.

A while ago, we made a model of the face of an ancient hominid. On it, we located every single bone and every single muscle. Our quality standards are not those of a news publication. People keep their copies of _National Geographic_ magazine for years and decades. That's why we stick to the same quality and accuracy standards that scientific publications follow. What we do is pure "precision journalism" even if that's a term that is usually applied just to statistical charts and the use of databases for news analysis.

Besides, all research we do for our project is firsthand. We read books and articles, but we also go directly to the sources and work with them on every step. Sometimes, experts can save the day, even in creative matters. It happened to us on a project about world population recently.

Q How so?

JV In 2011, world population was about to reach 7 billion people. We started working on a series of special stories that were going to be published throughout several issues of the magazine. However, we lacked an image that summarized how big a number that is. We had tons of data, many charts and maps, but we wanted to have also something that was precise and impactful.

One day, Bill Marr, our creative director, decided to take us to a bar to talk about the population project. There, in between gin and tonics, we shared a bunch of crazy ideas. One of them stood out. What if we focused our population graphic on the most common kind of person?

Q What would that person be like? Was that a data-based decision?

JV When you take a look at the population data sorted by sexes, ages, ethnicities, and countries, you see that the most common kind of person in the world is a 28-year-old male of the Han ethnicity, from China. That's the most numerous human group on Earth today. To get to that conclusion, we did a lot of sketches. For instance, we created a plot with 7,000 color dots, each representing 1 million people, and we divided it by countries (**Figure 10.15**).

The result was not bad, but it looked a bit dry and unsophisticated. Also the dots were so tiny that they were almost impossible to see. Besides, we did want to have people in the graphic, to make it look human. So John Tomanio, the senior graphics editor in charge of the story, thought: what if we change the dots for a grid of 7,000 tiny people, each a proxy for a million humans?

Q But you said that the focus was going to be the most common kind of person in the world.

JV It was, because the grid of little figures was not going to be randomly arranged. The concept was to have the tiny people organized in a specific way and dressed in color clothes that, when put together, formed the face of that 28-year-old Chinese

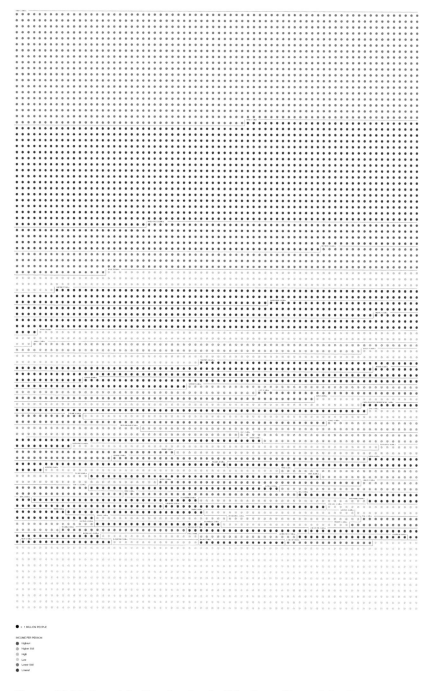

Figure 10.15 One of the first sketches for "The Face of Seven Billion" project. Each dot represents 1 million people.

male. So the little people, rendered in 3D by one of our partners, Bryan Christie, were going to be pixels of the final artwork. Bryan had made something similar for a *Newsweek* magazine cover in the past: He had drawn Barack Obama's face with little human figures. That's the look we wished our population poster to adopt.

At first, we went to our huge photo archive and painstakingly searched for a generic Chinese face, a photo that had good contrast and adequate lights and shades. We found a good one, and we did put the tiny 3D people in (**Figure 10.16**).

Figure 10.16 The second sketch for the "The Face of Seven Billion" project, based on a photograph of a real Chinese male.

Then we realized this approach was not correct: If we used this photograph, we would be bringing attention to a particular individual. Here's when we proved, once again, that great sources are the best asset an information graphics designer can have.

We were in touch with the Chinese Academy of Science, in Beijing. Based on 10 years of research, they were able to create a very particular kind of photograph for us. They brought together the passport photographs of 190,000 Han males of the right age. Then, they overlaid them, aggregated them, and averaged them. The outcome (**Figure 10.17**) is the face of the most common kind of person on Earth. This is true "big data," only that it's displayed as a photo-illustration, not as a chart or a graph.

Figure 10.17 The most common kind of person in the world in 2011. This is not a photograph of a real person, but a composite of more than 190,000 pictures averaged by the Chinese Academy of Science, in Beijing.

John Tomanio took that photograph, and he increased its size. Its pixels became visible. He sent the pixelated photograph to Bryan Christie, who distributed the 7,000 little figures on it, trying to match the color of each picture to the color of each particular pixel. For the final version (**Figure 10.18**), Bryan used 80 or 90 different 3D figures, placed on different angles and rotations. When we got to the end of the project, he had created 45 images like this one for us. As you can see, in our projects we don't usually stop until we have a graphic everybody feels comfortable with. We strive for perfection.

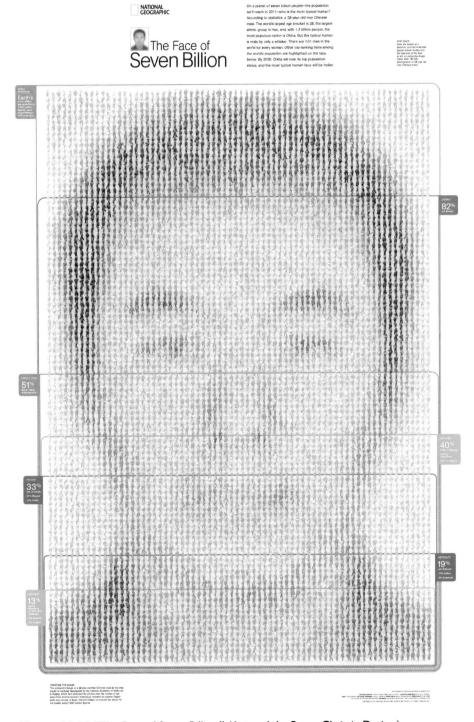

Figure 10.18 "The Face of Seven Billion." (Artwork by Bryan Christie Design.)

Q   **Fernando, one of your most impressive projects is about the Basilica of the Holy Family, in Barcelona. This infographic struck me for its beauty. You told me that the main illustration was a challenge, wasn't it?**

FB Not just the illustration, but the entire research process was a challenge. The Holy Family is one of the most iconic buildings in Spain. It started being built at the end of the nineteenth century, based on a plan by famous architect Antonio Gaudí, who died in 1926, having completed less than a third of his plans. The church has not been finished to this day, although Pope Benedict XVI consecrated it at the end of 2010. This is the excuse we found to spend some time on a project like this.

At the beginning, actually, this infographic was going to be relatively small, maybe two or three pages, but as we went deeper and deeper into the research, we realized we needed much more room. We ended up publishing a huge folder (**Figure 10.19**).

Q   **What made your bosses change their minds?**

FB Kaitlin Yarnall, deputy creative director for the magazine, and I spent four days in Barcelona, interviewing the architects who are currently working on the Holy Family. They are expecting to complete it by 2026.[6] When we visited their workshop, we realized that there were so many interesting angles to explore about this highly complex neogothic masterpiece, so many little details about its history, structure, style, ornamentation, that two pages were not nearly enough.

One of the main obstacles we faced this time was similar to the ones I found at Göbekli Tepe: It's really difficult to tell what Antonio Gaudí had in mind when he planned the basilica. The current architects don't have a complete model of the building, but many different partial models of its sections. I photographed them one by one (**Figure 10.20**).

Based on my photographs and notes, I developed a vector, perspective illustration (**Figure 10.21**) that I afterward traced with pencil (**Figure 10.22**) and retouched and colored in Photoshop (**Figure 10.23**). The final art is precise up to the tiniest details. In fact, we paid so much attention to those details during our research that we could even contribute a bit to meeting the 2026 deadline.

---

6 Read "Sagrada Familia gets final completion date," http://www.guardian.co.uk/world/2011/sep/22/sagrada-familia-final-completion-date.

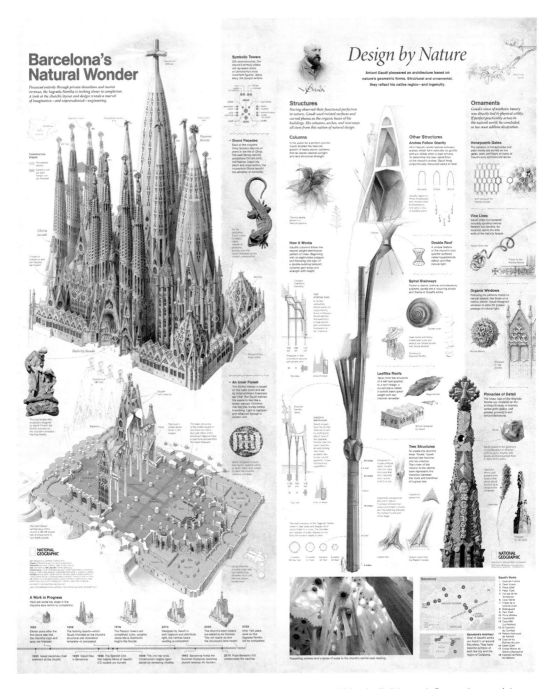

Figure 10.19 The Basilica of the Holy Family: "Barcelona's Natural Wonder." (*National Geographic* stock.)

Q That sounds intriguing. What do you mean?

FB When I was calculating sizes, lengths, and heights, I found that some floor plans and elevation models that the architects were using for one of the towers were not right. There was a five-yard mismatch between what those models showed and the actual height the tower should be. I expressed my concerns to the architects, and they tweaked their plans based on them. How great is that?

Figure 10.20 Fernando Baptista, photographing one of the partial models of the Basilica of the Holy Family.

Figure 10.21 One of the perspective studies Fernando Baptista drew for the Holy Family project.

Figure 10.22 A pencil
illustration of the basilica.

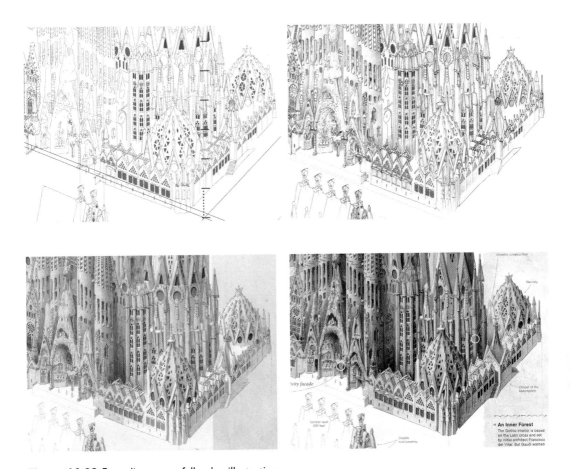

Figure 10.23 From line art to full-color illustration.

Profile 3
Steve Duenes and Xaquín G.V.
(*The New York Times*)

All the Infographics That Are Fit to Print

Steve Duenes is the graphics director at *The New York Times*, a position he has held since 2004. He manages a team of visual journalists who report and execute all of the print and interactive information graphics for the newspaper, website, and other platforms. He has spent time on the faculty at the School of Visual Arts in Manhattan and has been a contributing cartoonist at *The New Yorker*.

Xaquín G.V. has been a graphics editor at *The New York Times* since the 2008 Beijing Olympics. He started playing with graphics at *La Voz de Galicia* in 2000, while still an undergrad. In 2002, he moved to *El Mundo* (Spain), and three years later was heading the online graphics desk and having fun blurring the lines of interactive graphics and multimedia. In 2007, he worked as assistant art director at *Newsweek*.

Every morning, at around 7 a.m., a muffled thud on my front door announces the arrival of the print edition of *The New York Times*. The beginning of my day is organized around that moment. I usually wake up at 6.45 a.m., take a shower, prepare some coffee and, if the delivery person is not late, by the time I have completed those rituals, the newspaper will be waiting for me on the grass. I have kept that routine since the first day I lived in the U.S., back in 2005. When I had to give it up for two years—because I was in São Paulo, Brazil—I yearned for it.

Everybody in information graphics and visualization professes an almost religious reverence for *The New York Times*. I include myself in that crowd. When a big story breaks anywhere, say the killing of Bin Laden in Pakistan, the Deepwater Horizon oil spill in the Gulf of Mexico in 2010, or the earthquake and subsequent nuclear crisis in Fukushima, Japan, the eyes of many thousands of journalists and news designers focus on what the team led by Steve Duenes and Matthew Ericson does.

That team has become the standard for this industry. But what are its secrets? How are they able to maintain such a high and steady quality level? Why do they excel in almost every single project they undertake, both traditional infographics and complex visualizations of quantitative data? I conducted this interview with Steve, and with Xaquín G.V., one of the *Times's* graphics editors, to answer those questions.

Q   Steve, how does someone become the graphics director of *The New York Times*? I think this is something that intrigues many of our colleagues, as you are in a position to be one of the most influential people in this business.

Steve Duenes   In 1999, I came to *The New York Times* as the graphics editor for the Science section, which I still think is one of the best jobs in our field because science coverage is so visual and the *Times* is ambitious in the range of scientific disciplines it covers.

    I was quite happy in my niche in Science. I could take on as many graphics as I wanted, and I got to work with a pretty incredible staff of reporters and editors, plus I was collaborating with people on the graphics desk like Juan Velasco and Mika Gröndahl and Hannah Fairfield. It was a terrific time.

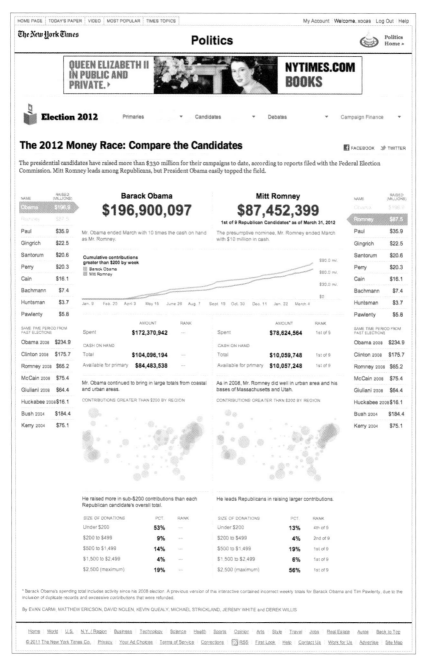

Figure 10.24 "The 2012 Money Race: Compare the Candidates," one of the many visualizations *The New York Times* publishes on a regular basis. http://elections.nytimes.com/2012/campaign-finance. Graphic by Evan Carmi, Matthew Ericson, David Nolen, Kevin Quealy, Michael Strickland, Jeremy White, and Derek Willis. (Reproduced with permission from *The New York Times*.)

Q   That sounds like a dream job, but you became a manager. Why?

SD The graphics director at the time was Charles Blow[7] who had been in that role for a while and had done it very well. He asked me to be his deputy in 2000 or 2001. By that time, I was already managing small teams of people in my role at the Science desk, but I was a little reluctant to spend all of my time managing. I enjoyed making my own graphics, and I liked the idea of being solely responsible for my work. If I accepted the position, I would be held accountable for the success or failure of a large group.

So, it took me a little time to wrap my head around what success would mean as a manager. There were people in the department, like Archie Tse, who convinced me that I'd do well. I felt very strongly about the department as a unit, and I decided I could have a positive impact. I realized that I'd have to let go of the control I had over my own graphics. Managing is obviously not about moving the hands of people you work with; it's about creating an environment where the best work gets done, and I had a few ideas about how to do that.

So I became the deputy, and did that for a while. I've been the graphics director since 2004.

Q   You both have experience working in newsrooms. What makes the graphics desk at *The New York Times* different from the ones in other publications?

Xaquín G.V. The size of the department is crucial. We have almost 30 people doing information graphics and visualizations here. However, it is not enough to have a lot of highly qualified professionals in a newsroom if they don't talk to each other. If I had to single out a factor that really defines what we do, I would say it's the culture of teamwork, collaboration, and open conversation that Steve and Matt Ericson—Steve's deputy—have instilled in the desk.

The Times encourages open conversation and sincere, constructive criticism. If someone is working on a project on a subject you care and know about, you must feel free to stop by and give your advice. On the other hand, you have to be open-minded enough to accept that same advice for your own projects and, moreover, be able to ask for suggestions from the people you know can help you. Say that you are working on a very complex data visualization. You should never publish it without getting input from Amanda Cox,[8] who has a master's degree in statistics.

---

7 Charles Blow is today an opinion writer at *The New York Times*. See http://topics.nytimes.com/top/opinion/editorialsandoped/oped/columnists/charles_m_blow/index.html.

8 To learn more about Amanda Cox: http://amandacox.tumblr.com/.

Figure 10.25 "Mapping America: Every City, Every Block," an immense map-based visualization based on data from the Census Bureau's American Community Survey. See http://projects.nytimes.com/census/2010/explorer. (Reproduced with permission from *The New York Times*. Map source: Google.)

Q   What are other factors that benefit your group?

SD There are many other factors, but two basic ideas stand out. A serious graphics group should be capable of high-level reporting, and everyone on the desk should have an impulse toward journalism. These are simple ideas, and they aren't unique to the *Times*, but we have explored them fairly deeply.

When I worked at the *Chicago Tribune*, there was real reporting going on within the graphics department, and it was an incredibly useful thing for me to witness and absorb. But the department was structured so "artists" and "graphics reporters" were separate. In some ways, it was an efficient structure, but it didn't allow people to cross over and really get better at things they couldn't already do. It was never a perfect fit for me.

At the *Times*, there is a lot of reporting that goes on, but it can come from anywhere. For example, Shan Carter is an exceptional developer and designer, but he's also a good reporter. He initiated and reported an interactive piece on Steve Jobs's patents last year. Why? Because he has those instincts and he knows how to find information, and there's an expectation that everyone on the desk will be involved in content—in gathering it, analyzing it, organizing it, and presenting it. Obviously, there are a few exceptional reporters in the department, but it's a desk full of curious people, so there's no reason to limit the kinds of questions they ask or the answers they pursue.

XGV Let me tell you a little story about that. When I was hired at the *Times*, I had a conversation with Rick Berke, the assistant managing editor. He told me that some of the best reporters in the newsroom were in the infographics desk. He was referring to people like Hannah Fairfield[9] and Archie Tse[10], who went to Lebanon in 2006 to cover the war with Israel and spent several months in Iraq in 2003. He is the only designer I know who got firsthand information when Saddam Hussein was captured in Tikrit. He actually entered Saddam's hole to take notes and draw an accurate sketch of it.

Q So you are not an "art" department. You don't consider yourselves just "artists."

SD Certainly, there is an "art" component to what we do, but we are not "graphic artists," and we are not a service group. We want to eliminate the passivity that suggests we should style a dummy headline and wait for the real journalist to fill it with meaning. We want to report and present the content ourselves. Very often, we work in parallel with other news departments. We pursue stories in ways that are similar to the Metro desk or the National desk, tasking reporters and organizing ourselves to pursue information. This was the drill, for instance, right after the Virginia Tech shootings, in April 2007 (**Figure 10.26**) and in response to many other breaking-news stories.

Q What would you recommend to a graphics director at a smaller news organization who is interested in reproducing what you have achieved at the *Times* but at a smaller scale? Let's say she can hire four or five people to build an infographics department. What kind of professional profiles should she look for?

XGV The first thing is that those four or five people have to be good journalists, be interested in current events, and be curious. That said, I would hire a good reporter, a good traditional designer, a high-end CGI artist and animator, and one or two excellent programmers and UI designers.

The reason I include a CGI artist in the group is that many people out there think that we at *The New York Times* are focusing too much on data visualization at

---

9 See Profile 4: Hannah Fairfield.

10 To learn about Archie Tse's experiences in reporting from Iraq, see http://www.udel.edu/PR/ UDaily/2004/nytimes031504.html.

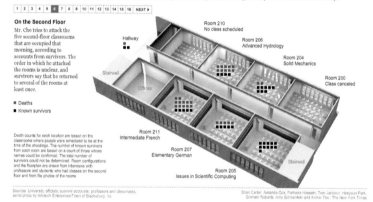

Figure 10.26 "Deadly Rampage at Virginia Tech," a breaking-news visual reconstruction of the shootings at Virginia Polytechnic Institute, in April 2007. Thirty-three people died, including the gunman. http://www.nytimes.com/2007/04/17/us/20070417_SHOOTING_GRAPHIC.html. (Reproduced with permission from *The New York Times*.)

the moment, and that's not true. In the past couple of years, we have done plenty of traditional linear explanation graphics, mixing 3D animation with video. I would mention one on Roger Federer, the tennis player (**Figure 10.27**), that reveals why his game is so precise (**Figure 10.28**). The best of our recent explanatory animations is one on baseball star Mariano Rivera (**Figure 10.29**), which won the Best of Show award at the Malofiej International Infographics competition in 2011.

Q **On your team, you have people who specialize in a particular area, such as statistical charts and cartography, and others, such as Xaquín, who have a more comprehensive knowledge of all the components of information graphics. Would you say that the right balance between generalists and specialists in a news graphics desk is half and half?**

SD You need a mix of generalists and specialists for sure, because there are different kinds of problems that desks will have to solve. Sometimes the solutions demand thinking that often comes from a person who has invested a lot of time focusing on development or cartography, or both. But there are other kinds of problems such as reporting challenges or situations that require a kind of visual improvisation. These solutions can come from anyone, but generalists tend to have a little more experience in the field and wider familiarity with what works and what doesn't.

Q **Can you give an example of a graphic in which the role of a generalist was decisive?**

XGV There are many. I can give you a fun one. A while ago, Steve told me to take a look at a story by Stephanie Clifford, a reporter at the Business Day desk. She was working with Dylan McClain, one of my colleagues, who is a specialist in charts. They were trying to show something that is common knowledge: Every fashion designer and every clothing chain has its own standards when it comes to sizes. There's not really a fixed standard.

What they had found out during the research, mainly at designers' websites, was that the disparities can be huge. If you are used to buying size 8 clothes from one store and you switch to a different store, it's likely you won't fit into size 8 anymore. Even within a single group of brands, such as Gap, which owns Banana Republic and Old Navy, there are shocking differences. For instance, a size 8 hip at Banana Republic equals a size 2 hip at Gap. More interestingly, a particular designer can use a double standard, and have slightly different bust, waist, and hip measures for her main line and for her mid-price line.

Figure 10.27 Frames from "Federer's Footwork: Artful and Efficient," a motion graphic on Roger Federer's technique. http://www.nytimes.com/interactive/2009/08/31/sports/tennis/20090831-roger-graphic.html. (Reproduced with permission from *The New York Times*.)

Figure 10.28 Before creating the 3D animation, the designers at *The New York Times* watched hours of footage of Federer's games. Then they drew arrows and lines on many frames to unveil the secrets of his game. (Reproduced with permission from *The New York Times*. Images obtained from Tennisplayer.net.)

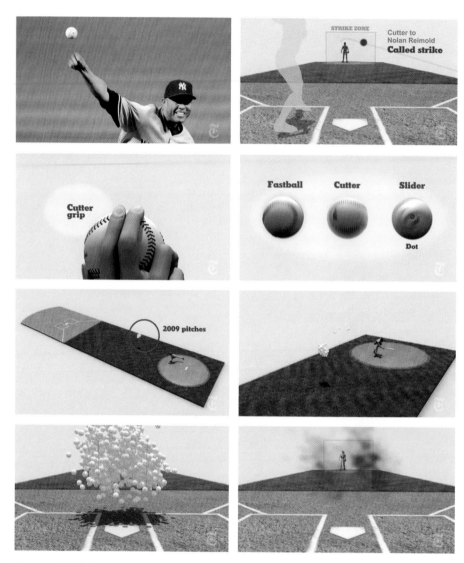

Figure 10.29 Frames from "How Mariano Rivera Dominates Hitters." http://www.nytimes.com/interactive/2010/06/29/magazine/rivera-pitches.html. (Based on motion capture research by New York University. Reproduced with permission from *The New York Times*.)

We wanted to do something engaging with the data. What we had at first was a series of bar charts, which are fine, but we wanted to find another way to present this information that kept the proportions but was eye-catching at the same time. I started playing around with the data in Processing[11] and, at one point, I encoded the figures with lines (**Figure 10.30**). That made the plot look like

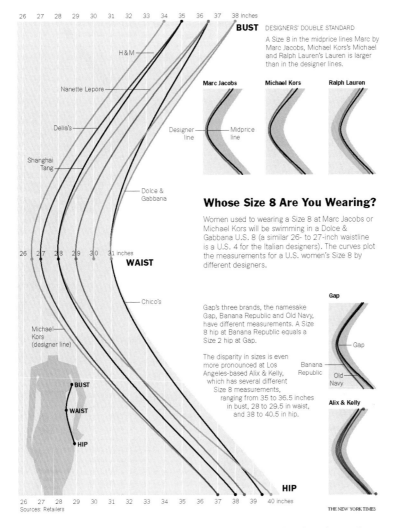

Figure 10.30 "Whose Size 8 Are You Wearing?" a graphic that shows that standard clothing sizes are not really standard. (Reproduced with permission from *The New York Times*.)

11 Processing is a programming language tailored for graphic designers (who are not usually fans of programming languages). Its first version was developed by Ben Fry, a specialist in information visualization: http://benfry.com/.

a woman's midsection. I must admit that clothes measurements are made based on the circumference of the body, not on a linear scale, so I cheated a little bit.

As a funny side note, a freelance designer and Web developer, Anna Powell-Smith, used our graphic as an inspiration for a project called "What Size Am I?" which is a database to find out what sizes fit you better, depending on your bust, waist, and hip circumferences.[12] I really like when people can build on your work and improve it. I recommend you check her tool out. It's fun to use.

Q   Based on that story, would you say that infographics generalists are crucial, but that they need to work side by side with specialists?

SD Well, it's possible for a generalist and specialist to be the same person, but that's kind of rare. Are generalists crucial? And is there a way of working that is ideal? I'd say yes, but my answer has to do with our mission at the *Times*. A smaller desk might have three scrappy generalists, and they might do incredible work. That's entirely possible.

Q   What does it take to get a job at the graphics desk at *The New York Times*?

SD The answer to that question is something that changes as the desk grows and adjusts, which is a process that shouldn't stop. We have people with academic and professional backgrounds that seemingly have nothing to do with information graphics. Really, the common characteristic is curiosity. It's a curiosity that leads to the pursuit of different methods of creating visual forms or it's a curiosity about current events.

For both students and professionals, we're definitely looking for people who can bring something special to the desk. These are people who excel in one area that helps us create innovative visualizations or people who have demonstrated a resourcefulness, technological or otherwise, in solving the kinds of problems we solve, which includes reporting or data collection, analysis and distillation, and clear, innovative presentation.

It's not hard to gain an understanding of what we do. You just have to look.

---

12 Anna Powell-Smith's take on standard sizing is in http://sizes.darkgreener.com/

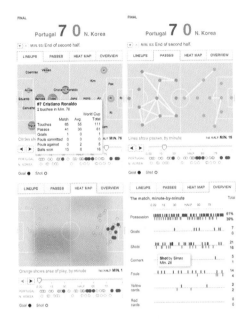

Figure 10.31 "World Cup Live," a series of graphics based on the 2010 Soccer World Cup games. These graphics display the main statistics and facts of each game during the competition, and were updated in real time. One example is at http://goal. blogs.nytimes.com/2010/07/11/world-cup-live-netherlands-vs-spain/. The data was provided by Match Analysis. (Reproduced with permission from *The New York Times*.)

Figure 10.32 A screenshot of Xaquin's desktop while he was working on a "World Cup Live" graphic. (Reproduced with permission from *The New York Times*.)

Profile 4
Hannah Fairfield
(*The Washington Post*)

Capital Infographics

When she was interviewed for this article, **Hannah Fairfield** was the graphics director at *The Washington Post*, a position she held from 2010–2012. She is currently a senior graphics editor for *The New York Times*, where she worked for 10 years before moving to *The Post*. She has two master's degrees from Columbia University and taught news graphics at the university's Graduate School of Journalism for six years.

The first time I saw Hannah Fairfield, she was sitting in a train, immersed in a cartography textbook. We both had been invited to speak at a conference in Spain. I was acquainted with her work, but we had not yet met. Even though I didn't know who she was at that moment, I immediately recognized a kindred spirit. Only a graphics enthusiast would be reading a book like that just for fun.

Hannah was a graphics editor at *The New York Times* when we first talked, but she was soon hired as the graphics director at *The Washington Post*. I was happy when I learned that news. For some years, she had done a lot of pieces for "Metrics," a Sunday business column she created at *The Times* that was based on a very bold use of charts, maps, and diagrams. In Chapter 8, I mentioned one of those graphics, about the relationship between the price of a gallon of gasoline and the amount of miles driven per capita each year. That section of the paper was a must-read for me when it was published.

I was interested in talking to Hannah not just because I admire her work as a reporter and a designer, but also because the current popularity of *The New York Times* in infographics sometimes overshadows other very important desks at other papers that are on equal footing with the Old Gray Lady in terms of experimentation with graphic forms and storytelling techniques. *The Washington Post*'s desk is undoubtedly one of them. Hannah returned to *The New York Times* in May 2012, but I decided to keep this interview as it is in the book because her team's work at the *Post* is simply amazing.

Q **You are the only infographics director I know who has such a strong background in science. How does this knowledge affect the way you approach your work in the newsroom?**

Hannah Fairfield As an undergraduate, I double majored in geoscience and English. I liked studying both because I think they complement each other. In college, I once wrote an essay on the role of geology in James Joyce's *Ulysses*. When I went to graduate school, I wasn't willing to give up either one of them, so I got dual master's degrees at Columbia University, one in geochemistry and one in journalism. I've always been interested in the connection between science and storytelling.

At Columbia's J-school, I discovered information graphics. I took a class called "Graphics in the Newsroom," taught by Jim McManus, who was the deputy graphics director at *The New York Times*. Jim's class was an epiphany for me because I realized that it was not just the intersection between science and writing that I wanted to explore. It was something deeper: I loved explaining complex issues, and I had just found a language that was powerful enough for that.

Jim saw my enthusiasm for graphics and taught me about good information design. I didn't have an art background, but I did have a strong basis in statistics and math. And at Columbia, I had learned how important reporting is for being a good storyteller. So the *Times* hired me right out of journalism school.

Q **A couple of years ago you moved to *The Washington Post* as the graphics director. How is the department organized?**

HF The team is strong because we have people with different skill sets who all work together extraordinarily well. We have reporters, designers, database editors, and developers—and many people on the graphics team have several or all of those skills. We have brilliant designer/developers like Wilson Andrews and Sisi Wei,

Discovery's last trek

After a year of decommissioning, NASA's space shuttle Discovery is ready for its final flight, to Washington for retirement at the Smithsonian's Steven F. Udvar-Hazy Center near Dulles Airport. Discovery donated some of its parts for NASA's next rocket, while other pieces will be scrutinized by engineers "to improve the reliability and safety" of next-generation spacecraft, said Kevin Templin, NASA's transition manager for the shuttles.

Discovery at the Steven F. Udvar-Hazy Center

Boeing aviation hangar

The Space shuttle will be on permanent display at the James S. McDonnell Space Hangar, a structure with a total display area of 48,222 sq. feet.

84.5 ft

James S. McDonnell Space Hangar

Orbital maneuvering system
Two pods housed thrusters to move Discovery to different orbits and to slow the craft for reentry. Before reinstalling the empty pods, crews sent them to New Mexico, where most of the components and all traces of toxic fuel were removed.

Front reaction control system
Thrusters in Discovery's nose maneuvered the craft in orbit and spun it around in a "backflip" to allow inspection of the heat-absorbing tiles. This mini van-sized section was removed, cleaned of all traces of toxic fuel and replaced.

Main engines
The three main engines, along with many valves, pipes, and regulators, were removed for reuse on NASA's next manned rocket, the Space Launch System. Three replica engine nozzles — leftover from NASA tests — were then bolted on. "You can't tell the difference," said Templin.

Robotic arm and airlock
The Canadian robotic arm used to sling spacewalkers and cargo has been removed and will be displayed next to Discovery. The airlock, which connected Discovery to the international space station while providing an exit to the payload bay, was removed before delivery.

Flight windows
Discovery sports nine double-pane windows. The outer panes were removed and sent to Johnson Space Center, where experts will study pits and scratches from micrometeorite impacts.

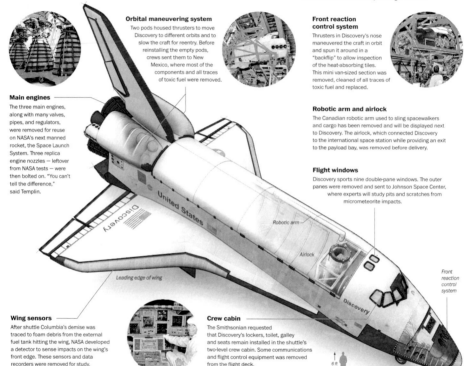

United States

Discovery

Robotic arm

Airlock

Leading edge of wing

Front reaction control system

Discovery

Wing sensors
After shuttle Columbia's demise was traced to foam debris from the external fuel tank hitting the wing, NASA developed a detector to sense impacts on the wing's front edge. These sensors and data recorders were removed for study.

Crew cabin
The Smithsonian requested that Discovery's lockers, toilet, galley and seats remain installed in the shuttle's two-level crew cabin. Some communications and flight control equipment was removed from the flight deck.

6 ft

Moving the Shuttle to Dulles

1. Discovery is towed from NASA's iconic 52-story Vehicle Assembly Building at Kennedy Space Center to the Mate/De-mate Device near the shuttle's runway.

MATE/DE-MATE DEVICE

2. The shuttle is lifted by a metal sling. The shuttle's taxi — a modified Boeing 747 — is rolled underneath.

SLING

STRUT

3. The shuttle is lowered and bolted to three mounting struts on the jumbo jet.

4. The 83-ton Discovery will fly piggyback from Florida to Dulles International Airport — site of the National Air and Space Museum's Steven F. Udvar-Hazy Center — on the morning of April 17, weather permitting.

5. Before landing, the tandem is scheduled to fly about 1,500 feet above the District and the region between 10 and 11 a.m.

6. Upon arrival at Dulles, the two-day de-mate process will begin. The pair will be towed between two cranes. A sling, suspended from cables attached to the cranes, will be fastened to Discovery. The shuttle will gently be hoisted above the 747. Its landing gear will be deployed and the shuttle will touch down one final time.

SLING

7. On April 19, Discovery will be towed into the James S. McDonnell Space Hangar, where it will replace the prototype shuttle Enterprise.

Sources: NASA, Smithsonian, reporting by Brian Vastag

ALBERTO CUADRA AND TODD LINDEMAN/THE WASHINGTON POST

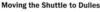

incredible traditional artists like Alberto Cuadra and Patterson Clark, gifted data visualizers like Todd Lindeman and Laura Stanton, and smart database editors like Dan Keating and Ted Mellnik. Everyone has good reporting skills. Reporting is a crucial skill for a strong department, so I try to encourage it as much as I can: the ability to communicate with editors and reporters in other desks and be able to find out what stories are happening during the day and rolling forward.

Q What changed in the newsroom when you were hired?

HF Years ago, the *Post*'s graphics department, like teams at most newspapers, was more service-oriented. Artists tended to wait for other desks to ask for graphics, charts, and maps, and bring information and possible ideas for layouts back to them. My vision was that the team needed more independence and autonomy in order to produce really creative, high-impact visual journalism. Based on my experience at *The New York Times*, I knew it could be done.

The graphics team was really enthusiastic about the change, but I had to win over some other parts of the newsroom. During the first few months, we spent a lot of time talking to editors and reporters from other departments, who brought very specific requests for the kind of infographics they wanted. "I really appreciate this idea you are bringing to us," I said over and over. "But let's talk about the story. We will read it, we will make a judgment, and I promise you we will provide the graphic that is right for it."

I was lucky I had the full support from high-level editors, because this is a pretty profound culture shift. Before I was hired, I was transparent about the fact that I wanted to bring some sweeping changes to the desk: If they wanted service, instead of the kind of autonomy I wanted to implement, they could have hired someone else.

Figure 10.33 (opposite) "Discovery's Last Trek" (Alberto Cuadra, Todd Lindeman, Emily Chow, Sisi Wei, for *The Washington Post*). Hannah Fairfield: "With all the excitement over having the Discovery space shuttle fly over D.C. on her way to the National Air and Space Museum, we tried to answer the main questions that everyone seemed to have. How does the shuttle ride piggyback on a 747? What parts of the shuttle get stripped off for research? We animated the online package [Figure 10.35] so that readers could watch how the shuttle is strapped on to the jet and also could rotate the shuttle to see all the parts that were removed. Those interactive features made the diagrams accessible and playful."

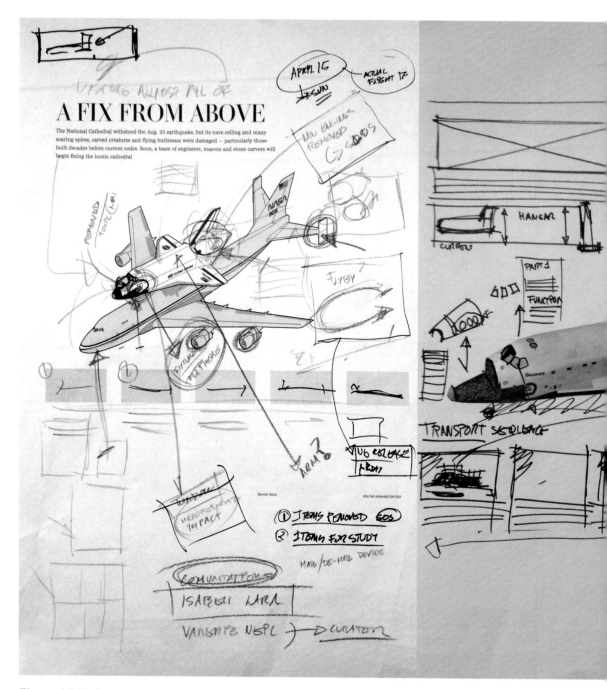

Figure 10.34 Sequence of three sketches for the "Discovery's Last Trek" infographic.

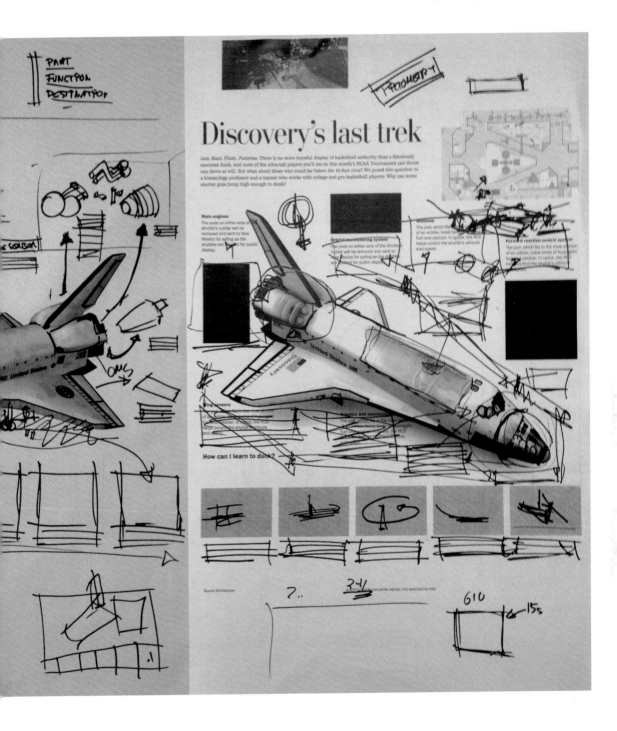

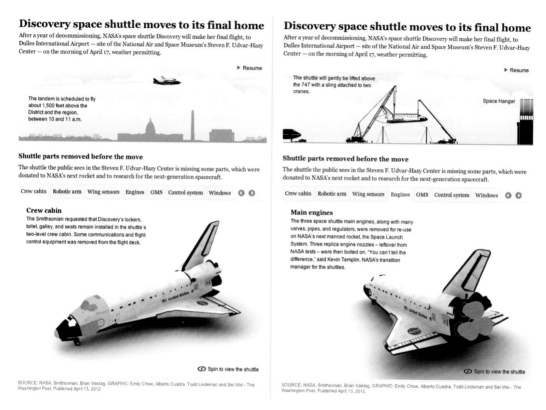

Figure 10.35 Online version of the Discovery's Last Trek infographic (http://www.washingtonpost.com/wp-srv/special/entertainment/discovery-space-shuttle/).

Q   What was the response from traditional journalists, writers, and editors?

HF The change was a success. First, it boosted the morale within the graphics department. I think that the team feels more valued in the newsroom now that they are able to do their own reporting and have full ownership of the graphics from idea through execution. It's not as much fun when somebody says, "I have an idea; please build it." When you can advance your own ideas—do the reporting, the planning, the design—and you do it in a team that enjoys the process as much as you do, the results are usually more creative and solid.

There was a little skepticism at first among some editors in the newsroom, but I was really careful to go to them and convey a clear message: "Trust us, and we will deliver."

Q How did you grow trust? The reason I am asking is that the reality in American newsrooms is not what designers in most other countries experience. In many Latin American and European newsrooms, for instance, infographics designers are second-class citizens, if you know what I mean.

HF You have to start with both sides. Inside the team, you can empower the infographics designers. Make very clear from the beginning that you expect them to be proactive, that the new standard includes a more engaged approach, and that you will fully support them.

And then, whenever an editor from a different desk comes to "order" a graphic, you say: "I will give this assignment to a person on the team who I completely trust. I know she will be able to deliver. You will not get what you ask for. You will get something that's even better."

So you have three people on that equation: the infographics artist; the traditional writer, editor, or reporter; and a graphics leader serving as a sort of bridge—at least in a first phase, when everybody is learning what their new roles are. That is a model that could work in any newsroom.

Q Would you recommend also that each person in an infographics department starts specializing in a particular area to promote teamwork?

HF I would not promote radical specialization, unless the department is really big. At *The Washington Post*, almost any graphics designer can do anything with a reasonable level of proficiency.

I mentioned Wilson Andrews and Alberto Cuadra before, and they are good examples of the kind of people who work here. They don't have narrow specializations, but they do have strengths. Wilson is a hugely talented designer/developer, and he is behind many of our high-impact interactives. Alberto is a wonderful illustrator; he can draw beautifully, model in 3D, and explain visual stories with ease with complex charts.

A manager's role in any graphics department is to play to people's strengths and give them projects where they can take advantage of those strengths. At the same time, managers can encourage them to start exploring new areas. Alberto, for instance, is now getting into motion graphics for the Web, and the team is doing more and more of them. Wilson is rapidly adding digital cartography to his powerful suite of skills.

Almost every big project we do has a highly collaborative team behind it. In a way, creating motion graphics is similar to creating a little documentary movie. A group of talented people get into a room and storyboard together, with everyone

Short guys can dunk

Jam. Slam. Flush. *Posterize.* There is no more forceful display of basketball authority than a fabulously executed dunk, and most of the ultra-tall players you'll see in this month's NCAA Tournament can throw one down at will. But what about those who stand far below the 10-foot rims? We posed this question to a kinesiology professor and a trainer who works with college and pro basketball players: Why can some shorter guys jump high enough to dunk?

One step at a time

Practicing over and over again trains the brain to activate muscles in a precise sequence so momentum travels in waves from shoulders to toes in a perfect kinetic chain.

1 Hands and arms swing forward and upward. (They don't need to be able to palm the basketball; many players dunk two-handed or cradle the ball against a forearm.)

2 Head raises and **trunk** extends.

3 Core engages. Legs, core muscles, even feet need to be strong. If one muscle group is under- or overdeveloped, the body won't accumulate as much force as it should.

4 Gluteus maximus contracts. The best dunkers have a high percentage of fast-twitch muscle fibers, which fire quickly, providing great power in short bursts.

5 Quadriceps contract. If you have shorter-than-average thighs for your height, you have the ideal mechanical setup for leaping, according to kinesiology professor Tim Anderson. It's a lever issue:

6 Calf muscles fire.

7 Small muscles in the **feet** give the final push. People who are very good at transferring forward momentum (running) to vertical momentum will dunk off one foot. Others need raw leg power to lift them, so they jump off two feet.

How can I learn to dunk?

Trade out your genes to grow a few inches taller and acquire a higher percentage of fast-twitch muscle fibers. If that ship has sailed, you have two options left, according to kinesiology professor Tim Anderson and trainer Jacob Ross.

Get stronger Ross suggests leg-strengthening exercises such as single-leg squats, regular squats, leg presses and calf extensions. Anderson recommends specifically strengthening your feet with toe raises and other barefoot exercises.

Practice jumping Plyometric exercises — they often have "jump" or "hop" in the title — require explosive movements that teach muscles in the chain to work together. (Caution: They can also be hard on untrained joints and tendons.)

Shorter femur, better jumper

When you jump, your thigh acts as a lever that propels your body weight upward. A shorter thigh resists movement less than a longer one. (To feel this, try a regular squat. Now imagine how much easier it would be to push yourself upward if your thighs were shorter.)

Long femur — Fulcrum — Takes more energy to lift

Short femur — Takes less energy to lift

Sources: Jacob Ross of EFT Sports Performance, who jumps off two feet to dunk; Tim Anderson of Fresno State, who blames deficient genes for his inability to dunk

BONNIE BERKOWITZ AND ALBERTO CUADRA /THE WASHINGTON POST

Figure 10.36 "Short Guys Can Dunk" (Bonnie Berkowitz, Alberto Cuadra, Sisi Wei/*The Washington Post*). Hannah Fairfield: "The intersection of sports and physics is fascinating. This was a classic how-it-works graphic on the cover of the Health and Science section. Online, we chose a very simple flip-book style animation that let the users step through the sequence."

Why short guys can dunk

We asked a kinesiology professor and a trainer who works with pro and college basketball players to explain why some shorter people can jump high enough to dunk. The answer? Genes and a lot of practice, which trains the brain to activate muscles in a precise sequence from shoulders to toes in an efficient kinetic chain.

1 2 3 4 5   Next »

Hands and arms swing forward and upward.

Head raises and trunk extends.

How can I learn to dunk?

 Trade out your genes to grow a few inches taller and acquire a higher percentage of fast-twitch muscle fibers. If that ship has sailed, you have two options left, according to kinesiology professor Tim Anderson and trainer Jacob Ross.

 Get stronger. Ross recommends leg-strengthening exercises such as squats and single-leg squats, leg presses and calf extensions. Anderson suggests specifically strengthening the feet with toe raises and other barefoot exercises.

 Practice jumping. Plyometric exercises — they often have "jump" or "hop" in the title — require explosive movements that teach muscles in the chain to work together. (Caution: They can also be hard on untrained joints and tendons.)

Why short guys can dunk

We asked a kinesiology professor and a trainer who works with pro and college basketball players to explain why some shorter people can jump high enough to dunk. The answer? Genes and a lot of practice, which trains the brain to activate muscles in a precise sequence from shoulders to toes in an efficient kinetic chain.

1 2 3 4 5   Next »

Core engages. Legs, core muscles, even feet need to be strong. If one muscle group is under- or overdeveloped, the body won't accumulate as much force as it should.

How can I learn to dunk?

 Trade out your genes to grow a few inches taller and acquire a higher percentage of fast-twitch muscle fibers. If that ship has sailed, you have two options left, according to kinesiology professor Tim Anderson and trainer Jacob Ross.

 Get stronger. Ross recommends leg-strengthening exercises such as squats and single-leg squats, leg presses and calf extensions. Anderson suggests specifically strengthening the feet with toe raises and other barefoot exercises.

 Practice jumping. Plyometric exercises — they often have "jump" or "hop" in the title — require explosive movements that teach muscles in the chain to work together. (Caution: They can also be hard on untrained joints and tendons.)

Why short guys can dunk

We asked a kinesiology professor and a trainer who works with pro and college basketball players to explain why some shorter people can jump high enough to dunk. The answer? Genes and a lot of practice, which trains the brain to activate muscles in a precise sequence from shoulders to toes in an efficient kinetic chain.

1 2 3 4 5   Next »

Gluteus maximus contracts. The best dunkers have a high percentage of fast-twitch muscle fibers, which fire quickly, providing great power in short bursts.

Quadriceps contract. If you have shorter-than-average thighs for your height, you have the ideal mechanical setup for leaping, see below for details.

How can I learn to dunk?

 Trade out your genes to grow a few inches taller and acquire a higher percentage of fast-twitch muscle fibers. If that ship has sailed, you have two options left, according to kinesiology professor Tim Anderson and trainer Jacob Ross.

 Get stronger. Ross recommends leg-strengthening exercises such as squats and single-leg squats, leg presses and calf extensions. Anderson suggests specifically strengthening the feet with toe raises and other barefoot exercises.

 Practice jumping. Plyometric exercises — they often have "jump" or "hop" in the title — require explosive movements that teach muscles in the chain to work together. (Caution: They can also be hard on untrained joints and tendons.)

Why short guys can dunk

We asked a kinesiology professor and a trainer who works with pro and college basketball players to explain why some shorter people can jump high enough to dunk. The answer? Genes and a lot of practice, which trains the brain to activate muscles in a precise sequence from shoulders to toes in an efficient kinetic chain.

1 2 3 4 5   Start over

The dunk. The players don't need to be able to palm the basketball; many players dunk two-handed or cradle the ball against a forearm.

How can I learn to dunk?

 Trade out your genes to grow a few inches taller and acquire a higher percentage of fast-twitch muscle fibers. If that ship has sailed, you have two options left, according to kinesiology professor Tim Anderson and trainer Jacob Ross.

 Get stronger. Ross recommends leg-strengthening exercises such as squats and single-leg squats, leg presses and calf extensions. Anderson suggests specifically strengthening the feet with toe raises and other barefoot exercises.

 Practice jumping. Plyometric exercises — they often have "jump" or "hop" in the title — require explosive movements that teach muscles in the chain to work together. (Caution: They can also be hard on untrained joints and tendons.)

Figure 10.37 Online version of the "Short Guys Can Dunk" infographic (http://www.washingtonpost.com/wp-srv/special/health/why-short-guys-can-dunk/).

focused on the content. Everyone contributes to the script and the design and the pacing from the very beginning, so everyone has ownership. The script informs the art, and the art informs further polishing of the script.

An example of this is a recent little project we made, both for print and the Web, about slam-dunking a basketball (**Figure 10.36**). Most people think that only tall players can dunk basketballs, but a short man can if he uses the right technique. Being able to dunk is related to how strong your muscles are and also how well you train in certain techniques that we explained in the graphic. It's a combination of sports and science, and the result was a fun design that looks a little bit like a flip-book.

Q   What lies ahead for the infographics desk at *The Washington Post*?

HF The team will go more deeply into what we have started: more autonomy, more ownership, more high-impact visual storytelling. We have made some outstanding standalone business graphics, many of them focused on the labor market. They tell a complex story through charts, maps, and other kinds of graphics (**Figure 10.38**). We want to do more of these because they are great storytelling tools.

The team may also reduce the amount of small graphics done every day, in order to focus on the big pieces. Today, we do half as many locator maps as we did last year. The reason is that before, every foreign story had to include a map, even if it was irrelevant. Today, we try to analyze if the story really needs a map to put it into context, and we make sure that the map is part of the storytelling.

Figure 10.38 (opposite) "Why the job hunt is so hard" (Todd Lindeman and Neil Irwin/ *The Washington Post*). Todd Lindeman: "The idea behind this graphic was to answer the question: Why are Americans having difficulty finding work? The main chart tells the broader story—that under certain economic conditions, the unemployment gap between those who are able to work but cannot find work and those who are employed will typically close over time following a recession. The results show, however, that the gap has widened substantially because the availability of jobs is not increasing as fast as the labor force. At the bottom of the graphic we focus in at a granular level and look at job opportunities within specific sectors—charts that underscore the struggle that people face when looking for jobs."

Why the job hunt is so hard

BY NEIL IRWIN AND TODD LINDEMAN

At the heart of America's economic woes is the growing gap between the number of people with jobs and the number who would have them if there were full employment. That gap has been increasing in recent months because job growth is stagnant while the population keeps rising. If the job market were healthy — that is, if the unemployment rate were 5 percent and the proportion of adults in the labor force were typical of earlier years — there would be 151 million workers employed in the United States. Instead, there are fewer than 140 million.

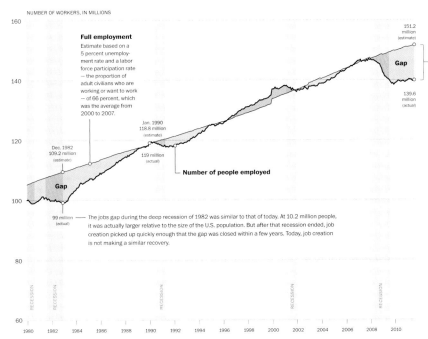

NUMBER OF WORKERS, IN MILLIONS

Full employment
Estimate based on a 5 percent unemployment rate and a labor force participation rate — the proportion of adult civilians who are working or want to work — of 66 percent, which was the average from 2000 to 2007.

151.2 million (estimate)

Gap

139.6 million (actual)

Jan. 1990
118.8 million
(estimate)

Dec. 1982
109.2 million
(estimate)

119 million
(actual)

Number of people employed

Gap

99 million (actual) — The jobs gap during the deep recession of 1982 was similar to that of today. At 10.2 million people, it was actually larger relative to the size of the U.S. population. But after that recession ended, job creation picked up quickly enough that the gap was closed within a few years. Today, job creation is not making a similar recovery.

The jobs gap

About **11.6 million** more people would be working under optimal conditions. Despite the steady growth of jobs in the private sector over the past year and the decline in the unemployment rate, the jobs gap is getting bigger. Last August, it was 10.9 million.

What's going on?

While the nation is adding jobs, it's happening too slowly to keep up with the growing population. And the unemployment rate has come down in part because people have dropped out of the labor force entirely, giving up looking for work out of frustration, so they're no longer counted among the unemployed.

Jobs created

Change in non-farm payroll employment since January.

IN THOUSANDS, SEASONALLY ADJUSTED

August: Zero job growth

*Data is preliminary

Jobs wanted vs. help wanted

The number of people looking for each available job varies widely from field to field. In construction, for instance, there are 16 prospective workers for each job opening, while in health care and education, there are only two for each opening.

JULY TOTALS, BY SELECT SECTORS

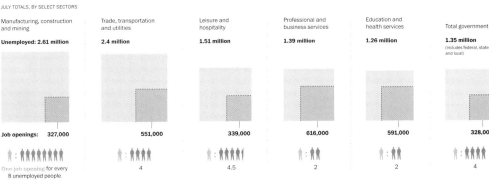

Manufacturing, construction and mining	Trade, transportation and utilities	Leisure and hospitality	Professional and business services	Education and health services	Total government
Unemployed: 2.61 million	2.4 million	1.51 million	1.39 million	1.26 million	1.35 million (includes federal, state and local)
Job openings: 327,000	551,000	339,000	616,000	591,000	328,000
One job opening for every 8 unemployed people	4	4.5	2	2	4

(There was one job opening for every 16 unemployed construction workers and one job opening for every 5.5 unemployed manufacturing workers. Numbers for mining unavailable.)

Note: July data is preliminary

Sources: U.S. Bureau of Labor Statistics, National Bureau of Economic Research

DATA

BY SECTOR, JULY 2011	JOB OPENINGS	TOTAL EMPLOYED	TOTAL UNEMPLOYED IN JULY	TOTAL UNEMPLOYED IN AUGUST
GOODS-PRODUCING	at least 327,000	18,087,000	2,608,000	2,572,000
Mining and logging	x	798,000	53,000	53,000
Construction	70,000	5,529,000	1,137,000	1,154,000
Manufacturing	257,000	11,760,000	1,418,000	1,365,000
PRIVATE-SERVICE PRODUCING	At least 2,097,000	91,066,000	7,907,000	10,340,000
Trade, transportation, and utilities	551,000	24,946,000	2,402,000	2,388,000
Retail trade	310,000	14,577,000	1,916,000	1,851,000
Wholesale trade	x	5,544,700		
Transportation and warehousing	x	4,272,600	486,000	537,000
Utilities	x	551,700		
Information	x	2,679,000	237,000	204,000
Financial activities	x	7,602,000	552,000	565,000
Professional and business services	616,000	17,183,000	1,389,000	1,440,000
Education and health services	591,000	19,990,000	1,263,000	1,371,000
Leisure and hospitality	339,000	13,214,000	1,510,000	1,399,000
Accommodation and food services	264,000	11,317,200		
Arts, entertainment, and recreation	75,000	1,896,000		
Other services*	x	5,452,000	554,000	585,000
Total private	2,900,000	109,153,000	10,515,000	12,912,000
Total government	328,000	21,979,000	1,349,000	1,271,000

Includes repair and maintenance; personal and laundry services; membership associations and organizations

FIRST IDEA

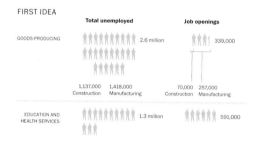

SECOND ATTEMPT

UNEMPLOYMENT AND JOB OPENINGS, BY SELECT SECTORS

Lead in for this series of charts goes here. Lead in for this series of charts goes here. In July, there was only one job opening for every five unemployed manufacturing workers. Construction jobs were even harder to find. Only 70,000 jobs were available for the nearly 1.1 million unemployed construction workers, or one opening for every 15 workers.

Figure 10.39 One of the sketches made for the "Why the job hunt is so hard" graphic.

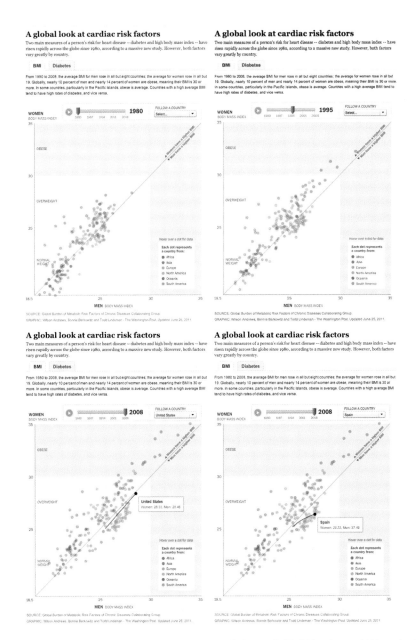

Figure 10.40 "A global look at cardiac risk factors" (Todd Lindeman, Wilson Andrews, Bonnie Berkowitz/ *The Washington Post*). Hannah Fairfield: "The headline for this project in print was 'Weight of the World,' a much more fun yet not search-engine-optimized headline. We had great data about body mass index and diabetes for most countries of the world each year since 1980, and it was astounding to see how so many countries had shifted toward obesity. When we charted men against women, we saw some stereotypes borne out: European women are thinner than European men. The interactive has a lot behind it, but the navigation is simple, and the visual story is very clear." (http://www.washingtonpost.com/wp-srv/special/health/weight-of-the-world-bmi/)

Q   You have made some hires recently. What kind of people were you looking for and what kind of professionals will you seek if there are more openings at *The Washington Post* in the future?

HF   The first thing I look for—the initial bar—is curiosity. The three recent hires on the graphics team at the *Post* were all incredibly curious and excited about how much the field of information graphics is changing and growing. They are also wonderful team members. This is the second bar. You don't see many graphics made by one single person nowadays. If you read the bylines on most of our graphics, you will notice that they are two, three, even four or five names long. This is a dynamic I want to encourage, because putting people with different strengths together can spark creativity.

The third factor is the skill to work across platforms. I look for people who are willing to think of projects in all forms that we publish in—print, on the Web, and on mobile devices. This affects the way you plan and execute any infographics project from the very beginning: what does a story look like on paper, on a computer screen, on an iPad, or on a cell phone? You have to be prepared to design for them all.

Profile 5
Jan Schwochow
(*Golden Section Graphics*)

Germanic Precision

Jan Schwochow is the executive creative director of the infographics agency Golden Section Graphics (http://www.golden-section-graphics.com/), based in Berlin, Germany. He has been an infographics designer for over 20 years. He is the former head of *STERN* and *MAX* magazines' infographics department in Hamburg. In 2004, he moved to Berlin to build up an infographic unit at the media company Kircher Burkhardt. Later, he started Golden Section Graphics. In 2010, he published the first issue of *IN GRAPHICS*, the magazine for visual people. Its articles are based on the experiences from the Golden Section Graphics team, which gets worldwide attention from work it produces for renowned media like *Die ZEIT*, *The New York Times Magazine*, and *GEO*.

The great psychologist Steven Pinker wrote once[13] that cultural stereotypes are much more accurate than you would like to think. You know how it goes: Spanish folks are, on average, likely to enjoy partying, soccer, and loud conversations (I am probably 100 standard deviations away from the average); Americans are

---

13 In his book *How the Mind Works*. New York: W.W. Norton & Company, 1997.

blunt and don't have a sense for verbal irony; Germans are serious, precise, and humorless. Jan Schwochow, who is German, is one of the most serious and precise infographics designers that I know. Fortunately, he is far from humorless, so he doesn't fulfill the stereotype 100 percent.

If there's an infographics designer that deserves to be called thorough, it's Jan. You will find out why in our conversation, but let me give you a heads up: Back in 2002, Jan delivered a groundbreaking talk at the Malofiej International Info-graphics Summit titled, "Have We Really Learned Anything?" referring to the fact that many news publications rush to produce information graphics whenever something big—such as a terrorist attack or a natural catastrophe—happens. In many cases, what they end up publishing is full of errors because they don't double-check their sources, and some even make up details.

Prior to that talk, Jan had gathered and compared more than 1,000 print and online information graphics about the 9/11 terrorist attacks. He focused on the planes that hit the World Trade Center. When he plotted the trajectories of the planes that each one of those infographics showed, he discovered that they were all different (**Figure 10.41**). Only a few newspapers and magazines got the trajectories right. He felt saddened, as he believes that the whole point of infographics, regardless of if they are statistical charts, maps, or explanation diagrams, is to be accurate.

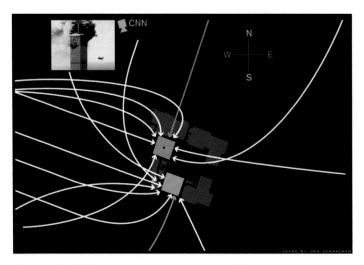

Figure 10.41 This graphic shows how many different newspapers traced the paths of the airplanes that hit the World Trade Center on 9/11 in their infographics. Most of them got the paths wrong. The orange and blue arrows are the real trajectories. Jan Schwochow was trying to make a point when he created this graphic: When facing a breaking-news story, infographics designers don't gather enough evidence to make an accurate reconstruction.

Q   What kind of professionals work for you at your company, Golden Section Graphics?

Jan Schwochow   I have 11 employees now, but the operation was not that large when I started back in 2007. My first employee was a great illustrator. I did the graphics, 3D design, and reporting, so it was a good mix. But we soon found ourselves receiving plenty of requests from clients, so we needed to expand. We started hiring people with other strengths. Today, all of us have generic skills in design, art, journalism, and so on, but each person specializes in something. So I have a programmer, a good animator who works mostly with After Effects, and a person who is an expert in Geographic Information Systems and mapping software. It's a pretty strong team.

Q   It's also much larger than your average news infographics desk.

JS   It certainly is, but we need to be this size. We keep a pretty brutal production pace. Just to give you an idea, one of the projects we have in our hands right now involves 1,000 letter-size infographics for a series of 150 travel books. Our client wants to produce them in just two years. If you do the math, and you take vacation time into account, you'll find that we have to produce an average of two pretty big graphics a day for the next 24 months. That includes doing the research, writing the copy, designing the layout, and doing illustrations and 3D models. And we have more clients than that one.

Work at our office is hectic. That's why I try to find some time for my own dreams. I love doing graphics just for myself or to be published in *InGraphics* magazine just for the sake of experimentation. I am always looking for good ideas that can be displayed as information graphics. Sometimes I find them in newspapers, in magazines, sometimes in books, and sometimes in films.

Q   One of your most famous "projects of love" was about the Berlin Wall. Why would you make a graphic about the Berlin Wall when everybody has published their own already, and you can find so much information about it in books, magazines, and on the Internet?

JS   That's exactly the point: There's a lot of information about the Berlin Wall out there. If you search in Google, you will find plenty of infographics that show you what the wall, the pits, the fences, and the towers looked like. But most of them are plainly wrong or have too many inaccuracies.

In 2009, when the 20th anniversary of the fall of the Berlin Wall was approaching, I was asked to produce a graphic about it for a local magazine. I started doing some research on my own and discovered many problems in the sources, plenty

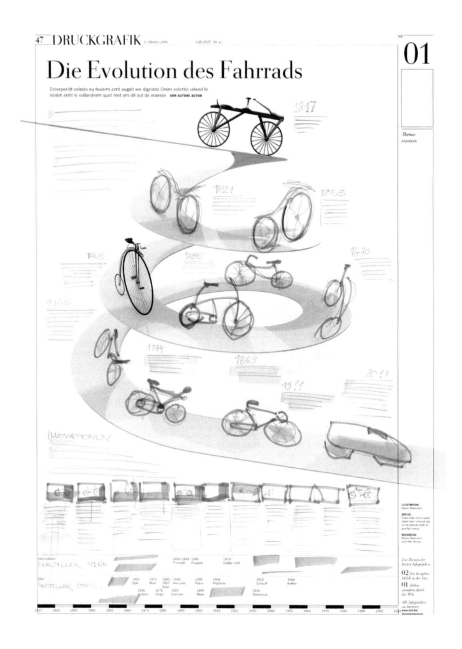

Figure 10.42 "The Evolution of the Bicycle," an example of the kind of infographics that Golden Section Graphics produces (opposite). Above, one of the very detailed sketches that are made in the production stages.

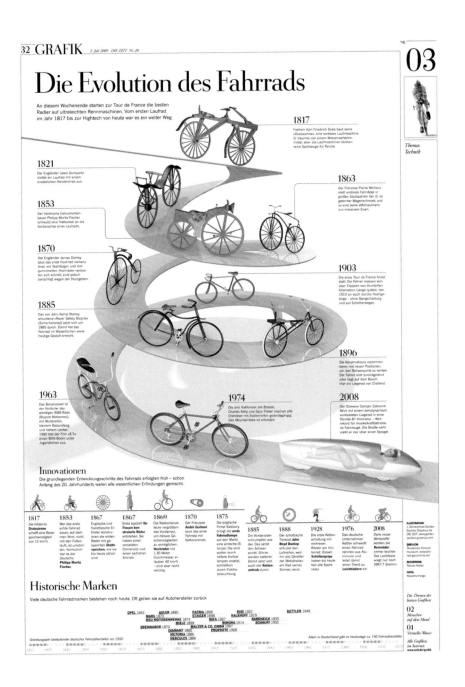

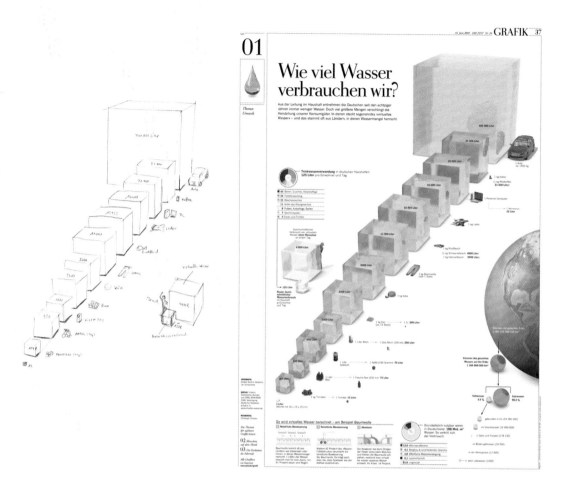

Figure 10.43 "How Much Water Do We Consume?" Infographic and draft, a project by Golden Section Infographics.

of contradictions. I hate incorrect infographics, so after we turned the project in to our client, I decided I needed to do something more ambitious on my own (**Figure 10.44**). I bought as many books as I could, walked around the remains of the wall, visited museums, and bought good images shot from airplanes between 1988 and 1989. I have a huge folder with all the research materials that I gathered.

In the end it took me two years to put all the pieces together. It was a lot of work to come up with an accurate map of what the Berlin Wall really looked like, but it was great fun. I guess that what this project shows is that you may

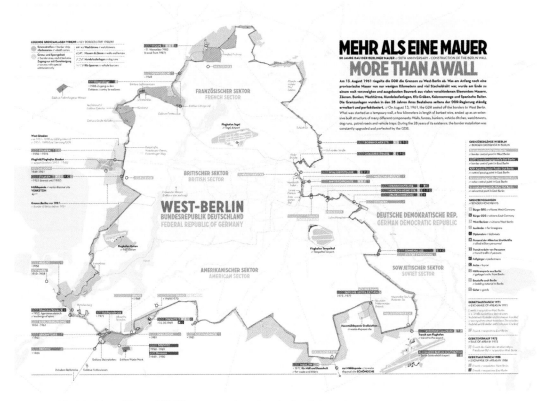

Figure 10.44 "More Than a Wall," a personal project by Jan Schwochow.

need some sort of unassailable passion to work in infographics. And you must also show respect for the facts and for the data. This business is not just about making pretty images, but about reproducing things as they really are or were.

Anyway, when I finished the project, we published it in *In Graphics*, the magazine my company produces, and we also printed it as a big table, 2 meters wide, that was used in the museum at the Glienicke Bridge, which used to be known as the bridge of the spies during the Cold War[14]. I may also use it in a book that I am planning to publish on the 25th anniversary of the end of the Berlin Wall.

---

14 The Glienicke Bridge stands over the Havel River, between Postdam and Berlin: http://www.glienicke-bridge.com/.

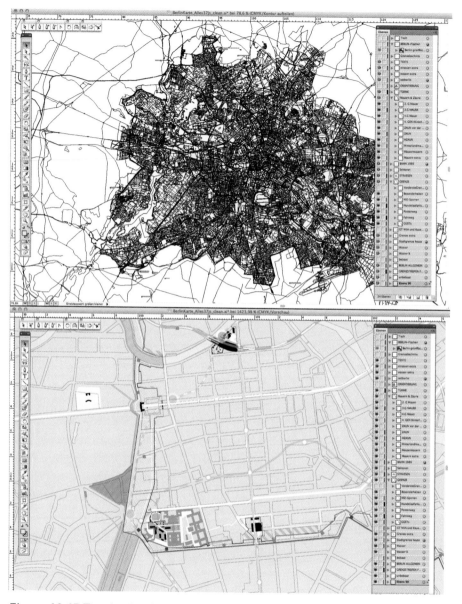

Figure 10.45 Two sketches for the Berlin Wall infographic.

Q It is amazing that a routine infographic led you to a personal project that spanned over two years.

JS That's how it's supposed to be. One of the key skills an infographics designer should develop is an eye for identifying when a story can be better told through visuals. A few years ago I read a book on Dieter Rams[15], one of the most well-known German functionalist designers, famous for his work for Braun. The book explained the influences Rams got from many other artists, industrial designers, and architects, but it was just text, text, and more text. While I was reading, an image sprang into my brain. I envisioned a timeline and some sort of node-based chart that showed those connections. I was doing a mental infographic that eventually became a real one (**Figure 10.46**).

I have always been a big fan of the Bauhaus school of design, so this project made a lot of sense to me, as the Bauhaus is at the center of German Modernism. In the graphic, you can trace the influences back to nineteenth-century Vienna, which was the cradle of Modernism, and see other connections some people are not aware of, such as the one with Russian Constructivism. Modernism extends all the way to the present, to Rams, and even to Apple's Jonathan Ive, the guy behind the iMac, the iPhone, and the iPad.

Maybe you will notice that I didn't become an infographics designer just to make money. I may get paid for this work in the future, as we may be able to sell it for some exhibition, but it is not something that I thought about when I began working on it. It won't win any international award either, as it is not that good as a piece of graphic design. But it is really dense, and it has a lot of interesting content, which I think is its main strength. It is not a graphic to see, but to explore. You can spend hours reading it. And I must say that I learned a lot reading about all the pioneers who I highlighted.

---

15 Dieter Rams embraced specific principles of design in the 1980s: Good design should be innovative, aesthetic, unobtrusive, honest, long-lasting, thorough, and make a product useful and understandable. See http://www.vitsoe.com/en/gb/about/dieterrams/gooddesign and http://www.telegraph.co.uk/technology/apple/8555503/Dieter-Rams-Apple-has-achieved-something-I-never-did.html.

Figure 10.46 "German Modernism: Architecture and Design," a timeline and connections chart that traces the history of German design back to the end of the nineteenth century.

Q That's the best part of our job, isn't it? To be able to pursue our own interests, spend time exploring unexpected paths, and gaining knowledge in the process.

JS Indeed. And you can do it not just with historical issues, as with my German Modernism and Berlin Wall projects, but with current events as well. Remember the 2002 Moscow Dubrovka Theatre crisis, when a group of Chechen terrorists took several hundred people as hostages?[16]

Q I do. It was a huge news story at the time. Many people were killed.

JS Those days, I was following the news very closely. I got tons of footage from TV news and, when I compared it to the infographics I was seeing in newspapers, magazines, and on the Web, I noticed they had a lot of mistakes. Four weeks after

16 The History Channel website has a good summary of the story: http://www.history.com/this-day-in-history/hostage-crisis-in-moscow-theater

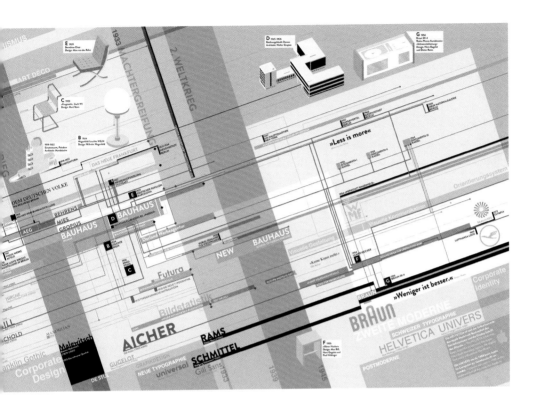

the crisis ended, after the theater was taken by Russian special forces, I decided that I wanted to do an infographic for *MAX*, a German magazine. The story was already a few weeks old. But I still needed to design the infographic to better understand what had happened (**Figure 10.47**).

I started by finding good satellite images of the area. Then, searching Russian newspapers for several days, I found a photographer who had made a documentary on the Dubrovka theater long before the hostage crisis. One of the things I have learned in 20 years working in infographics is that photographs and videos are crucial source materials if you want to be precise in re-creating a news story.

Q How were you able to draw the inside of the theater?

JS I got some help from a friend, an editor at *Stern* magazine. She had lived in Moscow for a while and got me information directly from the Moscow police. I didn't have access to really good floorplans of the building, so this part of the project was particularly hard to complete. I was lucky, though: One day, browsing through a Russian discussion forum, I got in touch with a young actor who had played at Dubrovka. I sent him an e-mail asking if he would help me make some corrections to the cutaway of the building. He was really kind, although he asked to be paid.

Q Did you pay him?

JS Not really, but he did ask me to get him a DVD from a heavy metal band, I don't remember which one, and ship it to Russia. And so I did.

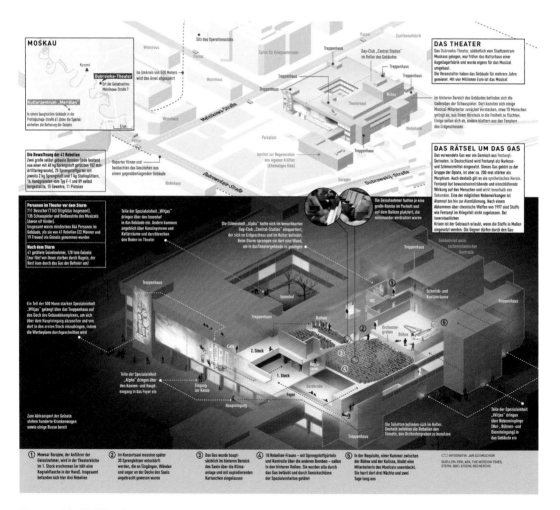

Figure 10.47 "The Dubrovka Theatre Hostage Crisis" infographic.

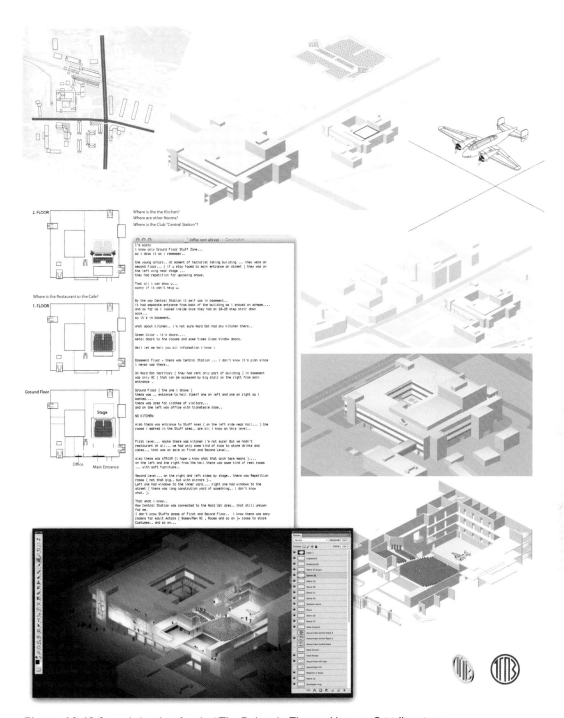

Figure 10.48 Several sketches for the "The Dubrovka Theatre Hostage Crisis" project.

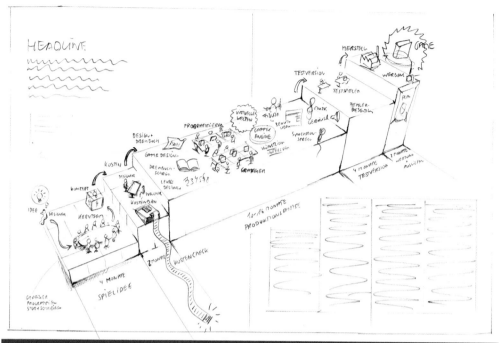

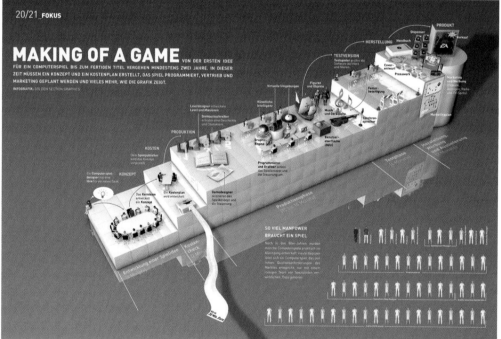

Figure 10.49 "The Making of a Video Game," by Golden Section Graphics. Infographic and sketch. Another example of the kind of work Schwochow's agency designs.

Profile 6
Geoff McGhee
(*Stanford University*)

Visualization in Academia

Geoff McGhee works on interactive data visualization and multimedia story-telling at the Bill Lane Center for the American West, a research institute at Stanford University. From 2000 to 2008, he worked as graphics editor, enterprise editor, chief multimedia producer, and video journalist at *The New York Times*. He has also worked at ABCNews.com and France's *Le Monde*. Geoff spent a Knight Fellowship year at Stanford in 2009–2010 researching data visualization, which resulted in the video documentary, "Journalism in the Age of Data." Geoff received his Master's degree in journalism from Columbia University in 1999.

All infographics designers and reporters I know are jacks-of-all-trades of some sort. They are forced to be: the current cutthroat job market forces out those who only generalize or only specialize. As the interviewees in the previous pages make clear, the best strategy seems to be to learn about everything and then go deeper into something: statistical charts, maps, illustrations, and so on.

Geoff McGhee is a one-of-a-kind jack-of-all-trades. At the beginning of this century, he was the only journalist producing interactive graphics at *The New York Times*. At the same time, he was educating himself in scripting languages. Then, he worked as a multimedia journalist, shooting and editing video stories, before moving to Paris to lead a team of designers, journalists, and developers at *Le Monde*. Finally, he came back to the U.S. to work at Stanford University.

I was interested in talking with Geoff because I have always felt that, when it comes to information graphics and visualization, there's a huge gap between newsrooms and academia. Managers in media organizations complain that universities don't train their undergraduates properly, and some academics grumble that professionals don't give educational institutions credit for the many innovations (software tools and new visualization techniques) that they foster.

Geoff is in a unique position to bridge that gap, as you are about to read. He is a professional embedded into one of the most respected universities in the world. He speaks the language of both seasoned practitioners and brainy intellectuals, so he acts as a translator between them.

Q   You were one of the pioneers in news information graphics, at ABC News and at *The New York Times*. What did you learn in those early days?

Geoff McGhee I think the key lesson that I learned even before going to the *Times* was how important it is to understand that Web graphics are extremely time and labor intensive: If you just toss them on the pile of 700-word news stories and throw them away after 6 hours—which is to say, take them down from the front pages—you've lost a huge amount of labor and potential audience. Online graphics are labor-intensive because they are, or should be, databases in essence, and not just narrow summaries of data.

In the early 2000s, the *Times's* print graphics desk was already well-established and producing exceptional work, especially since the paper's move to color in 1997 or 1998. The website, however, had been around since early 1996 and had not dedicated many resources to information graphics up to the point that I arrived in mid-summer of 2000.

One of my main duties at first was to translate print graphics into Web graphics. Working in print-to-online had a lot of drawbacks compared to the Web-original stuff I had been accustomed to produce at ABC. After a few years, we were able to produce some original content, of course, but it took a while. At the *Times*, I also became increasingly aware of how silly it was to bake quantitative information into a static raster image of a chart and wanted to start thinking about ways to serve and display data in a more dynamic way.

Q **Is that what eventually caused you to switch careers and go into academia?**

GM In part, yes. I moved to Stanford University after getting a Knight Foundation fellowship to spend a year taking classes and doing research. I had spent many years in newsrooms, and the idea of going back to school was a very appealing one. I felt I needed to learn about what's going on with information graphics and visualization.

When you are in media, you are aware of the many innovations that are being developed in academia—new tools, new techniques, new practices—but you don't usually have direct access to them. And the truth is that there are academics who study graphics and visualization, working for different institutions, who may not be journalists, but who are interested in what's going on in media. Take Robert Kosara, for instance.[17] A while ago, he wrote an article about how scientific visualization has a lot to learn from information graphics. Information graphics, I guess particularly for news, are sort of the state-of-the-art in terms of taking visual forms and telling a story with them.

So the reason those academics keep an eye on graphics in journalism is that they are used to the core idea of data viz, which is to preserve the source data as opposed to being some one-off snapshot of a particular point. But they also understand the need to make cogent points and to transmit meaning. That is the journalistic side. So I guess that my moving to academia was a result of my interest in bridging the gap between those two worlds: I am a professional journalist who has an interest in computer science, data, and visualization.

I think that the interest that certain researchers have in journalism is starting to bear fruit in a few different ways. One is that there are more people crossing over from computer science, from stats, and from more research-oriented fields, into media. There are also educational institutions that have started interdisciplinary programs, partnering programmers with journalists, like Medill at Northwestern University and also at Columbia.

Q **Can't that be done in newsrooms, bringing people with different skill sets together?**

GM Some publications are trying to replicate what some universities are doing. Think of *The New York Times* Research & Development Lab[18], for instance. They realize that a newsroom can also be a place for innovation. Not all companies

---

17 Robert Kosara is an associate professor of computer science at the University of North Carolina at Charlotte. He has a blog, http://eagereyes.org/, about information graphics and visualization.

18 See http://www.nytco.com/company/Innovation_and_Technology/ResearchandDevelopment. html.

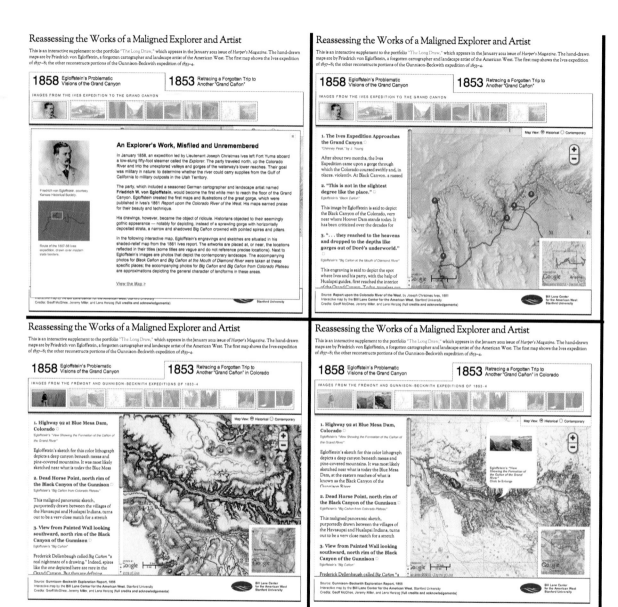

Figure 10.50 "Reassessing the Works of a Maligned Explorer and Artist," one of Geoff McGhee's projects for the Bill Lane Center for the American West, at Stanford University. A version of this graphic was published by *Harper's* magazine (http://harpers.org/media/free/2012-01-canyon.html). The graphic displays the maps drawn by Friedrich von Egloffstein, a German aristocrat who was part of the first expedition to reach the floor of the Grand Canyon, in 1857–1858. The interactive maps let readers see how different Egloffstein's drawings are when compared to reality.

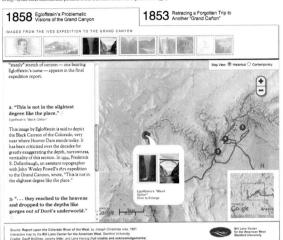

Reassessing the Works of a Maligned Explorer and Artist

This is an interactive supplement to the portfolio "The Long Draw," which appears in the January 2012 issue of *Harper's Magazine*. The hand-drawn maps are by Friedrich von Egloffstein, a forgotten cartographer and landscape artist of the American West. The first map shows the Ives expedition of 1857–8; the other reconstructs portions of the Gunnison-Beckwith expedition of 1853–4.

1858 Egloffstein's Problematic Visions of the Grand Canyon   **1853** Retracing a Forgotten Trip to Another "Grand Cañon"

IMAGES FROM THE IVES EXPEDITION TO THE GRAND CANYON

"stately" stretch of canyon — one bearing Egloffstein's name — appears in the final expedition report.

2. "This is not in the slightest degree like the place."
Egloffstein's "Black Cañon"

This image by Egloffstein is said to depict the Black Canyon of the Colorado, very near where Hoover Dam stands today. It has been criticized over the decades for greatly exaggerating the depth, narrowness, verticality of this section. In 1934, Frederick S. Dellenbaugh, an assistant topographer with John Wesley Powell's 1871 expedition to the Grand Canyon, wrote, "This is not in the slightest degree like the place."

3. "... they reached to the heavens and dropped to the depths like gorges out of Doré's underworld."

Map View: ● Historical ○ Contemporary

Egloffstein's "Black Cañon" Click to Enlarge

Source: Report upon the Colorado River of the West, by Joseph Christmas Ives, 1861
Interactive map by the Bill Lane Center for the American West, Stanford University
Credits: Geoff McGhee, Jeremy Miller, and Lena Herzog (full credits and acknowledgements)

Bill Lane Center for the American West, Stanford University

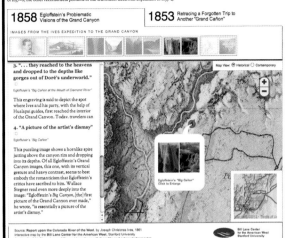

Reassessing the Works of a Maligned Explorer and Artist

This is an interactive supplement to the portfolio "The Long Draw," which appears in the January 2012 issue of *Harper's Magazine*. The hand-drawn maps are by Friedrich von Egloffstein, a forgotten cartographer and landscape artist of the American West. The first map shows the Ives expedition of 1857–8; the other reconstructs portions of the Gunnison-Beckwith expedition of 1853–4.

1858 Egloffstein's Problematic Visions of the Grand Canyon   **1853** Retracing a Forgotten Trip to Another "Grand Cañon"

IMAGES FROM THE IVES EXPEDITION TO THE GRAND CANYON

3. "... they reached to the heavens and dropped to the depths like gorges out of Doré's underworld."

Egloffstein's "Big Cañon at the Mouth of Diamond River"

This engraving is said to depict the spot where Ives and his party, with the help of Hualapai guides, first reached the interior of the Grand Canyon. Today, travelers can

4. "A picture of the artist's dismay"

Egloffstein's "Big Cañon"

This puzzling image shows a hornlike spire jutting above the canyon rim and dropping into its depths. Of all Egloffstein's Grand Canyon images, this one, with its vertical gesture and heavy contrast, seems to best embody the romanticism that Egloffstein's critics have ascribed to him. Wallace Stegner read even more deeply into the image: "Egloffstein's *Big Canyon*, [the] first picture of the Grand Canyon ever made," he wrote, "is essentially a picture of the artist's dismay."

Map View: ● Historical ○ Contemporary

Egloffstein's "Big Cañon" Click to Enlarge

Source: Report upon the Colorado River of the West, by Joseph Christmas Ives, 1861
Interactive map by the Bill Lane Center for the American West, Stanford University
Credits: Geoff McGhee, Jeremy Miller, and Lena Herzog (full credits and acknowledgements)

Bill Lane Center for the American West, Stanford University

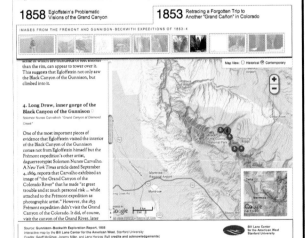

Reassessing the Works of a Maligned Explorer and Artist

This is an interactive supplement to the portfolio "The Long Draw," which appears in the January 2012 issue of *Harper's Magazine*. The hand-drawn maps are by Friedrich von Egloffstein, a forgotten cartographer and landscape artist of the American West. The first map shows the Ives expedition of 1857–8; the other reconstructs portions of the Gunnison-Beckwith expedition of 1853–4.

1858 Egloffstein's Problematic Visions of the Grand Canyon   **1853** Retracing a Forgotten Trip to Another "Grand Cañon" in Colorado

IMAGES FROM THE FRÉMONT AND GUNNISON-BECKWITH EXPEDITIONS OF 1853-4

some of which are hundreds of feet shorter than the rim, can appear to tower over it. This suggests that Egloffstein not only saw the Black Canyon of the Gunnison, but climbed into it.

4. Long Draw, inner gorge of the Black Canyon of the Gunnison
Solomon Nunes Carvalho's "Grand Canyon of Diamond Creek"

One of the most important pieces of evidence that Egloffstein visited the interior of the Black Canyon of the Gunnison comes not from Egloffstein himself but the Frémont expedition's other artist, daguerreotypist Solomon Nunes Carvalho. A *New York Times* article dated September 4, 1869, reports that Carvalho exhibited an image of "the Grand Canyon of the Colorado River" that he made "at great trouble and at much personal risk ... while attached to the Frémont expedition as photographic artist." However, the 1853 Frémont expedition didn't visit the Grand Canyon of the Colorado. It did, of course, visit the canyon of the Grand River, later

Map View: ○ Historical ● Contemporary

Source: Gunnison-Beckwith Exploration Report, 1855
Interactive map by the Bill Lane Center for the American West, Stanford University
Credits: Geoff McGhee, Jeremy Miller, and Lena Herzog (full credits and acknowledgements)

Bill Lane Center for the American West, Stanford University

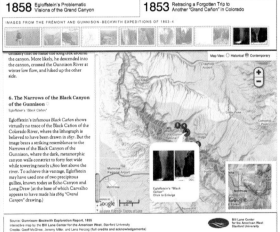

Reassessing the Works of a Maligned Explorer and Artist

This is an interactive supplement to the portfolio "The Long Draw," which appears in the January 2012 issue of *Harper's Magazine*. The hand-drawn maps are by Friedrich von Egloffstein, a forgotten cartographer and landscape artist of the American West. The first map shows the Ives expedition of 1857–8; the other reconstructs portions of the Gunnison-Beckwith expedition of 1853–4.

1858 Egloffstein's Problematic Visions of the Grand Canyon   **1853** Retracing a Forgotten Trip to Another "Grand Cañon" in Colorado

IMAGES FROM THE FRÉMONT AND GUNNISON-BECKWITH EXPEDITIONS OF 1853-4

unlikely that he made the long trek around the canyon. More likely, he descended into the canyon, crossed the Gunnison River at winter low flow, and hiked up the other side.

6. The Narrows of the Black Canyon of the Gunnison
Egloffstein's "Black Cañon"

Egloffstein's infamous *Black Cañon* shows virtually no trace of the Black Cañon of the Colorado River, where the lithograph is believed to have been drawn in 1857. But the image bears a striking resemblance to the Narrows of the Black Canyon of the Gunnison, where the dark, metamorphic canyon walls constrict to forty feet wide while towering nearly 1,800 feet above the river. To achieve this vantage, Egloffstein may have used one of two precipitous gullies, known today as Echo Canyon and Long Draw (at the base of which Carvalho appears to have made his 1869 "Grand Canyon" drawing).

Map View: ○ Historical ● Contemporary

Egloffstein's "Black Cañon" Click to Enlarge

Source: Gunnison-Beckwith Exploration Report, 1855
Interactive map by the Bill Lane Center for the American West, Stanford University
Credits: Geoff McGhee, Jeremy Miller, and Lena Herzog (full credits and acknowledgements)

Bill Lane Center for the American West, Stanford University

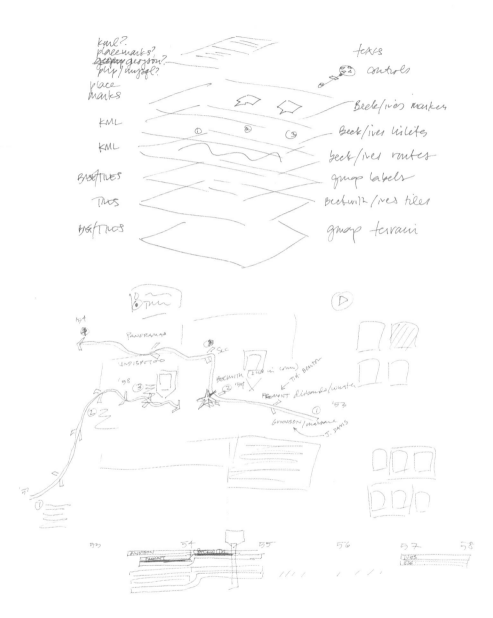

Figure 10.51 Early sketches for the "Maligned Explorer" interactive graphic.

can put together a research team, but at least they can bring in developers and engineers as part of the news product. Those people should not only be in the newsroom just in case the servers crash.

I tried to apply that idea when I worked for *Le Monde*. When I was hired, the expectations they had for me were significant. For instance, they wanted to develop an application for reporters and editors to use to generate maps and charts. I sympathized with that idea: Taking basic locator maps and simple charts from graphics editors and letting pretty much anybody create them is positive: It lets graphics people move up the value chain into more advanced storytelling and do more original reporting.

We ended up delivering the tool. It was pretty simple but it was completely built into the content management system. The only thing that the journalist needed to have on the desktop was the PDF with the data he or she wanted to use, or an Excel spreadsheet. Everything else happened inside the application: You uploaded the data and were able to generate the graphics. I guess that, after what I did at *The New York Times* and at *Le Monde*, coming to academia made a lot of sense: I was already doing some sort of research and development while at the newsroom, but I felt that I needed to have the right intellectual environment to really thrive at it.

Q   What are your duties at Stanford?

GM I participate in classes at the university, but my job is at the Bill Lane Center for the American West.[19] The main goal of the center is to work with historians, political scientists, climate scientists, and other scholars from many other areas, to promote public understanding of western North America. That includes parts of Canada, the U.S., and Mexico.

Just to give you an example of what we do, I would mention a project on the history of newspapers between the seventeenth and the twenty-first centuries (**Figure 10.53**). It all started as a part of the Bill Lane Center, called The Rural West Initiative. What this initiative does is to follow the path of President Teddy Roosevelt who, in 1909, conducted a landmark survey on the state of rural western America. The situation was not good at the beginning of the twentieth century: industrialization was sucking people into the cities and a lot of farm jobs were being eliminated by mechanization.

The question for President Roosevelt was, what is happening to rural America? We're losing jobs, the economic base is shrinking: Is it going to be a viable place in the future or is it going to become sort of hollowed out? And since he thought

---

19 http://west.stanford.edu/about.

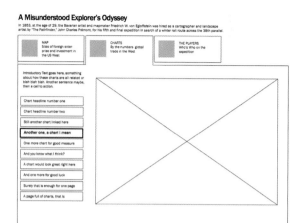

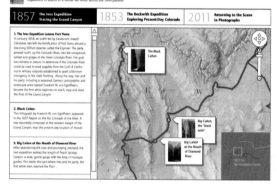

Figure 10.52 Layouts for the "Maligned Explorer" interactive graphics.

the rural West was part of the core of American identity, it was something that was very frightening to him. The question for us was, 100 years later, what has happened? Could we reapply some of the methodology and look at some of the same topics that they did in 1909, but in 2009?

One of the angles we wanted to look at was access to media. How did people in rural places get information in the past? And how do they get it now? We wanted to do some very ambitious stuff that we are still working on, like taking digitized newspaper articles from across history, run them through statistical analysis software that would read them for us and tell us how topics had changed over time. What were the subjects that people were interested in? How did they talk about them? But the first step of the project is what you can see online right now: a timeline of newspapers that uses a database from the Library of Congress.

Q Universities and educational and research institutions in general seem to be a good option for designers and journalists who have grown tired of the instability of media organizations.

GM Absolutely. Academics are increasingly interested in not only using the Web to transmit the description of their research but as a publication platform for their research and to open it up to make the research more of a collaborative exploration mission.

I think that is something that journalists can really help out with because academic communication has a certain protocol to it that is not necessarily open to a wider audience. Now that's not to say that Stanford engineering is going to be publishing its own *Popular Mechanics* magazine. But at the same time, I think more and more scholars are going to go more and more public with their work. And interactive data visualizations are powerful tools for reaching people more profoundly with their research and the content of what they do.

Q During your fellowship, you also produced "Journalism in the Age of Data," a groundbreaking video documentary about information visualization. How did that come about?

GM When I started my fellowship I took Jeffrey Heer's class on information visualization.[20] It was perfect for me, as I needed to adopt a rigorous approach to the field, studying Jacques Bertin, Edward Tufte, and the like, and learn about statistics, thematic mapping, and so on. At the same time, I had a travel budget, so it was my chance to go around and meet the people who were moving the field

---

20 http://hci.stanford.edu/jheer/.

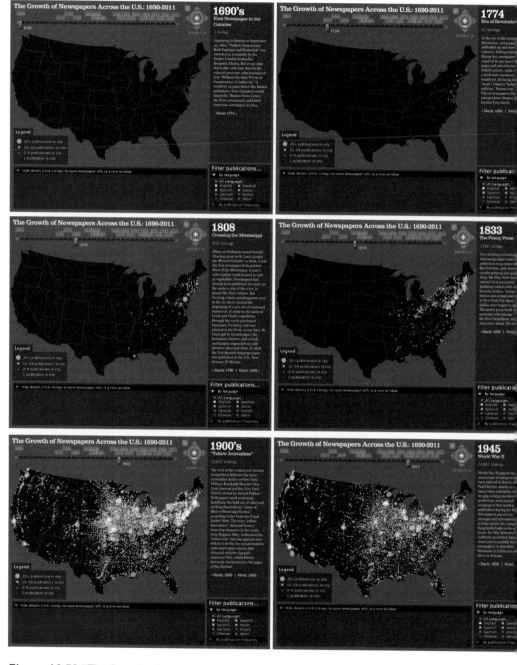

Figure 10.53 "The Growth of Newspapers Across the U.S.: 1690-2011." The Bill Lane Center for the American West, Stanford University (http://www.stanford.edu/group/ruralwest/cgi-bin/drupal/visualizations/us_newspapers).

forward or who had helped create it. It made sense to bring my camera with me and record those interviews.

One of the things that I discovered is that even the people who are doing the most way out and challenging, the most sophisticated types of visualization, are aware of the need to make data visualization more accessible, to help it mature as a communications medium.

After all, data visualization breaks down into two major categories: data visualization for exploring on your own, for analyzing and seeking out patterns; and data visualization for explanation. Algorithmic data visualization—where you're using computer code to "grow" charts and graphs from the source data—is a very powerful analytical tool, given that you have a basic understanding of the source data, and particularly if you have expertise in a particular domain, say, if you're a doctor looking at health care outcomes, for example.

Q   How do you turn those insights into explanatory visuals, so that other people can share in your discoveries? That's what information graphics have done for a long time. But they have traditionally been hand-crafted to show only the most pertinent information, with elegant and minimalist use of color and annotation to highlight the main points. Making computer-generated, interactive graphics that successfully impart meaning is a much more difficult task.

GM I'm happy to see academic specialists in info visualization taking a strong interest in interactive graphics done by journalists. For example, a couple of years ago, Jeff Heer and graduate student Edward Segel did a broad survey of interaction and storytelling techniques used by media organizations that drew some interesting lessons in how to guide users through an infographic story.[21] Out of that work, another student of Jeff's is now at work on a tool that will let you create "steps" in an interactive visualization—with control over zoom, center, selection and other variables—that can create a solid narrative experience, while still leaving the visualization open to nonlinear exploration as well.

To take another example, Ben Fry, the famous designer who developed the Processing visualization programming language, has plans of working with more journalists in the future through his firm, Fathom.[22] When I talked with him in 2010, you could sense that he was dissatisfied with the state of work that he was doing. I think he wants it to be less cold and clinical and more engaging on a human level.

---

21 http:/vis.stanford.edu/papers/narrative

22 See http://benfry.com/ and http://processing.org/ and http://fathom.info/

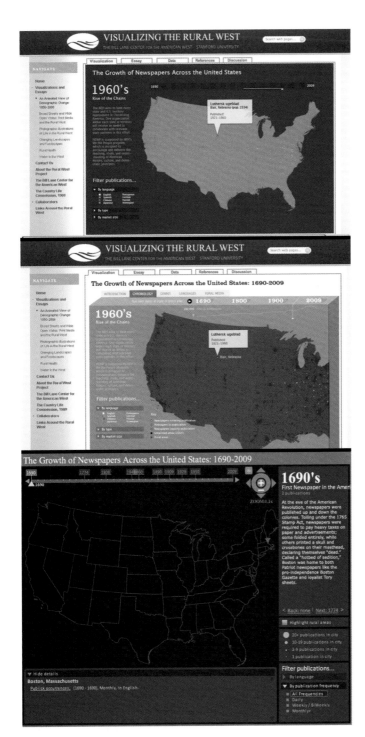

Figure 10.54 Several mock-ups for the "Growth of Newspapers" project.

Profile 7
Hans Rosling
(*Gapminder Foundation*)

Quantitative Humanism

Hans Rosling is a professor of International Health at the Karolinska Institute, in Sweden. He is also a world-famous medical doctor, statistician, and speaker. He has lectured on health and development at many important conferences, including TED. He is head of Gapminder, which produces software that helps visualize publicly available data and whose goal is to raise awareness of world health issues through the use of statistics and animations.

There are lives that change at a geological pace, imitating the sluggish drift of continents; there are other lives that change in a glorious instant. Hans Rosling's life changed one day in February of 2006. It happened two minutes into his first TED presentation, in Monterey, California, which perfectly mixed a great sense of pace and timing with an astonishing use of information graphics about population and economy trends. Unexpectedly, he because a superstar presenter about public health and international aid. Since then, he has presented at TED many more times, as well as given lectures around the world and served as an advisor to governments and public officials. I strongly recommend that you watch that presentation before you keep reading this profile.[23]

As you will immediately notice, what is most amazing about the way Hans Rosling presents is how he is able to blend with his graphics, to become an integral part of the colorful bubble charts and scatter plots that flow on his back (**Figure 10.55**). His words and actions help viewers make sense of the data being shown on screen.

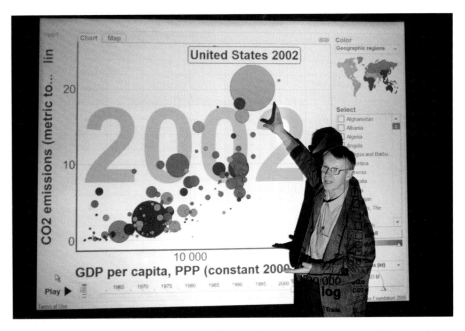

Figure 10.55 Hans Rosling, during one of his graphics-based presentations. Photograph by Stefan Nilsson for the Gapminder Foundation (www.gapminder.org).

Rosling has always been interested in popularizing statistics. The motto of the foundation he heads, Gapminder[24], is very clear about it: "Fighting the most devastating myths by building a fact-based world view that everyone understands."

In 2010, he produced an hour-long documentary for the BBC, titled *The Joy of Stats*, on the importance of statistics in daily life.[25] Its message: Statistics are not solely

23 TED stands for Technology, Entertainment, Design. It is the most influential set of conferences on innovative ideas. See Rosling's first presentation in http://www.ted.com/talks/lang/en/hans_rosling_shows_the_best_stats_you_ve_ever_seen.html

24 Visit http://www.gapminder.org/

25 *The Joy of Stats* is available online: http://www.gapminder.org/videos/the-joy-of-stats/

the realm of experts, but a simple, fun activity that has the potential to change the life of all citizens.

Hans Rosling is a medical doctor (he spent 20 years in Africa, most of them in Mozambique), but I would say that his motivations are those of a journalist. The "fact-based world view" he promotes could occupy the masthead of any good news publication. During our conversation, he insisted on his ideology, explained a few tricks behind his presentation style, and reflected on whether it's possible for graphic designers, journalists, programmers, and designers to work together under the same roof all with the goal of improving public understanding of complex issues.

Q   It is common to hear that we have more data today than we can handle, but that this situation does not necessarily lead to an informed citizenship. Is that statement true?

Hans Rosling The answer to that question needs to begin by explaining that different kinds of data exist, in different scales, and with the possibility of their being filtered in different ways. So follow me on.

The first data type usually generated in any study are microdata—detailed, granular data that are generally useless. Just to give you an example, in Sweden we have this database in which anyone can look for the price his neighbor's house was sold for a month ago. Those "micro" data are easy to spread: Just put them in a server and design a simple interface to access them. You don't have to worry that much about how to present them or organize them because we can assume that whoever accesses your tool will know beforehand what she is looking for. Think of this as the old Yellow Pages. You know what you need, your cousin's phone number, so you go directly to the page where it is, because names are organized alphabetically.

Q   You mean that the user knows what questions to ask of the database.

HR Exactly. But now let's go to another level. Imagine that what we want to see is not the price of your neighbor's house, but the trends in the real estate market and how they've changed over the years. Perhaps the user needs a tool to help him decide where to live, to identify the best neighborhoods with access to good hospitals, schools, and so on. In that case, the designer must aggregate the initial microdata in a form that makes sense, that forces patterns to become visible.

This is a challenge because it is not easy to do it correctly. Years ago, somebody designed a map of London divided into suburbs. The objective was to show the average risk of death because of heart attack in each of them. They took the hospital records and the total number of inhabitants, and associated them with postal codes. What the designers didn't consider was that the districts showing the greater risk of heart attacks were also those with a higher percentage of elderly inhabitants. They had not factored in that data, so what the map reflected was not the probability of dying of myocardial infarction, but where the young and old populations were concentrated.

Imagine that you use that map to choose where to live in London. It is likely that you will avoid those districts, thinking perhaps that they have more pollution or that the hospitals there are of poor quality. Who knows? But what you are actually doing is avoiding the places with a higher percentage of elderly people. That's the danger of putting together a user who doesn't know what to ask of the data, and a presentation that responds to the wrong questions.

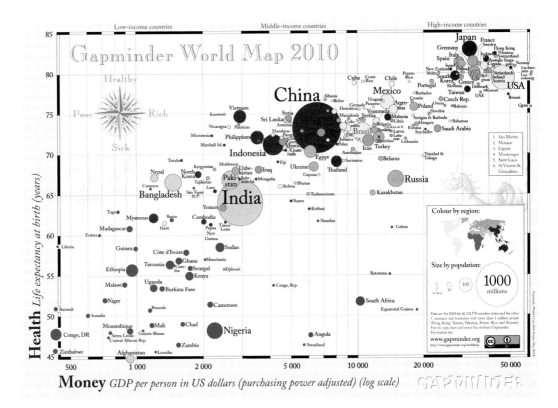

Figure 10.56 Life expectancy and GDP per person, in a scatter-plot. Gapminder Foundation (www.gapminder.org).

Q **So the form in which we filter the data is more important than the actual data.**

HR Yes. The best way to understand it is the weather forecast. What we see on television is the conclusion of a long process of tabulation, organization, simplification, and editing. Everything begins with the records taken by satellites and ground stations, which are sent to gigantic databases. The meteorologists then use mathematical models that help them to summarize and interpret the numbers to make predictions. Those predictions reach the television station, where another meteorologist filters them again. The result is the basis for a map, made in Adobe Illustrator or Photoshop, which the viewer sees at the end.

This idea of filtering data and transforming it into information, so that an ample public understands complex facts, is our goal at the Gapminder Foundation. If readers see only raw data, they will understand nothing. But if they access data after it's processed, the effect is very different. Data can take different forms to illuminate many subjects.

Q **That indeed seems to be the root of your foundation: to promote "a vision of the world based on facts," and to reveal "the beauty of statistics to improve the understanding of reality," to quote from the documentary you made for the BBC.**

HR I remember that when my son, Ola Rosling, my daughter-in-law Anna Rosling Rönnlund, and I founded Gapminder in February of 2005, we did it with one ideal in mind: "People have a pile of preconceived ideas on our planet that do not correspond with reality." In Sweden, it is common to think that in the majority of developing countries, the fertility rate is six or seven children per woman. But a glance at the data shows that, to mention only one case, women in Iran have fewer children on average than the Swedish! It's impossible to intuit that without seeing the numbers visually represented in a meaningful way.

Q **You have talked about the prejudices with which the inhabitants of rich countries see "the poor." You stated that you don't like the expression "developing country."**

HR It's not the expression in itself, but the simplistic idea that it is possible to divide the world into two groups: one group of a few millions of privileged people, and the "others." That way of thinking leads to putting countries as different as Somalia and Brazil in the same group, which is absurd. The data show that for the last 15 years, mortality in Brazil has fallen at double the rate of Sweden's in its entire history. Not to mention the economic differences within the country: The Brazilian government's distribution programs have reduced inequality considerably without stopping economic growth. It is a success.

Q   Why is the division of the world into two groups so extensive?

HR Part of it is racism, part of it is arrogance and, finally, part of it is a pessimistic view of reality. If someone is at once racist, arrogant, and pessimistic, it is very probable that she will think that the situation in poor countries can't change because of "culture" or "climate" or other factors not easily affected by human interventions. For example, she might think children in Africa lack normal intellectual development because of malaria, or that low-quality schools in India prevent students from reaching their full potential.

Or they might question the value of promoting sexual education and family planning in India and Bangladesh because both countries are "full of Hindus and Muslims who have too many children because of religion, therefore they are never going to change."

This enormous ignorance about the world is what we try to fight with our animated and interactive presentations.

Q   I believe that animation and interaction are not the only factors that explain the success of your conferences. It is also how you integrate with the animated graphics you show.

HR That, I believe, is the product of my years of experience as a doctor in Africa and a professor in Sweden. I have seen too many academic classes that have been catastrophic from the communicative point of view—the seated lecturer reading a paper or the bullet points of his PowerPoint slides. How boring is that? I have tried to learn from the reactions of my public, from regular people as well as from students and managers of companies.

When I am on the scene, I do not remain quiet. I also use a lot of analogies and metaphors, and borrow voice modulation tricks from sports broadcasters. Notice that when I am describing a chart it seems that I am describing a football game.

Q   What can designers and journalists learn from the success of Gapminder?

HR What I mentioned at the beginning of our conversation: Our main goal should be to transform complex data into information. Let me give you an analogy: Mozart was a wonderful composer; Steinway was the best piano maker of his time; and, today, there are a lot of musicians who use Steinway pianos to bring

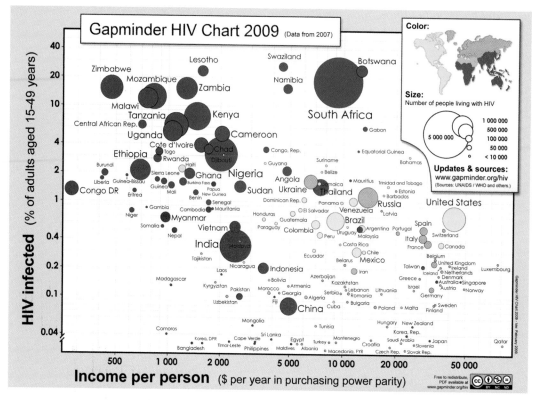

Figure 10.57 HIV rate of infection, compared to income per person. Gapminder Foundation (www.gapminder.org).

life to what Mozart once wrote. Those three people are equivalent to a statistician who gathers the data; the engineers at Google and Adobe who design the tool to filter, organize, and present them; and the designers who create the presentations that makes them understandable.

That is what Gapminder is. When those three kinds of people, the statistician, the engineer, and the designer, work together, you get the better results. This structure may not be applicable everywhere, though. When I spoke at some newspapers and magazines, I saw that they all face the same problem: journalists, designers, and programmers don't have coffee together. They speak different languages because they come from different cultures. It's like bringing together a Muslim, a Christian, and a Jew, leaving them alone, and hoping they will reach an agreement in matters of religion. You may need a translator in a situation like that.

Q   What lies ahead for Gapminder?

HR Our main goal is to give publicity to those databases that are crucial for a better understanding of the world. We don't want to gather all data available. Let's let Google do that. What we want to achieve is to select what is most relevant and present it in ways that can be informative and fun. The tools we are developing at this point go in that direction. It is my conviction that, by means of a better use of the current availability of data, it is possible to create a better world.

Profile 8
Moritz Stefaner

Truth and Beauty Operator

Moritz Stefaner works on the crossroads of data visualization, information aesthetics, and user interface design. With a background in cognitive science (a Bachelor's degree in science with distinction, University of Osnabrück) and interface design (M.A., University of Applied Sciences Potsdam), his work balances analytical and aesthetic aspects in mapping abstract and complex phenomena. He is especially interested in the visualization of large–scale human activity. In the past, he has helped clients like the Organization for Economic Cooperation and Development (OECD), the World Economic Forum, Skype, the German Press Agency (DPA), the International Federation of Soccer (FIFA), and the Max Planck Research Society to find insights and beauty in large data sets.

In 2010, he was nominated for the Design Award of the Federal Republic of Germany. His work has been exhibited at Venice Biennale of Architecture, SIGGRAPH, Ars Electronica Center and Max Planck Science Gallery. He is part of the advisory boards for the Places and Spaces Exhibit and the Digital Communities category at Prix Ars Electronica and serves as a reviewing expert for the Future and Emerging Technologies programme of the European Commission. He has co-authored books on the subjects covered in this book and has spoken and lectured on numerous occasions on the topic of information visualization.

Moritz Stefaner once thought about becoming an artist, but he wasn't accepted into art school when he applied. In his own words, that was a great thing because it gave him the chance to become an information designer, someone whose heart is split into two halves: that of the developer's and that of someone with a deep sensibility for aesthetics.

You can see that dual nature on any of his projects. They are informative, deep, precise, usable, and at the same time, they are also enjoyable, true gems for the eyes and the brain. Something similar can be said about his posts and articles, all collected in his website, http://well-formed-data.net. Take a look at it after reading our conversation, as he builds on some of the issues discussed here. You can find his project portfolio at http://moritz.stefaner.eu.

Q   You define yourself as a "truth and beauty operator." What does that mean?

Moritz Stefaner In the past, I used to tell clients and family I worked as a "free-lance information visualizer." That has way too many syllables. Also, I was always forced to explain what I actually did, as people don't really have much of a grasp on what it means. After I explained that I turn data into images and try to help people make sense of large data sets, I was often asked if I tended to prioritize truth or beauty, form or function: Do these compete in my projects? Do I have to trade off one against the other?

For me, truth and beauty have always been two sides of the same coin. What I want to highlight in my title is that I don't wish to trade truth for beauty or beauty for truth: I work with both. These are the two things that I will evaluate design solutions against: Are we helping to find out the truth? Are we doing it in an elegant way?

Q   So you cannot have truth without beauty, and vice versa.

MS I put truth and beauty at the same level. If you have only one without the other in a visualization project, you are not done yet.

Buckminster Fuller[26], the famous designer and systems theorist, said once that he didn't think about beauty when he started a design, engineering, or architectural project. He was just concerned with its functions; he wanted to find the right way to devise the product. But then, in the end, if the solution he came up with was not beautiful, he knew something was wrong. For Buckminster Fuller, in some sense, beauty was an indicator of functionality and of truth.

26 http://en.wikipedia.org/wiki/Buckminster_Fuller

Create Your Better Life Index

How do you define a better life? Use our interactive tool to see how your country performs on the topics you feel make for a better life.

Create Your Better Life Index

There is more to life than the cold numbers of GDP and economic statistics – This Index allows you to compare well-being across countries, based on 11 topics the OECD has identified as essential, in the areas of material living conditions and quality of life.

Find out more

April 27, 2011
Doing Better for Families
Read this report

April 7, 2011
Housing and the Economy: Policies for Renovation
Read this report

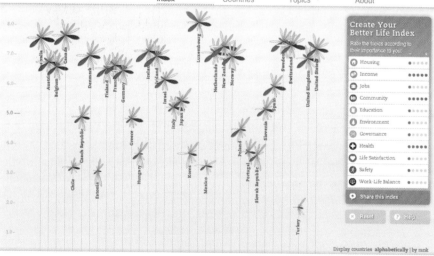

For me, design is much more than mere decoration. Scientists and engineering-focused people, the kind of professionals I usually work with, think of design as decorating a pre-existing structure. That is the wrong approach. Good design is tightly intertwined with the content it presents. It consists of thinking about what to show; what to leave out; what to highlight; how to structure information; what rhythm, visual flow, and pace, you want your story to have. That's design. I would say that structure dictates pretty much what comes out visually.

Q   You have a background in cognitive science. Has it influenced your work?

MS Big time. By studying science, I learned about methodology, formal systems, formal knowledge representation, data mining statistics, and language. Learning about how human language works is very important for visualization and information graphics because they are a language, too. They have a grammar, a syntax, and a vocabulary.

Interestingly, what I didn't use so much is what I learned about perception. You would think you would learn a lot of nice perception tricks if you study cognitive science, but most of the techniques that are relevant to visualization have been covered quite well already in the visualization and user interface design literature.

That said, cognitive science is an excellent basis for visualization or interface design. I would recommend learning about cognitive science to anybody who wants to move into our field.

Q   Let's talk about your workflow. What steps do you take to complete a project?

MS This is something I discuss with clients quite early in the process. I have even created a little diagram to explain it (**Figure 10.59**). When I start a visualization, first we define some high-level contents and goals: What do we want to achieve with the graphic? How will we know that it accomplishes what it should? How

Figure 10.58 (opposite) OECD Better Life Index, http://moritz.stefaner.eu/projects/oecd-better-life-index/ by Moritz Stefaner: "The OECD provides a forum in which governments can work together to share experiences and seek solutions to improve the economic and social well-being of people around the world. Together with the agency Raureif, I worked on an interactive application called 'Your Better Life Index.' It is designed to let the user visualize and compare some of the key factors, like education, housing, and environment, that contribute to well-being in OECD countries. Instead of presenting one authoritative country ranking, users can set their own priorities in a playful environment." (Created in collaboration with Raureif Creative Consultancy.)

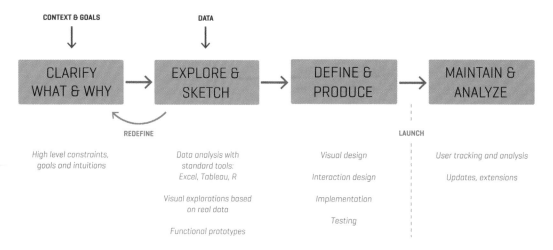

Figure 10.59 Moritz Stefaner's project workflow. (See the interview for an explanation.)

do we know when the project is done? At this stage, we don't think about the data or the visuals, just about challenges, goals, and strategies to overcome the former and reach the latter.

The second thing I need is data in raw form. I sketch many preliminary graphics with the data just to get a grip on it. I do these explorations with standard tools, such as Excel and Tableau[27], depending on the data sets. I usually try to produce as many sketches as possible that highlight individual parts of the data set and give me a sense of its texture. Is it very dense or is it sparse? Is it uniform or diverse? Do we have lots of different dimensions? Can they be reduced and summarized?

The most typical insight I get in these early steps is that people think they have a certain type of data, and it turns out they don't. Maybe they asked me to display the data on a world map, but they have data on only a few small countries, or the geography does not turn out to be the most important point. So I go back to the client and make alternative proposals.

I want to stress the importance of early sketches. If you are on the wrong track but you have only invested a day in them, then you are fine. You can easily throw them away and start over. But if you are on the wrong track and have invested six weeks in wonderfully rendered sketches, then you are in trouble.

---

27 http://www.tableausoftware.com/

Q **John Grimwade (featured in Profile 1) made a similar point about roughs when I talked with him. He draws many of his with a pencil, as doing so makes it cheap to fail.**

MS We designers tend to get committed to the things we invest work in. You get reluctant to throw them away and sometimes try to unconsciously convince yourself they are beautiful just because you have spent so much time on them. That's why it is also important that these first products are quickly produced and disposable, so you don't get attached to them. Refinement and tweaking comes later.

Besides helping you understand the data better, sketches are also useful to communicate to whomever works with you. I share some of my sketches with clients, after I annotate them. For instance, I might send over a PDF generated in Tableau, where I place little arrows with pop-up notes pointing out what I think is interesting or problematic.

While receiving feedback from clients and getting in touch with the data, my preliminary sketches gradually progress into custom-made visualizations. I usually create several functional prototypes based on real data and on my own code.

Q **What tools do you use for sketching prototypes?**

MS I use mostly Adobe Flash. It is still the best environment to produce visualizations. For more high-end projects, I have started playing with a combination of Java and Processing[28]. For web projects, I also use HTML 5 techniques, and frameworks such as d3 and Raphaël.

Q **There are designers, particularly traditional infographics artists, who contend that most data visualizations don't really tell a story. They argue that contemporary visualizers basically throw readers into an ocean of data and they let them on their own to navigate without any guidance. Do you think this is true?**

MS I think it's true, and I think it's positive and fantastic. The most fascinating thing about the rise of data visualization is exactly that anyone can explore all those large data sets without anyone telling us what the key insight is. We can look up our own hometown on a census map and look at exactly what the data points are and not just the averages in the county or the state.

In my work, I do not try to tell *a* story. I try to tell *thousands* of them. Obviously, you cannot present them all simultaneously or with the same priority, but still,

28 Processing is an open source programming language for visualization and graphics
http://processing.org/

Figure 10.60 Max Planck Research Networks: http://max-planck-research-networks.net. Moritz Stefaner: "This interactive multi-touch installation reveals how Max Planck Institutes collaborate with each other and with their international partners. A dynamic network provides a high-level map of the Max Planck Institutes and their connections. The size of the institute icons represents the number of scientific publications, and the width of the connecting lines represent the number of jointly published papers between two institutes. To create this visualization, we analyzed data from over 94,000 publications over the last 10 years. Touching an institute icon on the multi-touch screen centers the view around it and

highlights its most important collaboration partners, both in the collaboration network as well as on a world map. Visitors can move and zoom all views by touching and pinching (moving two fingers together or apart). The international flow of ideas is represented metaphorically by streams of energy particles being continuously exchanged between the institutions. The application is on display at the Max Planck Science Gallery, a highly interactive exhibition space presenting new forms of science communication in Berlin. (Created in collaboration with Christopher Warnow/Onformative.)

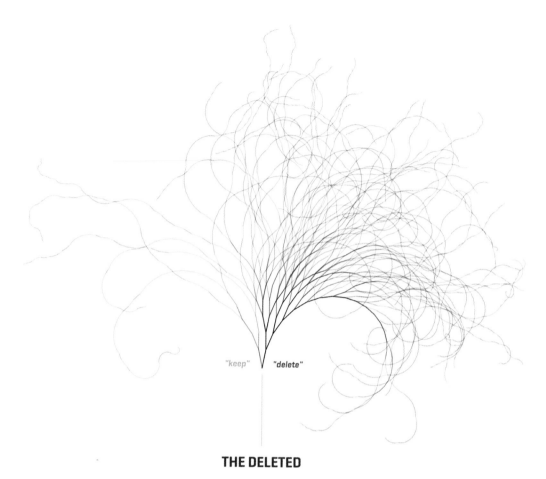

"keep"   "delete"

THE DELETED

The 100 longest **Article for Deletion (AfD)** discussions on Wikipedia,
which resulted in **deletion** of the article.

http://notabilia.net

Figure 10.61 Notabilia http://notabilia.net. Moritz Stefaner: "This is a visualization of deletion discussions on Wikipedia. Each discussion is represented by a thread starting at a shared root node, with curvature and coloring encoding the sequence of votes during the discussion. The work combines hard analysis of the phenomena around consensus finding in ad hoc communities with an allegorical treatment of the topic to foster serendipitous exploration of the domain." (Created in collaboration with Dario Taraborelli and Giovanni Luca Ciampaglia.)

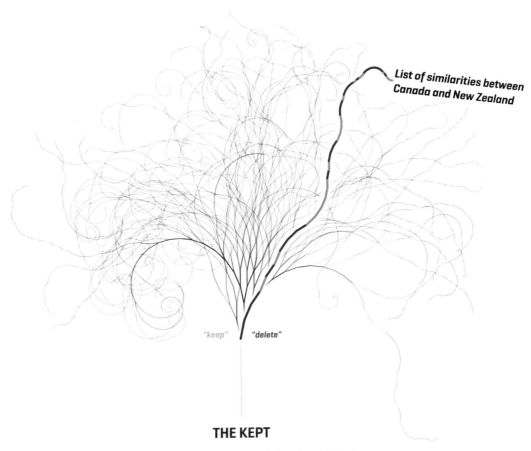

List of similarities between Canada and New Zealand

"keep"   *"delete"*

THE KEPT

The 100 longest **Article for Deletion (AfD)** discussions on Wikipedia,
which did **not** result in deletion of the article (i.e. it was kept, merged or redirected).

http://notabilia.net

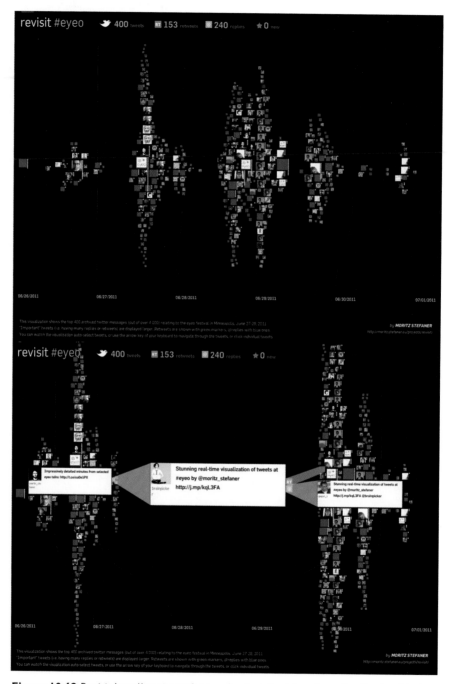

Figure 10.62 Revisit http://moritz.stefaner.eu/projects/revisit-twitter-visualization. Moritz Stefaner: "This is a real-time visualization of Twitter messages around a specific topic. The tool aligns all recent Twitter messages for a defined set of search terms along a timeline.

they can all be there, hidden in the raw data, waiting to be discovered through the interface of your presentation. I think this is the key difference of the genre of data visualization compared to, let's say, more traditional information graphics.

Q What advice would you give to students who want to get started in visualization?

MS If you want to produce information visualizations, you need to be able to work with the data directly. So you should learn about statistics and programming. Of course, you should also look into the arts, graphic design history, and visual language. If you master all those, then nothing can go wrong.

I would recommend to get used to producing 10 to 20 different solutions to each challenge, to draw many sketches for any project. You need to be honest about which ones work and which ones don't. Don't be afraid to fail. Sometimes you'll have a good hunch in the beginning, but more often you will need to look at many different variations of how to present the data using the right graphic forms. That's the other crucial component to be successful in this business: You need to design a lot to become a good designer.

Q Learning by doing?

MS Learning by doing and learning by transpiration!

Profile 9
Gregor Aisch (*driven-by-data.net*) and
Jan Willem Tulp (*TULP interactive*)

The Rising Stars

Gregor Aisch (http://driven-by-data.net) is a freelance visualization architect who combines skills in development, design, and data journalism. He has worked for clients such as General Electric and news organizations such as ZEIT Online.

Jan Willem Tulp (http://tulpinteractive.com) is a freelance information visualizer working from The Hague, The Netherlands. He works for clients around the world, and his visualizations range from static visualization in magazines like *Popular Science* and *Scientific American*, and interactive visualizations for the Web for clients such as the World Economic Forum, to internal visual analysis tools for clients such as the Amsterdam Airport and ING Investment Management.

Gregor Aisch and Jan Willem Tulp don't work together. In fact, they don't even live close to each other. Gregor works in Germany, and Jan Willem, in The Hague, The Netherlands. Nevertheless, I decided to talk to them together because I think their work is the most creative among the new breed of freelance information designers who seems to be flourishing in central Europe. Both of them have backgrounds in programming and computer science but, as in the case of Moritz

Stefaner (featured in Profile 8), their aesthetical sensibility is that of an artist. During our conversation, they were candid about the current shortcomings and challenges visualization faces, but they also proved to be optimistic about the power of visual displays of information to improve people's lives.

Q How did you become interested in visualization and graphics?

Gregor Aisch In 2004, I began to study computational visualistics at the University of Magdeburg[29], Germany. That course had a really broad range of topics. It included bits of computer science, psychology, education science, art, and an additional application subject which I could choose, like scientific or medical visualization. The major focus was to learn everything related to computers, images, and how humans interact with machines, both physical and virtual.

I would say I crossed paths with visualization, and it got my attention because I felt it allowed me to study something broad instead of becoming a narrow-minded specialist. I already had programmed Flash animations before going to college, and I had liked that a lot. After I graduated, I did things like designing and programming websites for a decade or so, until 2009, but then I made the decision to quit my job and became a visualization freelancer.

Jan Willem Tulp It's funny that my story is pretty similar to Gregor's. I have a B.A. in interaction design. I've always been interested in the synergy between design and technology, but spent nearly 10 years just in programming jobs after I graduated. Then, in 2009, I discovered there was something called "data visualization." For me, the pieces came together, as I found that it involved a lot of things I was curious about: advanced interaction, visual design, complex technology.

I got in touch with people like Moritz Stefaner and Ben Hosken, from Flink Labs[30], a visualization studio in Melbourne, Australia. I read many books, like Edward Tufte's and Stephen Few's. I went to conferences and started developing some projects in my spare time. The move for me was gradual; I didn't quit my full-time job immediately. But I am a freelancer today.

Q How did you find your first clients?

JWT Before officially starting as a freelancer, I wanted to have a lot of exposure, so that people knew I was into visualization. So I participated in some competitions, especially for www.visualizing.org. A few months before I actually opened

29 http://www.ovgu.de/en/home-p-1.html
30 http://www.flinklabs.com/

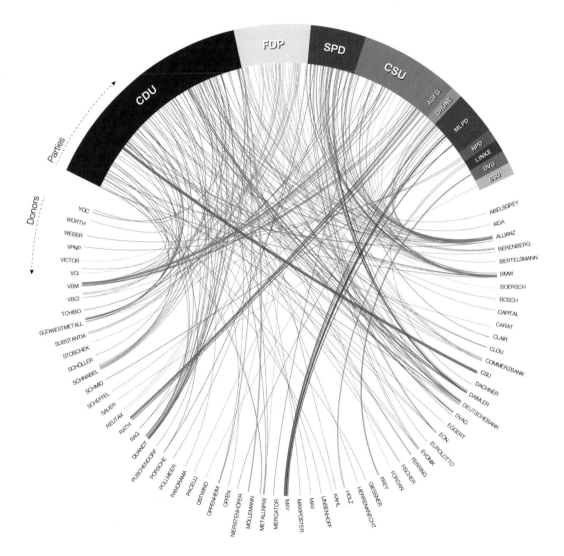

Figure 10.63 This radial convergence interactive graphic shows the money flow from private donators to parties in the German Bundestag. See the interactive version at http://labs.vis4.net/parteispenden/. By Gregor Aisch (driven-by-data.net).

my own business, I got some clients lined up. My first two were the Amsterdam Airport and the World Economic Forum.

GA I started to write about info vis topics in my blog. I was very interested in things like color theory, design, and so on. Then, I published some personal interactive visualizations. I got my first contract, with the German newspaper *Zeit Online*, after I published a project on donations to political parties (**Figure 10.63**) that I had done just to explore some data I had.

Q One of the things that I find curious about the visualization field is that there seems to be a lot of interest and talent in central Europe: The Netherlands, Germany, etc. Is the field as big and vibrant as it seems?

GA Visualization and infographics have a long tradition in central Europe. Just remember classics like Otto Neurath and Gerd Arntz, for instance. Some educational institutions, like the University of Konstanz[31], the University of Applied Sciences of Postdam[32], and the University of Magdeburg, have kept that tradition alive. However, the data vis freelancing scene is not as big as you would think. There are some other people doing visualization freelancing, such as Christopher Warnow[33], but not many local companies are interested in what we do. In the first year of my freelancing career, I worked mostly for clients overseas and in the UK. That led to strange situations sometimes, such as being hired by a U.S. company to design a visualization about energy in Germany (**Figure 10.64**).

Q Can you explain how you produce your projects?

JWT The process differs depending on the project. Some clients are really open and give me a lot of creative freedom. Others, magazines in particular, have a clearer idea of what they want, and they usually send an example picture of the kind of illustration they want for an article. The amount of preliminary exploration differs per project. The power of visualization is, of course, that it allows you to see what the data looks like. I always try to make my data visible as soon as possible, so I do a lot of prototyping and sketching.

To mention just one example, one of my first graphics was a visual tool for analyzing tax-free sales at the airport of Amsterdam (**Figure 10.65**). The airport officials had a huge data set that was updated constantly. They wanted to be able to study which stores sell more and less, and be able to filter the data by airline,

31 http://www.inf.uni-konstanz.de/gk/
32 http://design.fh-potsdam.de/studiengaenge/interfacedesign.html
33 http://christopherwarnow.com

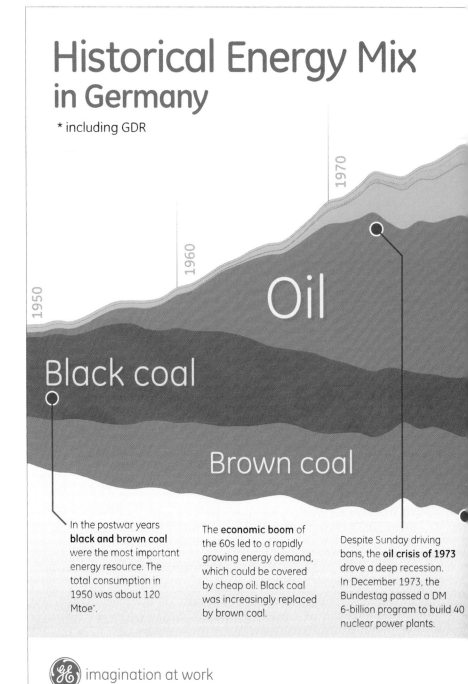

Figure 10.64 German Energy Landscape: http://driven-by-data.net/about/german-energy/#/0. By Gregor Aisch (driven-by-data.net).

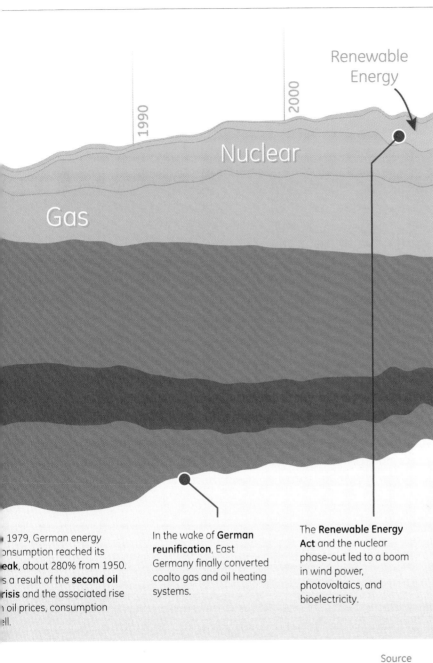

Renewable
Energy

Nuclear

Gas

1990

2000

1979, German energy
onsumption reached its
eak, about 280% from 1950.
s a result of the **second oil
risis** and the associated rise
oil prices, consumption
ell.

In the wake of **German
reunification**, East
Germany finally converted
coalto gas and oil heating
systems.

The **Renewable Energy
Act** and the nuclear
phase-out led to a boom
in wind power,
photovoltaics, and
bioelectricity.

Source
AG Energiebilanzen e.V.
Joachim Kahlert: Die Energiepolitik der DDR

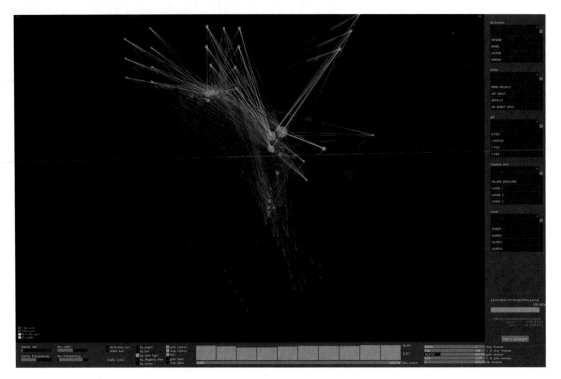

Figure 10.65 Visualization of tax-free sales at the Amsterdam Airport. These images were generated using random data. The actual data is not disclosed by the airport. By Jan Willem Tulp (TULP Interactive).

by time range, and so on. They already had a tool that let them plot the data in simple graphs, such as bar charts, but they wanted something more advanced. The fun part is that they mentioned that they wished to create something really sophisticated to convince all departments at the airport of the value of visualization.

A big part of the process for this project was regularly checking if the visualization was helping to answer the questions they had. I had many meetings with the airport analysts to show them what I had at each point. They were the ones who were going to use the tool, capturing screenshots of it to put in their regular reports, so we had to make sure that the graphics made sense. That was the priority: The tool should support sensible insights, and after that, it should look nice, too. It was stressed that it should not be just a fancy-looking tool, but it should be something of value to them.

I would like to mention that I try to write as much custom code as I can. There are some tools, like Tableau or Excel, that can do a lot. In many cases, they can help you get very valuable insights. But if you have more specific requests for

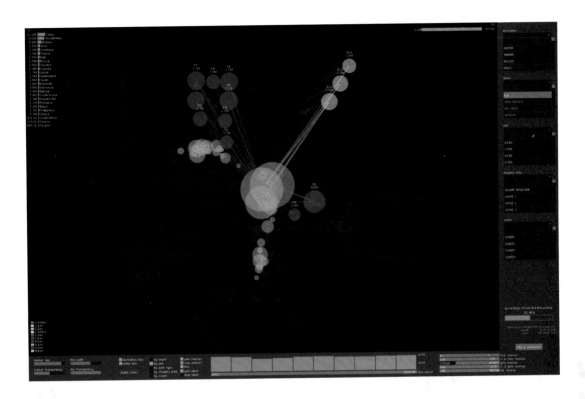

analysis, display, technology, integration with other tools, interaction, or more, then customized visualization tools are very valuable.

GA My own personal projects always start with a problem I identify, or a data set I am interested in exploring. Coming from a computer science background, I'm confronted with a lot of interesting stuff in economics, society, and politics, so visualizing key datasets of those domains is a way for me to learn new things. Sometimes, by doing that, I find something really interesting during these processes, a story which is worth publishing.

For instance, at the moment I'm very interested in the network of media corporations. There's a lot of talk about the role of mass media in our societies, so I believe it is crucial to learn about the corporations behind newspapers, magazines, and TV stations. So I did a bit of research and found a database of media ownership networks in Germany and started to visualize it using JavaScript and D3 (**Figure 10.66**).

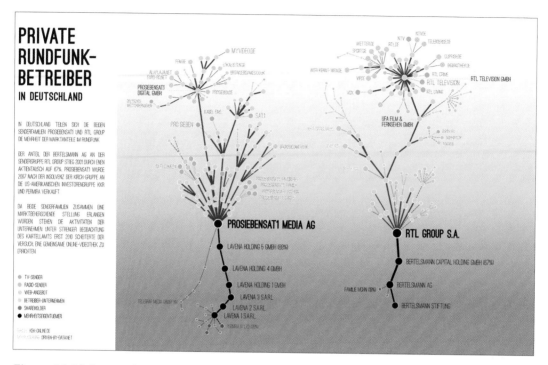

Figure 10.66 A network of media corporations in Germany, by Gregor Aisch (driven-by-data.net).

Q   Among the people you admire, who would you say have influenced you the most, and why?

GA Among the historical figures, I admire the work of Otto Neurath and Gerd Arntz[34]. That great ideal they promoted of developing a universal visual language to communicate across borders simply amazes me and drives my work even now. After Neurath's death, his wife, Marie Neurath, started to use ISOTYPE infographics to teach kids in developing countries that they should go to school, brush their teeth, care about pregnancy, and so on. Those are the kind of things that I love about visualization and infographics: The potential to help change the world for the better.

Neurath's work exemplified the power of natural visual metaphors. A plain bar chart, praised a lot for its efficiency in communicating numbers, also has the potential of scaring people away because it's also a very abstract representation. We should be aware that some people are not able to connect emotionally to highly

---

34 See Chapter 3: The Beauty Paradox.

efficient charts, but do feel attracted to, and understand, displays that include little pictograms, icons, and illustrations. Fun can promote learning.

Among the modern practitioners, I appreciate the work of David McCandless[35]. It is true he has done some commercial projects that have very little value in terms of communicating data, and he has been justly criticized for them[36]. Nevertheless, some of his more personal visualizations are quite engaging and worth seeing.

JWT There are two I'd like to mention: Moritz Stefaner and Jer Thorp[37]. I like Moritz's work because, as I've collaborated with him in some projects, I have seen that he can really justify every design decision he makes. He can elaborate very well on what he wants to communicate, and he is very skilled at emphasizing the core stories and the interesting parts in his visualizations.

The work of Jer Thorp is also very beautiful. His best graphics let you have a different perspective on the issues they cover and lead you to become aware of facts you didn't realize were there.

Q   If you had to highlight a project of yours above all the others, maybe one that you enjoyed designing, which one would that be?

JWT I would choose Ghost Counties (**Figure 10.67**). I made it for a challenge organized by Visualizing.org. They asked the participants to design a visualization based on census data on vacant homes per state and county, so the most obvious thing was to base it on a map. But they specifically asked us not to do that, unless you did something really different with that map. The winner would get a ticket to the Eyeo Festival[38]. At the end, I sketched a lot and designed something that is, at its core, a series of unorthodox scatter-plots (**Figure 10.68**).

GA I really like a visualization I made on a case of academic plagiarism (**Figure 10.69**). In February 2011, a law professor found traces of plagiarism in the Ph.D. dissertation of the German minister of defense Karl Theodor zu Guttenberg. At that time, zu Guttenberg was praised by the media as the new star in politics, the man who definitely would become the new chancellor. He had put himself on the stage willingly by, for example, taking his wife with him to official visits in Afghanistan and even arranging a TV talk show there. So it was very natural that the discovery of his plagiarism got big attention, particularly from the people who don't really like him.

---

35 http://www.davidmccandless.com/

36 Stephen Few has been one of the most outspoken critics of McCandless' projects. See http://www.perceptualedge.com/blog/?p=935 and http://www.perceptualedge.com/blog/?p=995

37 Jer Thorp is a Canadian digital artist, designer, and educator: http://blprnt.com/

38 http://eyeofestival.com/

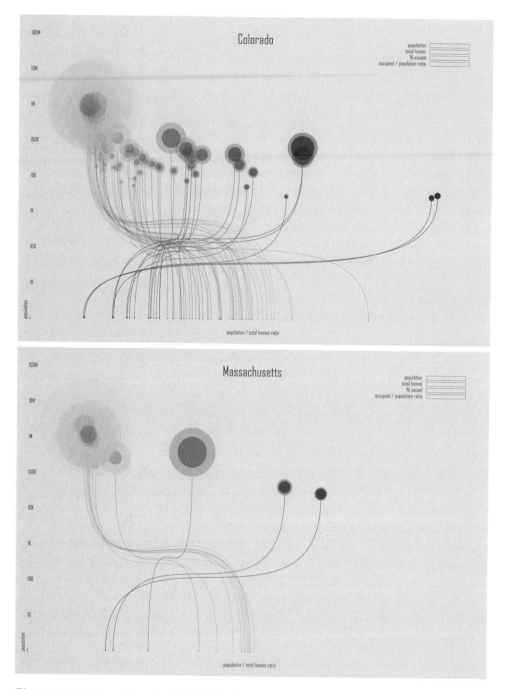

Figure 10.67 Ghost Counties, by Jan Willem Tulp (TULP Interactive). http://www.janwillemtulp.com/
eyeo/. Each line and bubble is a county in the state. The position on the vertical axis is proportional
to the population. The position on the horizontal axis is proportional to the ration between the
number of inhabitants and the total number of homes. When you roll over the circles, you get the
specific figures of total homes, vacant homes, and population.

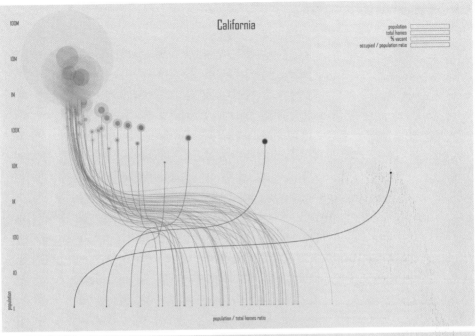

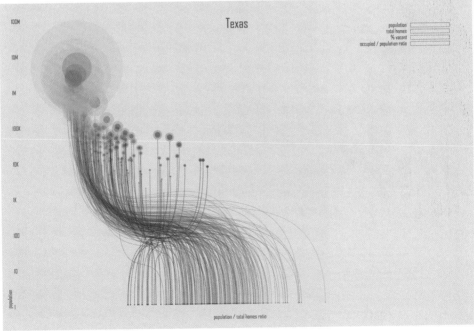

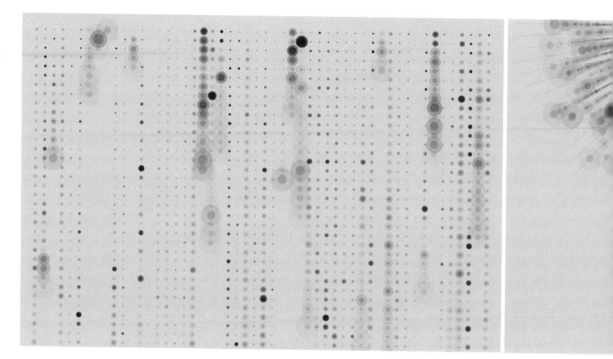

Ghost counties of Alaba

Figure 10.68 Jan Willem Tulp. Sketches for the Ghost Counties project.

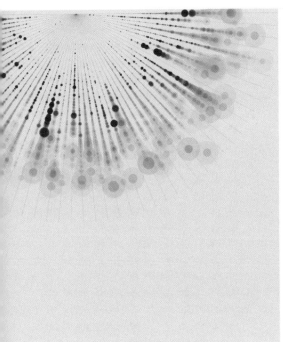
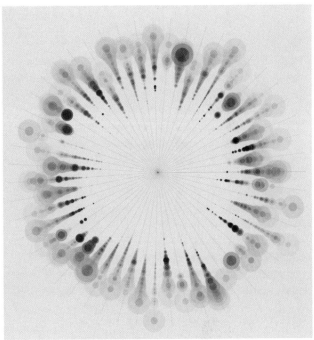

Ghost counties of Florida

Plagiarism in the PhD thesis
of Karl-Theodor Freiherr zu Guttenberg

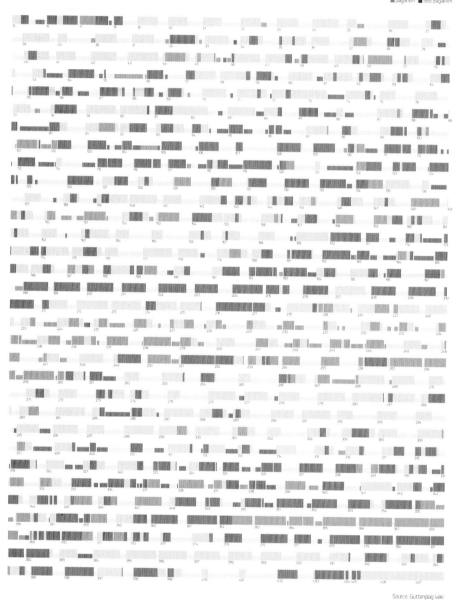

Source: Guttenplag Wiki

Figure 10.69 Visualizing Plagiarism. http://driven-by-data.net/about/plagiarism/. See the interview for an explanation. By Gregor Aisch (driven-by-data.net)

Over the next two weeks, an incredible crowd-sourced hunt on plagiarized parts in his dissertation took place. Every day, people found more evidence that his work, which was rated as summa cum laude, was blantly copied to criminal extents. But zu Guttenberg had no intention of stepping back.

Over those weeks, I followed the news intently. I spent the evenings in chat rooms, talking to anonymous people about the crowd-sourced process. For me, the most interesting thing was to get structured data that I could visualize. My intention was to show the full extent of plagiarism on a single page. The graphic I designed displays every single line in the dissertation, the plagiarized ones are highlighted in red. I felt like journalists would really need a good picture to understand what had happened. I managed to publish the project the very day before the minister finally resigned.

Profile 10
Stefanie Posavec
(*itsbeenreal.co.uk*)

Visualizing Literature

Stefanie Posavec, originally from Denver, Colorado, moved to London to complete an MA in Communication Design and never went home. Her studies focused mainly on the visualization of literature, which led to work as a book cover designer at Penguin Books UK, after which she went freelance. Her work spans from data visualization, information design, and data illustration to designing books and book covers for a variety of clients, including Penguin, Random House, Faber & Faber, *Information is Beautiful*, and *WIRED* magazine. Her personal projects focus on the visual representation of language and literature, and have been exhibited internationally, including at Millennium Galleries, Sheffield, ("On the Map," 2008), Somerset House, London ("Pick Me Up 2," 2011), and the Museum of Modern Art, New York, ("Talk to Me," 2011).

Stefanie Posavec works in the fringes between visualization and art. She has a background in graphic design and quite a bit of experience as a book cover designer for Penguin and other publishers, but her passion is in what lurks between those covers, in the pages of novels and poem collections.

Posavec's beautiful graphics can be considered translations: She transforms the words of language into colors, lines, and playful arrangements, with the goal of sharing her enthusiasm for literature with others and bringing attention to the books she cherishes. They are, in the words of Maria Popova, curator of www.brainpickings.org, "the most poetic pieces of visual meta-storytelling you'll ever see." Even if I usually try to dodge exaggeration, I feel compelled to agree.

Q   The projects you are most well known for are your literary visualizations, what you call your "Writing Without Words" graphics (Figure 10.70 and Figure 10.71). How did you come up with the idea of visualizing the words and sentences of books?

Stefanie Posavec "Writing Without Words" was the final year project for my MA, in London. I have always loved English. I was born in Denver, Colorado, and when I was a kid, I went to Catholic school. We spent a lot of time focusing on English grammar. I had six years of very intensive literature classes. I've been always interested in picking apart poems, novels, any piece of writing.

That's why I chose literature as a topic to visualize. Some of my preliminary ideas were really superficial, like trying to visualize compatibility in lonely-hearts ads. But then I realized I wanted to work on something I deeply cared about, literature, and mainly Jack Kerouac's *On The Road*. I loved that book when I was a teenager. I decided that if I was going to spend a year working on something, it would be better to spend it on a subject that was meaningful to me.

Q   How did you do the graphics? Did you use any script to count the words, organize them, sort them according to themes, etc.?

SP Believe it or not, I didn't. I did it all by hand. I could not get an electronic version of *On the Road,* and I couldn't figure out how to digitize the copy I had, either. So I ended up counting all the words one by one, and sorting them by key themes. I spent a lot of time going through the book and highlighting different sections (**Figure 10.72** and **Figure 10.73**).

I made the graphics in Illustrator. They were not generated with code. I know it's possible to do it using scripting, and there are wonderful tools for that, like Processing, but I don't know how to use them. I am aware that I need to automate, but sometimes I feel that it's important to spend that kind of time gathering your information by hand. It feels a little more natural. Also, it creates bonds with what you are working on: I had to read *On the Road* over and over again, so the outcome was as much a representation of the text as it is a representation of the novel in my head, of my experience of exploring it.

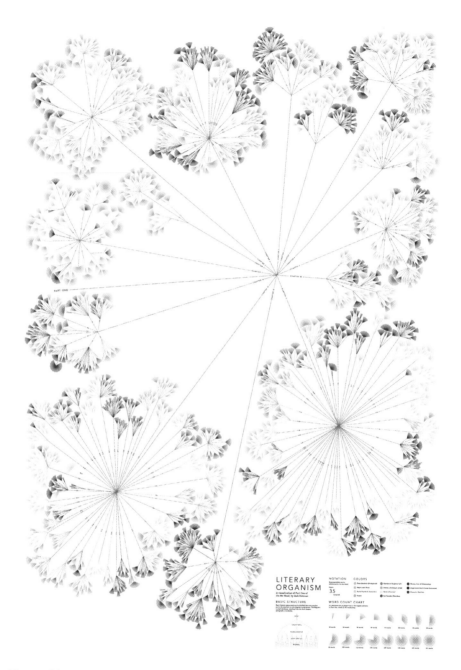

Figure 10.70 "Writing Without Words: Literary Organism." Stephanie Posavec, 2006. The structure of Part One of *On the Road*, by Jack Kerouac, visualized using a simple tree structure that has been worked with manually in order to give it a more organic feel. Here, Part One divides into chapters, chapters divide into paragraphs, paragraphs divide into sentences, and sentences divide into words. Everything is color-coded according to key themes in *On the Road*.

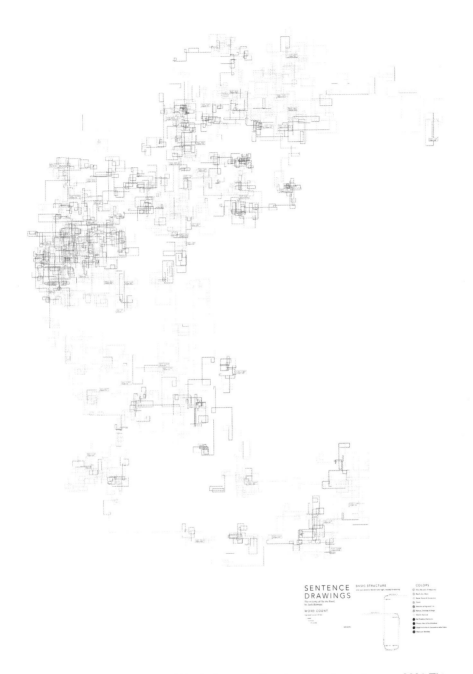

Figure 10.71 "Writing Without Words: Sentence Drawings." Stephanie Posavec, 2006. This is the entirety of *On the Road*, sentence by sentence. After the end of each sentence, the line turns right. The length of each segment of the line is proportional to the length of each sentence. Everything is color-coded according to key themes in the novel.

Figure 10.72 Stefanie Posavec's copy of *On the Road,* filled with color-coded highlights.

Q   Did you want to make a particular point with your graphics or did you just wish to create an art project?

SP To tell you the truth, my only goal was to be able to put the entirety of the book on the wall, maybe just with the intention of inspiring awe and wonder. After seeing the graphic, I wanted people to see *On the Road* in a different way.

As its name says, I consciously made *Literary Organism* feel organic. I am intrigued by the parallel between how books are cellular, and how plants and animals are cellular as well. I wanted to make that connection. With the circular arrangement of lines and colors, I also tried to convey the rhythm of the book. *On the Road* reads like a poem. So the graphic is not so much about insight, but about making you think differently about the book.

Q   You didn't have any background in visualization before your last year at graduate school. Where did you get your inspiration?

SP It comes back to when I was 19. In 2001, I got John Maeda's book *Maeda Media* and saw Martin Wattenberg's *The Shape of Song* visualizations, on what music

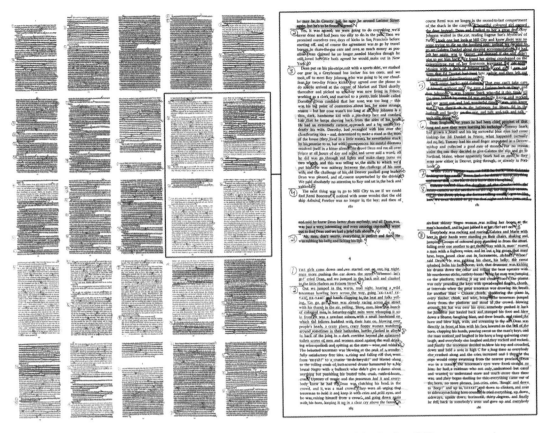

Figure 10.73 Highlights on several pages of Stefanie Posavec's copy of *On the Road*. When you see them displayed side by side, they work like a visualization that lets you see what key theme each portion of the book deals with.

looks like[38]. I was impressed by Wattenberg: I loved the simplicity of his work. So Maeda and Wattenberg were my main sources of inspiration at first. Today, I also like what Jer Thorp is doing[39]. He is really creative.

I also read some of Edward Tufte's books, but he didn't influence me as much. Actually, I find people like Tufte a bit intimidating, being so blunt and so firm about what is right and what is wrong in graphics.

---

38 Martin Wattenberg is an expert in data visualization. His *The Shape of Song* project is in http://bewitched.com/song.html.

39 http://blprnt.com/

Q Are there other novels you would like to visualize?

SP I tried to do something with *The Man Who Was Thursday*, by G.K. Chesterton because you can notice so many colors in it. The language that he used was really colorful. For a while, I thought about mapping out the colors in the book, brights, dazzling, and dark. I wouldn't mind doing something more comparative also, like looking at lots of different authors and putting them together side by side.

Another thing I have thought about over the years is to do a project inspired by the sentence diagrams which students in the U.S. use to learn grammar. They look really intriguing, and I would like to find a more beautiful way to show how sentences are little structures, displaying what words modify other words. I hope that I will find the time to work on all that.

Q You have also visualized Darwin's *On the Origin of Species*. As a long-time reader of science books, I found that project really eye-catching.

SP I produced the "(En)tangled Word Bank" (**Figure 10.74** and **Figure 10.75**) with my brother-in-law, Greg McInerny[40], who works for Microsoft. We thought about displaying the insertions and deletions in the six editions of Darwin's masterpiece. Greg is an ecologist, and we worked together on this project in 2009 to commemorate the 200th anniversary of Darwin's birth in 1809. He asked me, "Why don't we put together your methods and mine and come up with something nice?" We did it in our spare time. I did the design, and he wrote the code to generate the visuals.

At first we were aiming at scientists. Greg told me that many experts, even in the natural sciences, have never read *On the Origin of Species*. They know everything about evolution by natural selection, but most have never gone to the primary sources. But we also wanted to appeal to the general public. We wished to provoke awe and wonder again, to inspire them and draw attention to the book.

It's always about that awe and wonder for me. That's why I have decided to call myself a data illustrator, rather than a data visualizer. The reason is that I really like the idea of using data to communicate more subjective concepts about the topics I cover. Everything is accurate in my graphics, but they are not necessarily designed just for efficiency, they are not always what you would call information design.

---

40 http://research.microsoft.com/en-us/events/escience2011/speakers.aspx#McInerny

Figure 10.74 "(En)tangled Word Bank: Six Editions." Greg McInerny and Stefanie Posavec, 2009. Produced at Microsoft Research, Cambridge. Each diagram represents an edition of Charles Darwin's *On the Origin of Species* and is modeled on the "literary organism" structure used for Posavec's *On the Road* project. Within the diagram, chapters are divided into subchapters as in Darwin's original text, and these sub-chapters are divided into paragraph "leaves." The small wedge-shaped "leaflets" represent sentences. Each sentence is colored according to whether the sentence will survive to the next edition (blue) or whether it will be deleted and not be within the next edition (orange).

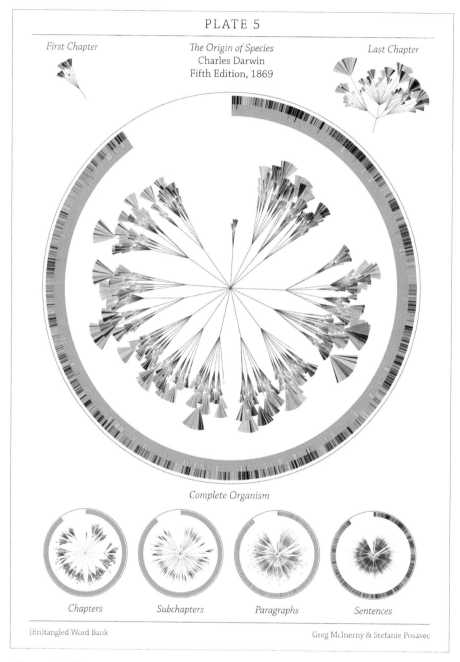

Figure 10.75 An example of the layout for each wheel of the "(En)tangled Word Bank: Six Editions." This represents the fifth edition of *On the Origin of Species*.

Bibliography

Arheim, Rudolf. *Visual Thinking*. Berkeley: University of California Press, 2004.

Arthur, Brian. *The Nature of Technology*. New York: Free Press, 2009.

Baigrie, Brian S. *Picturing Knowledge: Historical and Philosophical Problems Concerning the Use of Art in Science*. Toronto: University of Toronto Press, 1996.

Bateman, Scott, Regan Mandryk, Carl Gutwin,Aaron Genest, David McDine, and Christopher Brooks. "Useful Junk? The Effects of Visual Embellishment on Comprehension and Memorability of Charts." ACM Conference on Human Factors in Computing Systems, 2010.

Bertin, Jacques. *Semiology of Graphics: Diagrams, Networks, Maps*. Redland: ESRI Press, 2010.

Blasio, Anthony J. and Ann M. Bisantz. "A comparison of the effects of data-ink ratio on performance with dynamic displays in a monitoring task." *International Journal of Industrial Ergonomics*, 2010.

Card, Stuart K., Jock D. Mackinlay, Ben Shneiderman. *Information Visualization: Using Vision to Think*. San Francisco: Morgan Kaufmann, 1999.

Cleveland, William S. *The Elements of Graphing Data*. New Jersey: Hobart Press, 1993.

———. *Visualizing Data*. New Jersey: Hobart Press, 1993.

Costa, Joan. *La esquemática: visualizar la información*. Barcelona: Paidós, 1998.

Costa, Joan and Abraham Moles. *La imagen didáctica*. Barcelona: CEAC, 1991.

Damasio, Antonio. *Self Comes to Mind: Constructing the Conscious Brain*. New York: Pantheon Books, 2010.

Deacon, Terrence W. *The Symbolic Species: The Co-evolution of Language and the Brain*. New York: W.W. Norton & Company, 1997.

Dehaened, Stanislas. *Reading in the Brain: The Science and Evolution of a Human Invention*. New York: Viking, 2009.

Dennett, Daniel C. *Darwin's Dangerous Idea: Evolution and the Meanings of Life*. New York: Simon & Schuster, 1996.

Dent, Borden D. *Cartography: Thematic Map Design*. Boston: Addison-Wesley Publishing Company, 1985.

Ericson, Eric and Johan Pihl. *Design for Impact.* Princeton: Princeton University Press, 2003.

Few, Stephen. *Show Me the Numbers: Designing Tables and Graphs to Enlighten.* Burlingame: Analytics Press, 2004.

———. *Now You See It: Simple Visualization Techniques for Quantitative Analysis.* Burlingame: Analytics Press, 2009.

Friedenberg, Jay D. and Gordon Silverman. *Cognitive Science: An Introduction to the Study of Mind.* Thousand Oaks: Sage Publications, 2005.

Harris, Robert L. *Information Graphics: A Comprehensive Illustrated Reference.* New York: Oxford University Press, 2000.

Hoffman, Donald D. *Visual Intelligence: How We Create What We See.* New York: W.W. Norton & Company, 1999.

Holmes, Nigel. *Designer's Guide to Creating Charts and Diagrams.* New York: Watson-Guptill, 1991.

Inbar, Ohad, Noam Tractinsky, and Joachim Meyer. "Minimalism in information visualization: attitudes towards maximizing the data-ink ratio." ECCE '07 Proceedings of the 14th European conference on Cognitive ergonomics, 2010.

Jacob, Pierre and Marc Jeannerod. *Ways of Seeing: The Scope and Limits of Visual Cognition.* Oxford: Oxford University Press, 2003.

Jacobson, Robert. *Information Design.* Boston: MIT Press, 1999.

Johnson, Jeff. *Designing with the Mind in Mind: Simple Guide to Understanding User Interface Design Rules.* San Francisco: Morgan Kaufmann, 2010.

Johnson, Steven. *The Ghost Map: The Story of London's Most Terrifying Epidemic, and How It Changed Science, Cities, and the Modern World.* New York: Riverhead, 2006.

Kelly, Kevin. *What Technology Wants.* New York: Viking, 2010.

Koch, Tom. *Cartographies of Disease: Maps, Mapping and Medicine.* Redland: ESRI Press, 2005.

Kosslyn, Stephen M. *Image and Brain: The Resolution of the Imagery Debate.* Boston: MIT Press, 1996.

———. *Graph Design for the Eye and Mind.* New York: Oxford University Press, 2006.

Kosslyn, Stephen M., William L. Thomson, and Georgio Ganis. *The Case for Mental Imagery.* New York: Oxford University Press, 2009.

Krug, Steve. *Don't Make Me Think! A Common Sense Approach to Web Usability.* Berkeley: New Riders Press, 2005.

Lima, Manuel. *Visual Complexity: Mapping Patterns of Information.* New York: Princeton Architectural Press, 2011.

Maceachren, Alan M. *How Maps Work: Representation, Visualization, and Design.* New York: Guilford Press, 2004.

Malamed, Connie. *Visual Language for Designers: Principles for Creating Graphics That People Understand.* Beverly: Rockport Publishers, 2009.

Meyer, Philip. *Precision Journalism: A Reporter's Introduction to Social Science Methods.* Lanham: Rowman & Littlefield Publishers, 2002.

Monmonier, Mark. *How to Lie With Maps*. Chicago: University of Chicago Press, 1996.

Morozov, Evgeny. *The Net Delusion: The Dark Side of Internet Freedom*. New York: Public Affairs, 2011.

Neurath, Otto. *From Hieroglyphics to Isotype*. London: Hyphen Press, 2010.

Noë, Alva. *Action in Perception (Representation and Mind)*. Boston: MIT Press, 2006.

Norman, Donald A. *The Design of Everyday Things*. New York: Basic Books, 1988.

———. *Emotional Design: Why We Love (or Hate) Everyday Things*. New York: Perseus Books, 2004.

Palmer, Stephen E. *Vision Science: Photons to Phenomenology*. Boston: MIT Press, 1999.

Pinker, Steven. *How the Mind Works*. New York: W.W. Norton & Company, 1997.

Ramachandran, V. S. *The Tell-Tale Brain: A Neuroscientist's Quest for What Makes Us Human*. New York: W.W. Norton & Company, 2011.

Roam, Dan. *The Back of the Napkin: Solving Problems and Selling Ideas*. New York: Portfolio, 2008.

Robbins, Naomi B. *Creating More Effective Graphs*. Hoboken: Wiley, 2004.

Sharp, Helen, Yvonne Rogers, and Jenny Preece. *Interaction Design: Beyond Human-Computer Interaction*. West Sussex: Wiley, 2007.

Slocum, Terry A. *Thematic Cartography and Visualization*. Upper Saddle River: Prentice Hall, 1999.

Smith, Edward E. and Stephen M. Kosslyn. *Cognitive Psychology: Mind and Brain*. New Jersey: Pearson Education, 2007.

Spence, Robert. *Information Visualization: Design for Interaction*. Upper Saddle River: Prentice Hall, 2007.

Tractinsky, Noam and Joachim Meyer. "Chartjunk or goldgraph? Effects of presentation objectives and content desirability on information presentation." *MIS Quarterly 23*, 1999.

Tufte, Edward E. *The Visual Display of Quantitative Information*. Cheshire: Graphics Press, 1987.

———. *Envisioning Information*. Cheshire: Graphics Press, 1990.

———. *Visual Explanations*. Cheshire: Graphics Press, 1997.

Wainer, Howard. *Graphic Discovery: A Trout in the Milk and Other Visual Adventures*. Princeton: Princeton University Press, 2005.

Ware, Colin. *Information Visualization: Perception for Design*. San Francisco: Morgan Kauffman, 2004.

Wilkinson, Richard and Kate Pickett. *The Spirit Level: Why Greater Equality Makes Societies Stronger*. London: Bloomsbury Press, 2009.

Wurman, Richard Saul. *Information Anxiety 2*. New York: Que, 2000.

Wong, Dona M. *The Wall Street Journal Guide to Information Graphics: The Dos and Don'ts of Presenting Data, Facts, and Figures*. New York: W.W. Norton & Company, 2010.

Yau, Nathan. *Visualize This: The FlowingData Guide to Design, Visualization, and Statistics*. Hoboken: Wiley, 2011.

Index

WATCH READ CREATE

Unlimited online access to all Peachpit, Adobe Press, Apple Training and New Riders videos and books, as well as content from other leading publishers including: O'Reilly Media, Focal Press, Sams, Que, Total Training, John Wiley & Sons, Course Technology PTR, Class on Demand, VTC and more.

No time commitment or contract required! Sign up for one month or a year.
All for $19.99 a month

SIGN UP TODAY
peachpit.com/creativeedge

creative
edge